The Political Economy
of Hope and Fear

| Marcellus Andrews |

THE POLITICAL
ECONOMY OF
HOPE AND FEAR

CAPITALISM AND THE
BLACK CONDITION IN AMERICA

New York University Press

New York and London

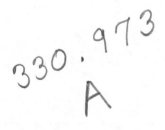

330.973
A

NEW YORK UNIVERSITY PRESS
New York and London

Library of Congress Cataloging-in-Publication Data
Andrews, Marcellus, 1956–
The political economy of hope and fear : capitalism and the
Black condition in America / Marcellus Andrews.
p.   cm.
Includes bibliographical references (p.   ) and index.
ISBN 0-8147-0679-7 (acid-free paper)
1. Afro-Americans—Economic conditions.   2. United
States—Economic conditions—1945–   3. Capitalism—United
States—History—20th century.   4. United States—Economic
policy.
I. Title.
E185.8.A77   1999
330.973'09—dc21   98-58107
CIP

New York University Press books are printed on acid-free paper,
and their binding materials are chosen for strength and durability.

Manufactured in the United States of America

10 9 8 7 6 5 4 3 2 1

CONTENTS

Contents

A PREFACE IN THREE PARTS

Economics as a Razor

This book is one economist's meditation on the economic fortunes of black Americans in the twilight of the Civil Rights movement. The limits of the Civil Rights dream in America are no longer in doubt. As long as basic questions of social justice remain in the shadows, genuine racial reconciliation between blacks and whites is not likely in this country, despite the curious talk about colorblindness that is in vogue among conservatives these days. The movement toward racial equality has faltered because Americans are uncertain about whether they really want to create a society that offers genuine equality of opportunity across color lines, much less basic security against poverty. The problem is that social class is a taboo subject among Americans since it is at odds with one of our most cherished and ludicrous national myths, namely, that each individual is solely responsible for his or her good or ill fortune in life. The condition of black people in America is an embarrassment for those politicians, pundits, preachers, and worried citizens who desperately want to believe this lie because it is all too clear that past abuse and current inequality can ruin innocent lives, thereby mocking all those who say that blacks are poor, dysfunctional, or intellectual failures because they have bad genes or bad cultures.

However, the "black problem" in modern America is complicated because there is no simple connection between color and economic well-being. The presence of a thriving black middle class and a seemingly permanent black underclass are evidence that the Civil Rights dream both succeeded and failed in transforming American life. Black athletes, actors, entertainers, artists, and writers have won wide acclaim among some segments of nonblack America at the same time that an unprecedented number of black men (1.7 million in 1997, or approximately 7% of the black male population) fill the nation's prisons and jails. The plight of poor black women is used by rightist scribblers and political hustlers for fun and profit as a symbol of the feckless nature of the race (we will have a great deal to say about these "conservatives" below). Politicians and thinkers use Martin Luther King's words about the coming of a colorblind society to eliminate all forms of race-based affirmative action in college admissions and employment, at the same time that residential segregation tightly links race and educational opportunity and major newspapers tell grim stories of routine racial discrimination at major Fortune 500 companies. In the spring of 1998, a black man in Jasper, Texas, was literally dismembered when a trio of white men tied him to the back of their truck and dragged him for two miles across country roads, severing his head from his body and tearing the rest of his body into seventy-five pieces. Blacks are still poorer, sicker, less well educated, and die younger than whites, despite all the talk of progress by "conservative" writers. Blacks are deeply ambivalent about the legitimacy of the police and courts in their lives, despite the fact that they are also far more likely to be victims of crime than whites, because they are subjected to all manner of racial abuse by the people sworn to protect them from abuse. It is fair to say that this state of affairs is not what Martin Luther King had in mind.

The important question for us is not whether the Civil Rights movement ended in America, but how economic forces have placed obstacles in the way of the nation's journey toward racial justice. It is important to remember that the Civil Rights movement, like any social movement, was bound to fade away someday. Had genuine racial reconciliation happened in America, the "movement" would have faded away as blacks and whites faced each other as friends, neighbors, lovers, business rivals, students, teachers, and eventually, family members in a post-racial order. The death of color and race as standards for judging the worth of human beings would have also meant the end of any and all forms of color preference in school admissions, hiring, promotions, elections, and other areas of public life. Of course, in the dream world of Martin Luther King, colorblind public policy would simply follow the spread of colorblind ways of living and working in society. But color is still a central force in American life, poisoning many of our dealings with each other because we cannot face the hideous legacy of American racism.

This book uses economic analysis as an intellectual scalpel to conduct an economic audit of the Civil Rights movement which shows that the movement toward racial justice in America was assassinated by free markets and the technological whirlwind driving capitalism worldwide rather than by organized racism per se. Racism is still an important and destructive influence on the economic fortunes of black people in America, but it is no longer the primary reason why black people are poorer than white people. Put bluntly, black Americans are generally poorer than white Americans because capitalism and racism combine to limit their access to education and knowledge, which in turn blocks their access to good jobs, decent health care, safe neighborhoods, and good lives. However, racism only abets the more basic problem: black people are poor now because they were so badly discriminated against by historic American racism that they were unprepared for the sea change in the American and world economy that has utterly transformed our lives over the past three decades. Black people were completely unprepared for, and unable to take advantage of, the shift in the structure of the American economy toward a knowledge- and technology-driven system that offers huge rewards to brains over brawn, because they remain an industrial labor force in a post-industrial country. Even if every racist white person in this country had a change of heart or moved abroad, most poor black people would be exactly where they are right now in the absence of major changes in government policy to address issues of poverty and economic inequality across color lines.

Our economic audit of American racial inequality will proceed in two stages. First, we present a brief but comprehensive portrait of the economic status of black Americans since the mid-1960s in order to orient ourselves and establish pertinent facts that then guide our succeeding discussions. For example, most Americans know that black Americans are, on average, poorer than white Americans, though surprisingly few seem to know that the largest group of poor people in this country (in absolute terms) is non-Hispanic whites. In 1996, a little over 36.4 million Americans lived in poverty, as defined by the official poverty line. Of these, 16.46 million were non-Hispanic whites (45.06% of the total poverty population), 8.18 million were white and Hispanic (22.4% of the total), 9.69 were black (26.5% of the total), and 1.45 million were Asian (4.06% of the total). At the same time, non-Hispanic whites were 8.6% of the total white population in 1996; poor blacks were

28.4% of all blacks (the lowest black poverty rate in American history); poor Hispanics (of all races) were 29.4% of all Hispanics; poor Asians were 14.5% of all Asians. These data tell us a number of important things that get lost in discussions about race in this country:

1. There are a lot of poor white people in America, so many in fact that one wonders how we manage to ignore them;
2. Though there are more white people than black people, black people suffer higher poverty rates than white people, while Hispanics have higher poverty rates than blacks;
3. The "model minority" myth tends to blind us all to the fact that Asians are, as a group, significantly poorer than whites, though not as poor as blacks or Hispanics.

This sort of information is very important, but it can't tell you very much in the absence of an analysis of the origins of inequality in a capitalist society and the relationship between racism and free markets. Therefore, our second task is to explore modern economic theory in order to present a coherent analytical scheme that can tie the facts together into a meaningful portrait of the link between color and economic well-being in America. This will require us to dip into pieces of economic analysis (though without the mathematics, cloudy jargon and bad prose that all too frequently get in the way of broad economic literacy) in order to benefit from the considerable insights of economists in these matters. One of the rewards of these brief excursions into economic thinking will be that we can learn how not to be fooled by economists, and especially by popular writers who falsely (but profitably) pose as social thinkers whose writing has such a terrible effect on public discussions on race. The general public is eager for simple, clear answers to difficult social dilemmas like the apparent link between race and poverty just noted above. Since America is a capitalist country, a large demand for answers to pressing social problems, backed up by significant amounts of consumer spending on popular books, encourages writers of even doubtful intellectual or moral legitimacy to try their hand at crafting simple answers to complex questions, for a price, even if the problems under review have no simple answers, or maybe no answers at all. Two particularly popular current approaches to the problem of racial inequality in modern times have filled this void, motivated by the possibility of profit. The first notion is that black people are an intellectually inferior subspecies that is short of brain power for biological reasons. This rather old, and frankly embarrassingly shallow explanation has recently been peddled by Charles Murray and the late Richard Herrnstein in their notorious tome *The Bell Curve*, which is sure to become known among future generations as a landmark contribution to American racist literature. The second offering in the simple-but-neat explanation of racial inequality, and especially black poverty, is Dinesh D'Souza's long and cheeky book *The End of Racism*, which manages to snarl at black people as the worthless spawn of a morally and intellectually defective "culture," while piously insisting that the author is an objective, colorblind truth sayer whose love of America requires straight talk about THOSE people.

Economic analysis is the perfect tool for breaking these fables apart, thereby exposing the logical flaws and leaps into the lunar side of some right-wing racist subculture that hold these "arguments" together. These books should be deep embarrassments to their publisher (though the "ka-ching" of the cash register can apparently assuage guilt over peddling this sort of antiblack filth) and are further proof that there is not much relationship between the intellectual merits of an argument and its popularity. Sadly, we must consider the arguments of these volumes in some detail because one or another variant of each is popular with the public, the politicians, and the media.

Simple-minded arguments about race and inequality crowd out more complex analyses, thereby relieving the public of the need to think deeply about hard things, or worse, face up to the possibility that the social system we cherish is basically unfair to poor people and black people in ways that cannot be wished away or painlessly changed. Yet, complex arguments are usually rather boring to attend to, with the result that they rarely get much of a hearing even if they are usually right. One of our primary tasks is to replace racist screeds like *The Bell Curve* and *The End of Racism* with sound economic arguments that are relatively simple to understand and yet serious enough to encompass divergent points of view. However, the reader should know that this essay will not end with easy or happy prescriptions about how black people are the saintly victims of evil white people in bad capitalist America. Instead, we will see why the capitalist rules of the game in

| 5 |

America have necessarily compounded the suffering of so many blacks while offering other blacks more opportunities than they have ever had.

This is not an encyclopedic review of economists' writings about race. A number of journal articles, textbooks, and treatises give a good account of the diversity of perspectives among economists on these matters. Instead, this book draws on the work of economists and other social thinkers to provide a coherent and intellectually respectable account of the relationship between color and economic well-being to an intelligent, curious, but perhaps economically naive reader. Our goal is to paint an intellectually defensible—and decidedly anticonservative— picture of the complicated ties between race and economic well-being in late twentieth-century America. Very little of the substance of the essay will be new to economists (though the mathematical models of the long-term consequences of racial discrimination for permanent inequality across color lines after apartheid will be interesting to theoretically minded readers who doubt some of the arguments made in chapter 2). Still, I hope that the analysis will command some respect and assent from other economists, though I know it will make some people very angry. Nonetheless, the primary audience for this book is the confused man or woman who still thinks that reason and argument can help us escape the dangerous place we seem to have drifted into before we declare war on each other.

Conservative and Anti-conservative

The term "anti-conservative" calls for some explanation, in part because of the considerable ambiguity and elasticity of the word "conservative" in American political discourse. The use of the term "conservative," without modifiers, refers to a set of commitments to private property, free markets, minimal state regulation in economic affairs, and a skeptical outlook about the legitimacy and desirability of public action to offset the economic inequalities associated with free markets, social custom, or a history of racial hostility and abuse. This stance, which is most succinctly described in Milton Friedman's classic statement of libertarian capitalist principles in *Capitalism and Freedom*, is deeply suspicious of the idea of social justice, in part because of doubts about the very idea of "equality" as well as worries about the possibility that the centralization of power in the name of collective action to promote fairness and social decency must result in the diminution or even destruction of individual liberty. This stance has an old and venerable history dating back at least to the writings of John Stuart Mill whose *On Liberty* and *Principles of Political Economy* are landmark contributions to political and moral philosophy as well as economics. These principles are called "conservative" here only because Americans refer to them as such, even though logic and history would eschew such intellectual and verbal sloppiness.

In turn, this book is anti-conservative in the narrow sense that it is inspired by a commitment to search for viable approaches to promote economic and social equality in the context of a market economy. Specifically, an underlying theme of the book, which is fully explored in the last chapter, is that conservative economic and social policy in the United States has had a destructive effect on the economic well-being of blacks, particularly poor blacks, precisely because its commitment to free market capitalism in an American context necessarily accepts the tendency for markets to cater to the segregationist demands of the white majority. Further, conservative policy has partially dismantled the welfare state at a time of rapid economic change that has left large numbers of low-income people across the color spectrum, but especially black people, with little hope of achieving a middle-class life in a technology-driven world. The net result of conservative approaches has been the emergence of a new color class system on the basis of free market principles that locks millions of black people into a cycle of poverty, violence, and despair. This system works because the white suburban majority uses its buying power to separate itself from blacks, and its voting power to restrict the extent to which government policy can be used to promote genuine equal opportunity and poverty relief, particularly in matters of education, health care, housing, and income support for the poor. Conservative free market visions *must* ratify this outcome so long as lightly regulated capitalism is seen as the best guarantee of economic progress.

It is important for the reader to remember that there is nothing inherently racist about conservative principles, despite the tendency for contemporary political argument to conflate race hatred and pro-market economics. Classical liberals or "conservatives" value individual liberty above all else. Private property and free markets are valuable for classical liberals because these institutions secure maximum individual autonomy from all other institutions that might seek to restrict freedom of thought and action. The only legitimate infringements on individual liberty for classical liberals are those regulations and institutions to protect the nation's boundaries by an adequate national defense and the protection of private property (including opposition to slavery) through a stable system of law, including police and courts. Classical liberals view all other projects of government with suspicion (which does not mean that these projects—schools, health care, and even redistribution—are automatically wrong by classical liberal lights) to the extent that they require collective action that centralizes power in the hands of the State. John Gray's summary of classical liberal thinking in his small but powerful volume, *Liberalism*, demonstrates that

> The early classical liberals were concerned primarily, almost exclusively, with coercive or prescriptive governmental involvement in the economy. They attacked tariffs and regulations which imposed legal constraints on economic activity, and for the most part they were content if such constraints were removed. They did *not*, in other words, demand a complete withdrawal of government from economic life. This is not an inconsistent position once it is understood that government activity may take coercive or non-coercive forms. . . . A government activity may be non-authoritative, and so permissible, if—as with governmental support for scientific research—it imposes no coercive burdens on private initiatives in the areas in which it operates. . . . On this interpretation of laissez faire, governmental activity may encompass any manner of service functions—even including a welfare state—provided these functions be conducted in a non-coercive fashion.[1]

This should make it clear that conservatives must be fierce opponents of any form of organized racism, especially apartheid, but also forms of racial hierarchy and domination that involve the subordination of individuals to group action or group identity.

The tendency for some Americans to equate "conservative" with "racist" comes from two sources. First, many people who fervently believe in the idea of race and racial hierarchy also believe in pieces of the classical liberal agenda, though there is nothing within classical liberal thought to support the idea that race or color or religion should matter in our dealings with each other. Hence, many men and women who oppose government initiatives to promote equality on "conservative" grounds are frequently also racists. This conflation is unfortunate, in part because it limits our political imaginations and undermines the possibility of clear political thought. We would do better to call people who simultaneously hold racist and classical liberal views racist-conservatives or white nationalist conservatives, or simply racist hypocrites.

Second, many nonracist-conservatives are willing to live in a society with wide disparities in income, wealth, and life chances across class and color lines. This means that many conservatives are also willing to accommodate themselves to the primary legacy of historical racism in the United States—systematically unequal life chances and living standards between blacks and Native Americans on the one side and whites on the other. There is no good reason for referring to conservatives with a high tolerance for economic and social inequality as racists, no matter how obnoxious or vicious one might find their preferences to be. Many of us on the Left have a bad habit of lumping all conservatives together, thereby obscuring important distinctions between these people. This failure to make distinctions is, in its own way, a failure of nerve precisely because it reflects a refusal to see the world as a complex place which defies simple categories.

Finally, the reader should know that the anti-conservative stance of the author does not mean that arguments by serious conservative economists, philosophers, sociologists, and legal scholars on race in American life are automatically exempted from consideration. Indeed, one of the purposes of this book is to undermine simple-minded ideological posturing that gets in the way of serious thinking about race and economics.

A Note on the Vocabulary of Color

One more point about language is in order. Recent immigration from Asia and Latin America has altered the link between color and prosperity in America. America has never been a two-toned society, despite the obsessive talk about the "crisis in black and white." One of the most important developments in American life has been the gradual emergence of a vast new body of knowledge created by scholars, writers, and artists that explores the ways that the struggles of Asian, Latino, and Native American men and women have molded the politics and culture of the United States. Historians, sociologists, legal scholars, literary critics, and scholars in other disciplines are writing men and women of Asian and Hispanic descent into the nation's history and public culture, thereby overthrowing the shameful but all too comfortable black/white hegemony over racial discourse. American science, arts and letters, music, and cinema as well as cuisine are being transformed by writers, artists, scientists, musicians, filmmakers, and chefs whose work is inspired by sensibilities whose insights and accents are from different shores that cannot be traced to the sick and sad dance in black and white that has warped our public culture and private dealings. These unfamiliar voices among intellectuals and artists pose difficult challenges for citizens and politicians all too ready to slip into the comfortable grooves of racial animosity that, curiously, offer an odd sort of security by providing a predictable structure to conventional thinking about color in America.

Latino and Asian immigration have, in different ways, shown the tacit agreement between blacks and whites about the contours of racial dialogue and the substance of racial controversy to be a fraud. For instance, the term "Latino" hides a powerful truth: Latinos are a multiracial, multi-ethnic, mixed race "group" that is largely defined by language, not color or culture. The attempt to collapse Mexican, Cuban, Dominican, Puerto Rican, Brazilian, Nicaraguan, and Panamanian immigrants and their children into a single category is ridiculous. Similarly, the term "Asian" is a bureaucratic dodge that barely improves on the racist label "Oriental" that Americans have long used to lump together people as diverse—and in many ways bitterly opposed—as Chinese, Japanese, Koreans, Filipinos, Thai, and Vietnamese. This labeling process is surely another example of the ways in which black/white conflict has tried to squeeze the experience of others into familiar and ill-suited grooves. The labels "black" or "African American" are part of the residue of an especially brutal form of slavery that intentionally wiped away ethnicity and language in order to reduce the diverse groups of people who formed the human cargo of the trans-Atlantic slave trade to a human mass defined solely by their color, just as "white" has been used to signify a human state consistent with freedom, selfhood, and human possibility.

The gradual emergence of "Latinos" and "Asians" as visible and assertive minority groups will force Americans to face a basic fact about "race" and "racial" conflict: the discriminatory behavior of the white majority toward "Others" defines the nature of majority-minority strife. In time, the traditional, color-based conflict pioneered by whites and blacks, with its obsessive concern for racial purity in private and intimate life, will probably merge with a "creole" form of racialism that is common throughout the Caribbean and Latin America. In this new, "multicultural" America, the link between color and well-being will be reflected in the racial customs and sexual taboos of the white majority about love and marriage across the color line. Dark skin and poverty will remain linked because families are formed on the basis of class as well as color. Nonetheless, the superficial changes in the particular hues arranged in the American color wheel, brought on perhaps by the emergence of a "mixed race" middle class, will only testify to the flexibility of the "racial" system to absorb new peoples and ideas while maintaining the connection between color and well-being.

This work focuses on the complicated and bitter relationship between blacks and whites in the last years of the twentieth century. However, this focus on blacks, and to a lesser extent Latinos, is not meant to suggest that black economic deprivation vis-à-vis whites is the only form of racial inequality in this country. The central thesis of this book is that despised racial minorities, in this case blacks and Latinos, find themselves in a new kind of racial system where the free market conspires with populism to create powerful barriers to minority economic and social development. This new type of racial system, which is the successor to the old apartheid system, has emerged in response to the demands of an economically powerful racial majority—whites—for social distance from blacks and Latinos in a modern, technology-driven world economy. However, the particular racial identities of the powerful and weak social groups is not very important, except, of course, to the men and women who are suffering in these new circumstances. What matters is that the United States is in the midst of a momentous social change where a color-coded class system is emerging without the help of formal apartheid, on the basis of the capitalist rules of the economic game. Please do not put too much stock in the vocabulary of color used in this work. Anyone, including the white poor, who can be designated as Other, and whose social identity and life chances can be shaped by the whims and petty hatreds of others, is a victim of the new order.

This book was born in the aftermath of the first round in a series of fights between myself and black fascists (who have the good sense to call themselves "afro-centrists") at Wellesley College in 1992. *The Political Economy of Hope and Fear* speaks to the anger and frustration that black people, especially young black people, feel in the face of assaults against affirmative action which they perceive as the nation's abandonment of racial equality as a worthy objective. I have found that placing the dilemmas and miseries that blacks face in a larger economic context kills off the romance of nationalism among us, replacing the twisted utopianism of black fascism with a realistic, and deeply sad, view of the economic and social barriers to the well-being of black Americans. The book offers an alternative to black nationalist hate-mongering by connecting the revived racism of conservative America to the gales of economic change that are blowing throughout the world.

Three remarkable young women from Wellesley College provided superb research assistance in various stages of this study. Indrani Muhkerjee worked on the first, awful drafts of this volume. Poor Indrani worked cheerfully as I tried out theme after theme before finally settling on the risky strategy of a work for noneconomists on race and modern capitalism in America. Indrani was always willing to challenge my interpretations of arguments and data, thereby making me think more clearly about what I was trying to say. She reminded me that I was not writing this book for economists or specialists, but for intelligent readers who know little economics but who are desperate to learn about the unhappy relationship between blacks and capitalism in America.

Lilian Quah helped me unearth loads of data, run lots of regressions, and simulated my ridiculously complex (though very helpful) mathematical models that were subsequently eliminated from this volume (instead making their way into another, rather technical book for economists who care about theory and race). Lilian was also a stickler for prose style, ready with a sharp quip if my writing slipped into that dreadful, sludgy style that economists slip into from time to time.

Zoe Robbins worked on later versions of the book, helping me refine my analysis in various ways and demanding that I stay true to leftist principles. It is hard for a middle-aged black man to remain upbeat about racial matters when white nationalists and market conservatives form an alliance to gain control of Congress, thereby sacrificing the well-being of blacks in the process. Zoe, from Sedgwick, Maine, reminded me that she comes from a place where poor whites have been neglected and wounded and abused by those in power. I have always tried to remember that race is not only a base superstition but also an illusion that can trap the citizen, politician, and scholar alike.

This book was completed during my sabbatical from Wellesley during the 1997–1998 academic year. I had the good fortune to work as a fellow at the Institute on Race and Social Division at Boston University, under the directorship of Glenn Loury. Loury is one of those rare intellectuals in American life who want to get to the root of social problems, without worrying too much about who is offended or why. I had the chance to spend ten months fighting with Loury debating various aspects of my thinking on race and economics that were gradually incorporated into the manuscript. Alas, I fear that Loury will not like this book much, in part because I am implacably angry about the misery that American conservatives (of all political parties) have visited on black people over the past two decades but also because of honest disagreements over matters of economic theory and policy. Loury is so smart that one must be either bold or foolish to disagree with him in public. Time will tell.

Two more acknowledgments. My greatest teacher is my son. Inflexible people bound by rigid notions of age and hierarchy will find this notion strange. Too bad for them: Isaiah Andrews is a miraculous being whose only problem is that more people do not know him.

Kanwal Singh is equally marvelous. Kanwal came into my life at a most fortunate time. Physicists are surely wonderful people, but so few of them care passionately about life, love, literature, and freedom the way she does. The usual practice of authors is to absolve their soul mates of responsibility for their errors. I will follow this tradition, though I am sure that she would have spotted my mistakes, and inspired correction immediately, had I completed the manuscript in time.

ONE

The Color of Prosperity

*A Few Facts about Black Economic Well-
Being in America*

Color and Well-Being in America

Race in America is a complicated and embarrassing riddle. Americans rightly tell themselves that their allegiance to the values of fairness, hard work, responsibility, and individual liberty has created a generally free and rich society. Yet, economic well-being is linked to race in this country, so much so that we cannot really lump all Americans together when comparing them to citizens of other nations. It is certainly true that, on average, all Americans, no matter their color, are rich compared to most other people in the world. Though the American people can no longer boast that they enjoy the world's highest standard of living, it is still true that, as the United Nations tells us in its latest report on human development, Americans are still among the more prosperous people in the world.[1]

The United Nations Human Development Report, a yearly analysis of the economic and social well-being of the citizens of its member states, notes that the level of income per person in the US in 1994 (the latest year that data are available for cross-national comparisons) was $16,555.[2] However, the US Census Bureau reports that the level of income per person for Asians, blacks, Hispanics, and whites in 1994 was as shown in Table 1.1. If we were to treat each of the above-listed "racial" groups as a separate subnational group (a dubious procedure in the case of Asians and Latinos but possibly less so in the case of blacks for reasons we will explore shortly) and then try to place each group within the UN's listing of per person income figures for all

Table 1.1 Income per Person by Race in the
US in 1994[3]

Group	Income per Person	Ratio to US Average
US Average	$16,555	1.00
Asians	16,902	1.02
Blacks	10,650	0.643
Hispanics	9,435	0.569
Whites	17,611	1.06

member states in 1994, we would find that white Americans have the highest level of income per person in the world, closely followed by Asian Americans. By contrast, the level of income per person for black Americans in 1994 was roughly equivalent to that of the average New Zealander (whose income was 63.8% of the US level in 1994), while Hispanics had a level of income per person roughly equivalent to that of the average Spaniard (54.2%).[4]

Many will object to this comparison of the average income of citizens in each UN member state to the average income of Americans in four of the five "official" racial categories used by the US Census Bureau, because it falsely separates Americans into "racially" defined subnations. This procedure suggests that Americans live in largely distinct racial enclaves that can be equated with distinct governmental units. There is little doubt that this objection makes sense for whites, Asians, and to a certain extent Hispanics. Studies of racial segregation and isolation clearly show that Asian Americans and Hispanic Americans face relatively low degrees of racial segregation when compared to blacks, who still tend to be clustered together no matter their levels of family income or education. Douglass Massey and Nancy Denton's comprehensive study of the impact of residential segregation on the well-being of black Americans, *American Apartheid*, shows that blacks still face high degrees of residential segregation despite the considerable improvement in black access to housing and housing finance brought about by anti-discrimination legislation and fair housing policies. One of the most depressing, and most surprising, aspects of American residential segregation is the extent to which social class has little effect on the degree of black residential isolation. Statistical analyses of the 1980 Census and later data show that high-income blacks in major metropolitan areas experience similar degrees of residential segregation as low-income blacks.[5] Though a growing proportion of blacks are moving into the suburbs (reflecting the growth of the black middle class), these suburban areas tend to be black enclaves that are, in many cases, poor outlying suburban districts.[6] The American commitment to local government provision and financing of many health, welfare, educational, and public safety services means that residential segregation also leads to the distribution of important public resources by race, particularly for blacks. Hence, treating black Americans as a distinct subnational group is consistent with the facts about the residential segregation of blacks.

There is a tendency for American discussions of racial inequality to forget about the fact that most Americans are quite rich, so the above comparison should help us put American racial inequalities into perspective. Blacks and Latinos rightly resent and object to economic and social conditions that leave them with smaller incomes and fewer life chances than their white and Asian countrymen. Still, we must remember that New Zealand and Spain are rich countries by any reckoning.

Yet, a central concern about the knot between race and economic well-being in America is that black people remain poorer than white people, despite the end of the old apartheid system in the South and the considerable retreat of the culture of Negrophobia among whites everywhere. Figure 1.1(a) shows family poverty rates for blacks and whites between 1967 and 1996, while Figure 1.1(b) shows the ratio between black and white family poverty rates over the same period. Figure 1.1(a) illustrates the well-known fact that black poverty rates are much higher than white poverty rates. However, Figure 1.1(b) shows that the ratio of black to white family poverty rates has been declining over time. Indeed, one of the most basic, and lamentable, facts about the American economy is that black unemployment rates are much more sensitive to swings in economic activity than are white unemployment rates. When economic times are good, black unemployment rates come down far faster than white unemployment rates, though black unemployment rates are also much higher than white unemployment rates in times of recession. However, when economic times are bad, black unemployment rates rise far faster than white unemployment rates. Nonetheless, Figure 1.1(b) presents a slightly hopeful picture:

Figure 1.1(a): Percentage of Black and White Families in Poverty:
1967–1996

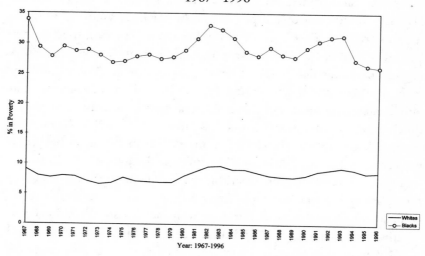

Figure 1.1(b): Ratio of Black to White Family Poverty Rates:
1967–1996

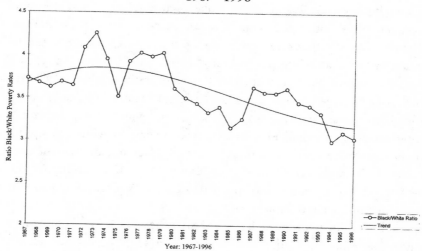

black family poverty is gradually (though all too slowly) falling relative to white family poverty.

A careful look at Figure 1.1(b) may lead the reader to ask an obvious question: why is there so much hand wringing about black poverty when the data suggest that black people are slowly (admittedly too slowly) becoming less poor relative to whites? The decline in white family poverty rates from over 16% to a little over 10%, or the drop in poverty rates for black families from over 35% to a little over 28% in thirty years is a remarkable achievement that should be *celebrated* rather than disparaged. While there is much to be done about poverty in America, there is little reason for pretending that things are as bad as they've ever been, or worse, pretending that the liberal program of reducing poverty was a gigantic waste of money, time, and effort.

Nevertheless, the apparent decline in black and white family poverty rates noted above is a bit misleading. Figure 1.1(a) tells us that a smaller percentage of both black and white families are poor in the 1990s than in the 1960s, while Figure 1.1(b) says that blacks are, when compared to whites, relatively less poor in the 1990s than they were in the 1960s. However, the poor in general, and the black poor in particular, are no better off now than they were in the 1960s. Even worse, poor people are much worse off relative to middle- and upper-class Americans in the 1990s than in the 1960s.

One of the best ways to understand what is happening to the distribution of economic well-being of Americans across class and color lines is to break the population up into different income groups and study what happens to each group over time. Imagine that we could arrange all American families along a spectrum from the lowest to the highest level of family income each year. We might then divide the population of families into five equal size groups, called quintiles by statisticians (it's an ugly but useful name) and compute the average income within each group. For example, if there were one hundred families in the population, then each quintile group would consist of twenty families. Note that since we have arranged these families from the poorest to the richest, we can see that the average level of family income in the first group of twenty families, here called the first quintile, is lower than the average income of families in the second quintile, and so on up to the fifth quintile.

Tables 1.2(a) through 1.2(c) show average family income in each quintile for selected years from 1967 through 1996 for whites, blacks, and Hispanics adjusted for inflation (in 1996 dollars). Table 1.2(a) shows that the inflation-adjusted incomes of poor and working-class white families in the first and second quintiles rose significantly between 1967 and 1980, only to stagnate thereafter. Indeed, the incomes of the poorest white families in the first quintile actually fell a small bit (by 4.6%) between 1980 and 1996. By contrast, the incomes of middle- and high-income whites have risen appreciably since the 1960s, with especially dramatic increases in family income in the fourth and fifth quintiles in the 1980s.

Tables 1.2(b) and 1.2(c) present a roughly similar picture of growing inequality for blacks and Hispanics, respectively, with two important differences. First, both black and Latino families in the first quintile experienced large absolute declines in their incomes between 1980 and 1996 in contrast to the rather small decline in the incomes of poor white families. While the poor may have gotten poorer in America over the past two decades, it is clear that the black and Latino poor have suffered far more than the white poor. Second, these data indicate that Latino families experienced falling incomes across a far wider class spectrum than either blacks or whites. Only Latino families in the fifth quintile enjoy higher, inflation-adjusted incomes in the mid-1990s than in 1980, while middle- and upper-income black and white families have enjoyed growing incomes over the same period. We will show shortly why Latino family incomes have lagged behind both black and white family incomes over this period, including a brief review of the role of documented and undocumented immigration in determining the economic well-being of Latino families. However, our brief look at the evidence implies that the decline in poverty among blacks and Hispanics has been accompanied by both an increase in the severity of poverty for those who remain poor and growing inequality between the rich and poor within and between racial groups.

The decline in average incomes for first-quintile families is due to important changes in the American job market and in the structure of American families. First, there has been a significant increase over the past two decades in the number of families headed by women, regardless of race. Table 1.3 presents the percentage of white, black, and

Table 1.2(a) Quintile Family Income Averages. Whites, for Selected Years

Year	1st (Lowest)	2nd	3rd (Middle)	4th	5th (Highest)
1967	$11,657	$25,277	$35,369	$46,962	$82,599
1970	12,746	27,326	38,564	51,507	88,384
1980	13,732	28,587	41,972	57,457	96,140
1990	13,632	29,696	44,430	63,040	116,536
1995	13,241	28,781	44,011	63,483	126,379
1996	13,097	29,059	44,784	64,272	129,773

Table 1.2(b) Quintile Family Income Averages. Blacks, for Selected Years

Year	1st (Lowest)	2nd	3rd (Middle)	4th	5th (Highest)
1967	$6,047	$13,170	$19,840	$29,214	$49,116
1970	6,489	14,964	23,778	35,255	60,902
1980	6,467	14,512	24,237	38,361	67,120
1990	5,438	14,198	25,798	41,811	78,174
1995	5,687	15,298	26,689	42,226	85,176
1996	5,651	15,180	26,594	42,621	84,627

Table 1.2(c) Quintile Family Income Averages. Hispanics, for Selected Years

Year	1st (Lowest)	2nd	3rd (Middle)	4th	5th (Highest)
1967	(NA)	(NA)	(NA)	(NA)	(NA)
1970	(NA)	(NA)	(NA)	(NA)	(NA)
1980	$8,303	$18,012	$28,112	$41,412	$72,157
1990	7,568	17,192	28,145	42,622	80,443
1995	6,881	15,959	25,291	39,060	80,900
1996	7,139	16,481	26,215	40,814	87,309

Hispanic families that are headed by women for selected years between 1980 and 1997. Women heading these families also tend to be younger than the heads of single male and two-parent families and to have lower levels of educational attainment and lower wages than their single male or married male counterparts, with the result that families headed by single women tend to be poorer than two-parent families. In addition, the percentage of young male high school graduates whose incomes are below the income threshold that defines poverty for a family of four has risen steadily since the early 1970s across the color spectrum. Table 1.4

| 21 |

Table 1.3 Percentage of White, Black, and
Hispanic Families with Own Children under 18
Headed by Women, 1980–1997

Year	Whites	Blacks	Hispanics
1980	15.1%	48.7%	24.0%
1985	17.8%	56.7%	28.2%
1990	18.8%	56.2%	29.3%
1995	20.9%	58.2%	31.0%
1997	21.1%	57.5%	30.8%

Source: US Census Bureau, Table FM-2, All Parent/Child
Situations: By Type, Race, and Hispanic Origin

Table 1.4 Percentage of Men Aged 25–34 with
Annual Earnings Below the Poverty Line for a
Family of Four

Year	White	Hispanic	Black
1949	33.9%	49.9%	66.1%
1969	8.6%	15.6%	19.9%
1991	29.5%	47.5%	52.5%

Source: Danziger and Gottschalk (1995), pp. 85–86

shows the percentage of white, black, and Hispanic men between the ages of 25 and 34 whose incomes fell below the poverty line for a family of four in 1949, 1969, and 1991. While increased labor force participation for women of all races offset the lower male wages on family income after the early 1970s, the general rise in divorce rates across the income spectrum puts poor families at greater risk of declining incomes.

The growth of wage inequality across color and ethnic lines also reflects an underlying shift in the fortunes of skilled and unskilled workers since the late 1960s. Highly educated workers, particularly workers with a college education, have seen their wages rise substantially. There was a time, particularly from the mid-1970s through the early 1980s, when the economic benefits of higher education were low enough that many men and women chose against continuing their education past high school.[7] The rise in the relative wages of skilled workers over the whole post–World War II period, and particularly since 1980, has been driven by the rapid growth in the demand for skilled labor (relative to the supply of skilled labor), despite the fact that the proportion of college-educated workers in the labor force has increased substantially over the same period.[8] This rise in the demand for skilled workers is primarily the result of changes in technology that favor educated workers over their modestly educated counterparts. One consequence of the relative decline in demand for unskilled labor is that families headed by women have lost ground, despite the fact that a slightly larger fraction of these women have been working.[9]

While some analysts claim that the increased openness of the American economy to international trade has had a large negative impact on unskilled workers, most economists doubt that trade can account for more than a small part of growing wage inequality for two reasons. First, the rapid growth in the demand for skilled labor (relative to unskilled workers) predates the increasing importance of international trade in recent years. Second, the rise in the demand for skilled labor has been occurring in all industries rather than being restricted to sectors where trade is especially important. Indeed, there is some evidence that the growth in the demand for skilled workers has accelerated in the 1980s and 1990s, thereby leading to faster increases in the wages of skilled workers relative to unskilled workers.[10] These changes in technology, which we consider in greater detail in chapter 3, have led to a decline in the job prospects and wages of modestly educated workers, who are disproportionately black and Latino. Finally, the increase in the supply of unskilled workers as a result of immigration has led to a rise in the pool of unskilled workers at a time when the demand for these workers is flagging.[11]

It is important to note that the stalled incomes of poor and working-class families does not necessarily mean that their absolute living standards are completely stagnant. The ongoing march of technology, combined with the genius of American consumer capitalism, has certainly led to the creation of cheap, high-quality goods—from color televisions and microwaves through dishwashers and cars to computers—that are within the reach of working and middle-income families. Indeed, one of the triumphs of American capitalism is precisely its capacity to bring an ever wider array of goods and services into the lives of millions of people with modest educations and incomes, thereby lending a democratic counterweight to the rhythms of free markets which generate inequality. Nonetheless, we must face the fact that measured poverty is deepening for poor people of color at the same time that the gap between the rich and the poor is growing within racial groups.

These trends go a long way toward explaining the trends in family income noted above. Families in the lower quintiles tend to be supported by poorly educated married adults or by single women in declining labor markets and occupations, while upper-middle- and upper-income families in the fourth and fifth quintiles are supported by well-educated workers in growing sectors of the economy. Further, poor black families tend to be supported by modestly schooled adults concentrated in occupations that have been adversely affected by technology, trade, and immigration. However, the improving prospects of black middle- and upper-class families discussed earlier is in part due to blacks' increased access to high-quality schooling that followed the end of apartheid as well as a result of affirmative action in employment and college admissions. Figures 1.2(a) and 1.2(b) show the change in the percentage of black and white adults over the age of 25 who have completed at least four years of college between 1967 and 1996 and the ratio of the fraction of whites who have achieved advanced education relative to the ratio for similarly trained blacks, respectively. This ratio, hereafter referred to as the college-knowledge gap, is a rough measure of the extent to which advanced schooling is more widely diffused across the white adult population than the black. Figure 1.2(a) shows that the fraction of adults who have completed college between 1967 and 1996 has risen greatly for blacks and whites alike, while Figure 1.2(b) shows that blacks are gradually closing the college-knowledge gap vis-à-vis whites (where the smooth line is a type of trend line).[12] These graphs tell us that blacks have managed to break into high wage employment by acquiring technical knowledge and skills in ever greater numbers. Note that the sharp decline in the knowledge gap between blacks and whites slowed a bit in the mid- to late 1980s, which is a cause for concern, but not for great despair. Indeed, the growth of a college-educated black middle class means that blacks now have a permanent, though still disproportionately small place in the nation's most advanced economic and intellectual spheres.

Though blacks are on average still far poorer than whites, the growth of a prosperous black middle class is one of the great social advance-

Figure 1.2(a): Percentage of Whites and Blacks over 25 with Four or More Years of Higher Education

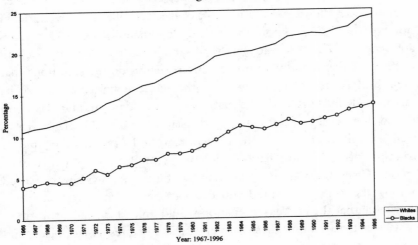

Figure 1.2(b): Ratio of White to Black Percentage of Adults over 25 with Four or More Years of Higher Education

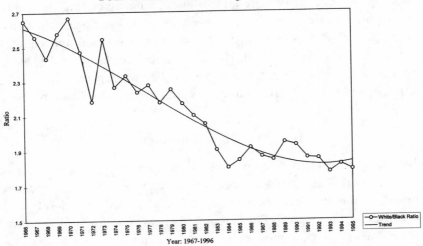

ments in the nation's history. The gradual decline in black poverty also means that black people are more prosperous than they have ever been in America: if slightly more than 25% of black families are now mired in poverty, we must also note that slightly less than *75%* of black families are *not* poor. This is fabulous news for an abused people who have had to bear their suffering with dignity and patience, on the slim hope that their protests might one day force the white majority to realize its racism and finally relent. The existence of this dark middle class, and the swelling ranks of the Latino and Asian American middle classes as well, is brilliant testimony to the courage and passion of people to triumph over the humiliation, violence, and deep scars inflicted by racism. Given the abundant talent and ambition that has always existed among the ranks of colored and despised peoples in America, it was inevitable that the end of segregation would unleash a brilliant storm of creative activity among these former restricted castes. Asian, black, and Latino artists, musicians, writers, actors, film-makers, scholars, and teachers are completely reshaping the intellectual landscape of this nation, thereby changing America's understanding of itself and creating, perhaps for the first time, a genuinely democratic American culture. The fabulous possibilities that have opened up for young people of color in business and the professions, with or without affirmative action, will lead, hopefully, to the gradual incorporation of people of color into the highest councils of state and business, thereby ending the white monopoly on private and public power. In time, and despite the fierce resistance of white supremacists in conservative political and cultural circles, America will eventually see itself and be seen by the world as an amazing "colored" country that blends the children of Africa, Asia, Europe, and Latin America into a spicy, beautiful, and brilliant people.

Two Black Americas

But the path toward a democratic and integrated colored America is full of dangers and pitfalls, especially the danger of social meltdown posed by the fact that color and well-being are still too tightly tied together in this country. For better or for worse, the minority middle classes are as much a product of liberal social policy as they are the product of the labors and ambitions of formerly captive people making good in a time of new freedom. The slow death of segregation was accomplished over the objections of a substantial minority of white Americans whose privileges and prerogatives as members of the "master race" were sacrificed to the cause of racial equality. While liberals did manage to mortally wound the old racial regime by passing anti-discrimination laws and voting rights acts, they could not force reluctant and resentful whites to accept their "darker" neighbors as equals. The habits of white superiority—and particularly the belief in black inferiority, criminality, and immorality—have proven to be quite resilient and tenacious, making customary discrimination a powerful force in business and politics to this day.

The problem that poor black people face is that they live in an economic world that has little use for their labor and in a country whose commitment to free markets includes a high tolerance for economic inequality. These people have become part of the American economic underclass because their lack of skills or high-quality schooling has rendered them largely unemployable in the legal economy. Orlando Patterson, one of America's premier intellectuals and social analysts, has observed that our tendency to talk about the "black" underclass is profoundly misleading because it shifts our attention away from important problems of unemployment and social class that are simply beyond race.[13] America's history of racial discrimination and racial oppression is certainly the ultimate reason that blacks are poorer, sicker, and less learned than whites (though there are a number of proponents of biological and cultural theories of social inequality who would dispute this claim). Yet, it is hard to claim that poor black people are in bad shape because of widespread anti-black discrimination.

One of the problems with the term "underclass" is that it has become associated with the idea of an alien population whose values, beliefs, and behavior are so perverse and destructive as to constitute a different order of humanity. This projection of "otherness" onto the American underclass prevents many of us from noticing that these men and women are suffering from chronic unemployment and deep poverty, frequently in urban or rural areas that experience high rates of crime and drug abuse. Children in these areas experience high rates of educational failure; school truancy is commonplace, and high school dropout rates are high. Rates of childbearing among teenagers and unmarried poor adult women are very high while marriage rates are low. Many of the places where poor people are forced to live are dirty and dangerous, despite the best efforts of residents of these areas to improve their living conditions. Journalistic descriptions of poor people in high-poverty urban neighborhoods focus on extreme instances of crime and violence, or indolence, cruelty, or sloth in order to capture the attention of the suburban reading public.

Once the lurid fantasy of an evil and alien underclass is put aside in favor of economic analysis, we see that the underclass is just a population of chronically unemployed people who cannot escape conditions of low wages and joblessness and whose children are all too likely to inherit their poverty. The shift in the composition of jobs toward technical and highly educated workers means that badly schooled people face bleak job prospects, without much ability to move from weak to more prosperous sectors of the labor market. In turn, chronic unemployment undermines family relationships and community ties by wrecking adult self-esteem, fostering dependence on others, discouraging initiative, and promoting hopelessness.[14] Low wages means that poor people cannot afford important resources for themselves or their children, including decent-quality housing, schooling, health care, or education that can break the cycle of poverty and dependency. There is little mystery why neighborhoods with high concentrations of poor and unemployed people tend to be places with high crime rates, low levels of academic achievement, high rates of divorce, and high rates of teenage childbearing. Poor neighborhoods and regions can become sites of continuing failure, and therefore sites of social dysfunction, because the disappearance of essential sustaining rituals and activities—especially regular work and the responsibilities and discipline that go with it—leave adults and children prey to boredom, depression, anger, cruelty, and all the problems that come with these emotions.

The other black America, the nonpoor majority, faces a very different set of challenges. Working-class black people, those with modest educational attainments who drive trucks, taxis, and buses, deliver the mail, cook food, clean offices, assemble autos, pour steel, type memos, or care for other people's children, are proud but insecure people. The Civil Rights movement opened up opportunities for these people, from the late 1960s onward, at just the time the American economy was undergoing radical structure change. So many working-class blacks are in occupations that offer limited options for advancement or that are open to potential competition from immigrant labor. Other working-class blacks are at the mercy of new technologies that require better educated workers. The collapse in the real wages of most American workers during the 1980s and early 1990s, and especially low-wage black workers, has sharply curtailed the blue-collar road to the middle class for these workers, even if it has not ejected them from the economy altogether.

The other part of nonpoor black America, black college educated workers, are in an odd social position. On the one hand, this group of workers is the most economically secure group of black people in American history. Their college training gives them access to stable jobs and higher wages than blacks have ever had. Even though affirmative action is likely to be ended in favor of some dubious notion of "colorblind" merit in a racially divided country, college-educated blacks will be in a position to compete for good schools and good jobs to the extent that anti-discrimination laws are rigorously enforced and that middle-class blacks are able to improve their ability to earn high scores on standardized tests. Yet, middle-class black people are being assailed and insulted for doing poorly on standardized tests. Indeed, many conservatives claim that poor black performance on these tests means that blacks are stupid, or at best, that blacks have not "earned" the right to attend elite universities or gain access to lucrative professions because they have failed to demonstrate the appropriate degree of "merit." Table 1.5 and Figure 1.3 show the distribution of SAT (Scholastic Aptitude Test) scores by race for college-bound seniors in 1996. Figure 1.3 shows that the bulk of black students have lower scores than whites, with only a small fraction of the black student population scoring above 1200 points on the combined scale. For example, if elite colleges and universities choose to follow a colorblind admissions policy that used a 1200 score on the SAT as the cut-off for determining their applicant pool, then these data imply that 31.3% of Asians, 24.9% of whites, 10.2% of Hispanics and 5.5% of blacks would be considered for admission.

Table 1.5 Distribution of SAT Scores by Race for College-Bound Seniors in 1996. (Cell entries are in percentage terms; each column adds up to 100%)

Combined Score	Asian	Black	Hispanic	White
400–480	1.4	2.7	1.7	0.3
500–580	2.4	5.3	3.5	0.8
600–680	4.5	10.4	8.0	2.6
700–780	7.7	18.9	14.5	6.4
800–880	10.9	21.0	18.5	12.1
900–980	13.9	18.2	19.0	17.9
1000–1080	14.2	11.5	14.5	18.5
1100–1180	13.7	6.6	10.1	16.5
1200–1280	12.2	3.4	5.9	12.4
1300–1380	9.0	1.4	2.7	7.3
1400–1480	6.2	0.5	1.1	3.5
1500–1600	3.9	0.2	0.5	1.7

Source: The College Board

Table 1.6 shows the distribution of SAT scores by race and income class for entering college freshmen in 1996. The table clearly shows that blacks have lower SAT scores regardless of social class, and that black children from high-income families have lower scores than poor Asian and white students. Middle-class blacks find themselves accused of being the unqualified and incompetent beneficiaries of affirmative action policies in college admissions and employment that may have contributed to the growth of the black middle classes, but at the cost of "colorblind" admissions, hiring, and promotion policies that reward effort and achievement without regard to race. Indeed, middle-class blacks are being criticized by conservatives in the words of Martin Luther King, Jr., for relying on policies that judge people by the color of their skin rather than the content of their character . . . and their test score (the very same conservatives who opposed the end of segregation and the liberal rollback of hysterical Negrophobia in public and private life).

This is a curious situation because the apparent improvement in black well-being since the end of segregation in the early 1960s has given way to a new and complex reality. The black underclass is trapped by low wages, unemployment, and the usual links between poverty and

Figure 1.3: Distribution of Total SAT Scores for Blacks and Whites

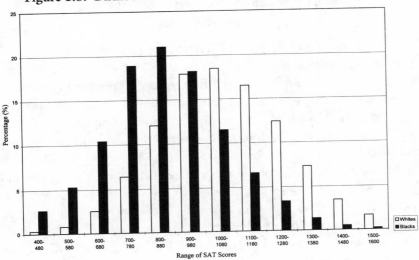

deprivation in capitalist economies. Working-class black people are muddling through an economy that no longer offers the prospect of middle-class life to hard-working but modestly educated adults. The fact of a growing black middle class is welcomed as proof that America has overcome its racist heritage, but is also scorned as a sign that the unqualified, undeserving, just plain dumb black people have gotten better jobs and lives than they have "earned," as shown by their low test scores. What is going on here?

Table 1.6 Mean Combined SAT Scores by Race and Family Income in 1996

Income	Asian	Blacks	Hispanics	Whites
Under 10,000	916	760	818	967
10,000–20,000	965	817	864	966
20,000–30,000	1012	848	896	1004
30,000–40,000	1039	868	925	1014
40,000–50,000	1067	888	955	1030
50,000–60,000	1089	907	967	1042
60,000–70,000	1103	913	986	1059
70,000–80,000	1121	927	997	1072
80,000–100,000	1149	970	1011	1090
Over 100,000	1186	1007	1049	1129

"Merit," Economic Change, and the Racial Blame Game

The existence of an economic underclass, trapped by a combination of poverty and destructive behavior that simply reinforces the harmful effects of low incomes and poor job prospects, is bewildering to many Americans, who have a difficult time accepting the idea of a "poverty trap." American political and economic mythology celebrates the capacity of free markets and vigorous competition to continually overturn social hierarchies among free, white citizens. The grudging admission of blacks into the zone of liberties protected by the Constitution and into American capitalism on terms of formal equality brings with it a belief that success or failure in economic and academic competition is, in the end, a reflection of the talent, preparation, and effort of individuals. Though we have seen that many black Americans have made a spectacular journey from great poverty to growing prosperity, the fact that black poverty rates are still over three times those of whites is a rebuke to popular forms of individualism. The recent nightmare of violence and death that swept through poor, mostly minority sections of American cities in the war to control markets for crack cocaine in the late 1980s and early 1990s has fed the disdain of suburban whites for the black underclass. The idea that poor blacks, and poor people in general, are "trapped" by a combination of merit-based forms of selection for schooling and jobs, combined with the maelstrom of technology-driven capitalist development, suggests that free markets are a potential barrier to racial equality.

Many writers and politicians claim that poverty, joblessness, and all the problems associated with these conditions are the result of a combination of deficient morals and initiative on the part of the poor, compounded by the legacy of foolish liberal social policy. A commonly accepted argument in politics and policy circles is that generous social welfare policies have actually made poverty worse by undermining the incentive of poor people to seek work, study hard, and avoid destructive sexual behavior by breaking the link between work and income. This argument has carried the day among the conservative politicians who control Congress and sit in the White House (party affiliation is hardly meaningful in this matter), so much so that American social policy has actually incorporated a number of punitive measures to force aid recipients back into the labor market. Yet, there is little evidence that previous forms of welfare policy had much effect on recipients' work habits, or on the marriage and divorce rates of poor people, or on the fertility of poor teenagers.

Other writers, including conservatives like Charles Murray, whose book *Losing Ground: American Social Policy, 1950–1980* was an important catalyst for modern attempts to restrict welfare spending, have proposed other, more "fundamentalist" explanations for the origins of the underclass. There are two kinds of right-"fundamentalist" explanations for black poverty: (1) the black underclass is a class of men and women whose poverty and unemployment in a modern, technologically dynamic America reflects their low IQs which, unfortunately, are due to genetic bad luck and (2) the black underclass is the result of a perverse, anti-academic black culture that denigrates intellectual success and glorifies violence, sexual libertinism, a casual attitude toward child rearing, and crime. The first explanation, that poor black people are in trouble because black people are dumb by nature, has been most forcefully stated by Richard Herrnstein and Charles Murray in their recent contribution to world hate literature *The Bell Curve*, while the second argument has also been widely disseminated in Dinesh D'Souza's *The End of Racism*.

We will examine both of these arguments more closely in a few moments. The arguments are important, despite their obvious and numerous flaws, because each claims that a significant remnant of the black American population (or maybe even the majority, depending on how you read these works) is poor because it is a failure rather than the other way around. According to each of these arguments, race and economic backwardness are linked because black people are dumb by nature, or made stupid by culture, but in any case because there is something wrong with them.

Genes

The Bell Curve's central thesis is that many of our most pressing social problems, from income inequality across class and color lines through crime, reflect basic differences in the intellectual abilities of people to cope with the complex tasks associated with life in a modern society.[15] In turn, intellectual differences between successful and unsuccessful people are primarily, though not exclusively, due to genetically based differences in raw cognitive capacities that can be accurately measured by various types of IQ tests. Finally, raw cognitive abilities are passed across the generations through families, with the result that social hierarchies are reproduced over time because low IQ parents tend to have low IQ children.

Though *The Bell Curve* artfully declaims that black people and Latinos are poorer than white people because they're dumber than white people, Murray and Herrnstein's most basic claim is that racial inequality is simply a special instance of a general tendency for social institutions to reflect Nature-based inequality among individuals and racial groups. According to Murray and Herrnstein, racial inequality is a social problem because Americans are unwilling to acknowledge the "fact" that some people, especially blacks and Latinos, are just not smart enough to make it in a modern, technology-driven market society.[16] Intellectually inferior races could get by in the past, where a strong back and good character were all that was necessary to make a living in a simpler industrial society. But times have changed: technology places a premium on intelligence and blacks and Latinos just don't have enough of it. If blacks and Latinos would only accept their fate as less intelligent, and therefore less well-off members of the American nation, then most *racial* problems would disappear, leaving society with the profound but ultimately nonracial question of how to care for our poorer and dumber brothers and sisters.[17]

Indeed, the primary social problem of modern times, at least in the eyes of the authors of *The Bell Curve*, is that liberals and others who resist the idea that economic inequality is rooted in "intelligence" insist on trying to use social policy to override nature's decree that some races are smarter and more intellectually competent than others, thereby sowing the seeds of discontent among the lower classes. If we endorsed a conservative pluralism that accepted cultural diversity, and that saw economic inequality as yet another expression of cultural diversity, we could move beyond the current impasse where we mistake the economic differences between the "races" for a social problem that can somehow be fixed by policy.

In the last chapter of *The Bell Curve*, "A Place for Everyone," Murray and Herrnstein make a case for a new feudalism, where the smart and the dumb support each other in their roles as shepherds and sheep in a brave new technological world.[18] This chapter, with its emphasis on the need for society to promote and enforce simple rules of conduct (so as to not overtax the limited abilities of the dull among us), and its denigration of equality in favor of an ethos of peaceful submission to the decrees of a natural hierarchy, is a chilling apology for a caste society. The irony here is that many members of the planter class in the American South prior to and during the Civil War justified the institutions of slavery for all people, not only blacks, on the basis of a concern for the less intelligent and imprudent.[19] That modern writers like Murray and Herrnstein would seriously suggest that policy and social rules need to be simplified in order to allow the dumb and dark to get by in the world is reminiscent of the vicious doctrines of the planter class.

The Bell Curve has not fared very well among serious scholars and critics. Like Murray's earlier and extremely popular book on social policy *Losing Ground*, which claimed that the programs of the Great Society combined with liberalism in law, education, and social mores to undermine the power of social and moral norms to regulate the behavior of the poor, thereby making poverty worse and encouraging the growth of the underclass, careful study of *The Bell Curve* reveals that the authors' statistical analyses were rather shoddy.[20] Though many popular accounts of the so-called "Bell Curve Wars" pretend that liberal zealots inside and outside the academy have heaped scorn on *The Bell Curve* because it dares to point out that class-based inequality reflects differences in intelligence between individuals and racial groups, careful analysts of various political persuasions have found so many serious errors of fact, method, and judgment in the book that few serious people bother to defend it.

Our primary purpose in mentioning *The Bell Curve* is not to rehash the controversy or to review the criticisms of the various protagonists in the argument. There are a number of excellent books written by critics of *The Bell Curve* that deal with every aspect of the argument. Rather, it is important that we remember why the central question that Murray and Herrnstein raised once more—over the relative contributions of genes versus social environment in the creation of intellectual abilities—is an explosive and important social question whose answer affects our understanding of how economic classes are formed, how the rewards and pain of modern life are distributed across class and racial lines, and the limits of social policy to promote equality or at least reduce suffering.

One of the things that is sometimes lost in the loud arguments about the origins of intelligence and the link between intelligence and social class is that Murray and Herrnstein's basic claim—that the evolution of modern society has put a premium on cognitive abilities—is essentially correct. There is a burgeoning academic literature on the growing importance of education, particularly college education, in modern economic life and as a primary cause of increasing wage inequality in the United States and in a large number of the technologically advanced, market-oriented societies of Asia, Europe, and North America. We have already seen how the value of education, in terms of higher wages and lower unemployment rates for college-trained workers, has increased substantially over the past two decades. The inequality resulting from a shift in the demand for labor toward well-educated workers and away from modestly schooled labor is certainly a problem in a society that worries about the social consequences of income inequality. However, this difficulty need not lead to grave anxiety about the possibilities of social peace or social equality in a society that combines a well-functioning labor market with adequate public policy to facilitate worker education and training, as well as provides an effective social safety net for the nation's citizens. It is important to remember that growing wage inequality in a well-functioning market economy is usually a signal that young people should invest in education and delay their entry into the job market. Further, growing wage inequality of the kind we are considering should also encourage current low-wage workers to invest in improving their skills, either by attending a limited number of courses or by returning to school for more advanced technical education. In both cases, the fact that the return to education has increased should lead to a gradual increase in the supply of well-educated workers and a fall in the ranks of unskilled workers.

Of course, market economies rarely function as smoothly as the rhetoric of free market advocates implies. One of the most basic propositions in economics is that a free market economy, left to its own devices, will tend to undersupply education to its citizens. The reason for this type of market failure is known to every competent undergraduate economics major: the wage differences between skilled and unskilled workers only partially reflect the value of greater levels of schooling to society. Increasing the number of skilled workers raises the overall productive capacity of the economy, reduces the social costs of low wages, unemployment, and inequality—including poor support, the direct and indirect costs of crime to private citizens and criminal justice expenditures—and increases the ability of the work force to adapt to changes in new technologies and to absorb new scientific and technical information, among other things. The typical student/worker will only consider the direct increase in his or her long-term income associated with schooling, just as the typical private school will only consider the contributions that potential new students bring to the institution (principally the increased value of the endowment and the improved academic reputation of the institution). In turn, banks and other sources of education loans will only consider their own narrow interests in granting or refusing to lend money to finance education. Since private schools and commercial banks pay scant attention to the broader, social benefits of schooling to society as a whole, they will generally fund too small a number of students' education choices, thereby leading to a shortage of students and schooling relative to the socially optimal level. Banks will withhold loans from bright but financially strapped students because these borrowers are high-risk investment opportunities compared to wealthier students with more modest intellectual abilities. These basic considerations are the primary justification for public schools, and even in this conservative era, for the public funding of primary, secondary, and college education.

This short digression on market failure and education is important because it tells us that a primary barrier to the movement of workers from low-wage to high-wage jobs is that poorer families and low-wage workers may not be able to purchase the schooling that they need. *The Bell Curve*, however, is effectively claiming the primary problem in modern, technology-driven American society is not that some workers and families need help adjusting to the new order, but that low-wage workers are incapable of succeeding in a sophisticated economic world. If some groups of people, especially black people, are too stupid to succeed at complex technical tasks, then no amount of government help, high-quality schooling, equal educational opportunity, or even affirmative action can overcome Nature's basic decree that some folks are just too dim to do well. Yet, our brief analysis of markets and wages has pointed out that wage inequality is a persistent long-term problem for any number of reasons, for example that low-wage and poor workers and their children do not have access to good schools that can adequately prepare them for rigorous academic competition. While there may be some unclear connection between genes and intelligence, there is a much clearer link between wage inequality, schooling, and access to education. *The Bell Curve* wants us to believe that the fact that children tend to inherit the class status of their parents is biologically determined. Yet, modern science, and even *The Bell Curve*, tell us that social class itself shapes the intellectual abilities of children.

Culture

For those who feel a bit uneasy about Murray and Herrnstein's claim that blacks and Latinos are intellectually inferior to whites by virtue of lousy genes, but who still need to blame our darker and Spanish-speaking neighbors for "their" deficiencies, there is always the "cultural" explanation for society's racial problems. One popular, profitable, and very long account of the cultural origins of racial inequality is Dinesh D'Souza's own contribution to hate literature, *The End of Racism*. D'Souza has no sympathy with the view that black folks or members of any other racial group are dumb by nature.[21] Indeed, D'Souza goes to some lengths to claim that the problem isn't with what black people are (genetically) but rather with what black people do.[22]

D'Souza sets himself the task of explaining the nature of modern American racism in the era after the victory of the Civil Rights movement over government-sponsored racial oppression. *The End of Racism* is comprehensive in the sense that it tries to account for the origins and current state of racism as a social force in American life. This leads D'Souza to provide brief sketches of the beginnings of Western racism, the impact of slavery and segregation on black life, the legitimacy of IQ tests and a whole plethora of standardized tests of intelligence, and what he sees as the political economy of victim-mongering and special pleading by black middle-class devotees of affirmative action, among other things. Though *The End of Racism* is a very long book, with seemingly endless digressions and gratuitous racial insults about the morality, civility, and decency of black people, D'Souza's most coherent (if that is the word) "analysis" of racial inequality is contained in chapters 8, 11, and 12 of the volume. D'Souza's central theses can be reduced to five direct statements:

1. Black Americans are, on average, poorer than white Americans because they have failed to acquire the appropriate forms and levels of education and technical knowledge, as well as to learn how to negotiate the rituals and social conventions of a technologically sophisticated market economy. (Pages 289–302)

2. Blacks exhibit low levels of intellectual and academic achievement compared to whites, Asians, and Hispanics, even after accounting for the impact of income and social class on the IQ levels and SAT scores of black children. Upper-middle-class black children have lower SAT scores than poor Asian children; the gap in scores is greater between upper-class whites, Asians, and blacks than between poorer children across color lines. Other tests of intellectual and cognitive ability repeatedly show that blacks, as a group, are the least intellectually capable racial group in American life. In turn, low levels of academic achievement are the primary reason for the relatively poor performance of blacks in the job market and in all arenas of endeavor tied to intellectual achievement. (Pages 302–317)

3. The primary reason for low levels of black intellectual and academic achievement is not that blacks are an intellectually inferior subspecies by virtue of their genetic inheritance, but that the cultural inheritance of black Americans cripples them in a highly competitive academic and economic system. D'Souza believes that black Americans are burdened by a maladaptive oppositional culture that views learning, intellectual achievement, delayed gratification, sexual restraint—especially among the young—marriage, and abhorrence of violence as signs of capitulation to an oppressive white American regime. This oppositional culture is one of the negative legacies of slavery and segregation that traps blacks in

self-defeating patterns of behavior and result in the tangle of social pathologies associated with the black underclass. (Pages 477–486)

4. This oppositional culture is responsible for the high rates of crime, disdain for study and achievement, high rates of teenage child-bearing, low marriage rates, high rates of welfare dependency and reliance on other forms of public assistance, and general misery of the black underclass. In addition, black middle-class men and women are infected by remnants of this culture, which is an essential element of black nationalist critiques of American society as irredeemably racist. Further evidence of this culture is contained in black teenage consumer culture—rap music, black popular film, the presumed repudiation of proper English by black students. (D'Souza would surely include the recent controversy over "ebonics" in this litany of failure; ibid)

5. Liberal commitments to "cultural relativism"—which D'Souza identifies with the work of anthropologist Franz Boas who claimed that all "cultures" are equally legitimate—along with black apologists for black failure have insulated black people from the power of rigorous academic and economic competition to force black communities to adjust their "civilization" to the requirements for success in modern times. Black complaints of "racism" in the post–Civil Rights era are an excuse for avoiding the hard work of competing in the open arenas of free markets and modern schools. Similarly, affirmative action in employment and college admissions is a special privilege that illegitimately grants blacks valuable assets that should properly be acquired through fair competition. (Pages 487–524)

According to D'Souza, blacks (especially) are victims of their own bad culture which promotes bad behavior and values. Black people are violent, lazy, lousy at learning, break the law, drink too much, do drugs, are sex obsessed, and raise children really badly because, well, that's just what they do.[23] Of course, people from better cultures, that is, people whose ways of living make them well suited to earn high incomes, do well in school, and stay out of jail, are perfectly right to discriminate against dangerous, foul, and ignorant black people because "good" people must defend themselves. If and when black people stop being so silly and badly behaved and adopt more civilized ways of living, then they will be respectable and acceptable to the rest of society. At that point, says D'Souza, racism will disappear.[24]

A number of reviewers have picked apart D'Souza's arguments, showing that he has paid little or no attention to the facts, based his "arguments" on anecdotes and innuendo rather than solid research, misunderstood rudimentary economics (does this mean that he is the victim of a particular "civilizational gap"?), and let his own animus toward blacks overwhelm the judgment and subtle insights that one associates (or at any rate would like to associate) with a Dartmouth education. Economist Glenn Loury has written a number of scathing reviews of D'Souza's work that point out the intellectual problems with *The End of Racism*. Indeed, Loury's criticisms proved so fundamental and damaging that D'Souza was forced to respond (fitfully, with lots of sneering and little else) in the paperback edition of *The End of Racism*.[25]

The reader may have noticed that D'Souza's entire argument rests with the claim that blacks are the unfortunate inheritors of a defective culture that they are having difficulty sloughing off in favor of better ways of living and working. D'Souza claims that this terrible culture has its origins in slavery and apartheid, which means that its noxious effects should have been seen throughout the post–Civil Rights period. Yet, the data we presented above suggest that black people are, on average, much better off now than they have ever been while poor black people are far poorer than they were thirty years ago. It seems tough to explain both of the events with a single "cultural" explanation. Are poor black people suffering more because the perverse "oppositional" culture that chains them to their awful ways has somehow deepened over the past thirty years? Does this mean that "bad black culture"—whatever that is—is only afflicting an ever smaller minority of black people, particularly poor black people? Why? Is the growing black middle and upper class the end product of "good black culture"? But since black middle class people have far higher rates of childbearing outside of marriage than whites and Asians, and since these same folks' children do not seem to do as well in school and on standardized tests as whites or Asians, are they the victims of a "better-but-not-good-enough black culture"?[26]

The racist lunacy of D'Souza's tome should now be quite clear.

D'Souza treats "culture" like a golden nugget, or a poison pill that exists isolated from conditions of wealth and poverty, social inclusion and oppression, relations between racial "groups" or the historical circumstances that provide the raw material from which men and women try to fashion honorable lives. D'Souza makes the same mistake that the typical bigot makes when he or she assumes that "culture" is a discrete parcel that each generation plants into the psyches of its children, who then act out the imperatives of the cultural scripts like bad actors. Accordingly, this cultural script can change if the older generation wants change to occur. For example, D'Souza asserts that he does not subscribe to the belief that cultures are hermetically sealed off little nodes that are unaffected by history, politics, and the larger society (p. 483). However, once the idea that "cultures" are evolving systems of meaning has been conceded, D'Souza's argument, and all other cultural arguments about black economic and educational performance, fall apart.

There could be all sorts of reasons why poor black people don't do very well in school. Indeed, there is a raging debate on precisely this question among brilliant and subtle scholars. Most scholars now believe that academic achievement is driven by a complex tapestry of forces including: parents' attitudes toward achievement in school; the larger community's attitudes toward learning and intellectual life; the complex interplay between religious belief, critical thought, and the life of the mind; the political and social conditions of the child's ethnic and racial group in the community; the quantity and quality of economic resources devoted to schooling; the quality of instruction, and many other factors.[27]

The logical problem with D'Souza's argument is characteristic of a significant part of popular conservative thinking about race. D'Souza's text is imbued with a powerful, common, and utterly false idea, namely that the grades people earn in school and the incomes they earn in labor markets reflect the intellectual and economic "competence" of their "cultures." The claim that black people are failing in schools because they are the unfortunate inheritors of an intellectually enfeebled culture ignores one of the most fundamental findings of social scientists who study education: the best predictor of the educational achievements of children is the level of education attained by their parents. In other words, the children of college graduates tend to be college graduates, children of high school graduates complete college at lower rates, and so on. This fact should have caused D'Souza to put his pen down and think a moment. Could the relatively low rates of academic achievement among blacks (despite the phenomenal increase in black high school and college completion rates over the past thirty years as noted earlier) be a legacy of discrimination and segregation in just the same way the blacks have relatively low rates of home ownership because historic discrimination in mortgage lending and housing markets blocked black home buying?[28] Figure 1.2(a) above showed that only 4% of black adults over the age of 25 had completed four years or more of college in 1967. This means that a very limited number of black parents would be in a position to pass on valuable information about academic success in college to their children. Indeed, only 29.5% of black adults over the age of 25 had completed high school in 1967, so that relatively few black parents would have been in a position to help their children succeed in secondary school. Is it reasonable to say that such a small fraction of black people graduated from high school in 1967 because their "culture" encouraged them to refuse to go to school? Clearly not. Even a casual acquaintance with American history would indicate that black adults in 1967 were largely deprived of education as a consequence of the systematic policy of limited schooling pursued by state governments in the South. Is there any reason to attribute the fact that in 1996 74.3% of blacks over 25 had completed high school or that 13.6% of blacks over 25 had completed college to deficient black achievement rooted in a perverse black intellectual "culture"? Compared to whom? To whites, who had not been subjected to the same government-backed restrictions on access to education? To Asian immigrants, many of whom had to take lower-wage jobs after arriving in America despite the fact that they had advanced professional and doctoral degrees that were not recognized by American universities and professional societies?

Markets and schools are not simply arenas that rank and reward the abilities of "cultures," but also create competencies and abilities by directing educational resources toward some people and away from others. Black people were systematically excluded from adequate quality schooling for many years, which deprived current and future generations of the skills required for success in academic competition. Education is a process where students learn the particular lessons of the day and the most important lessons, which are why school is important and how to succeed in school. In other words, going to school creates a "taste" for school that is then passed on to future generations. It is ludicrous to claim that schooling does not help shape "culture" if this word refers to habits of mind and intellectual outlooks that are bequeathed to subsequent generations within families and via communal institutions (churches, neighborhood associations, clubs, political groups, and other elements of civil society). Blacks have made enormous strides in closing the knowledge gap with whites. The problem is that black people began with such a large handicap that is made worse by the fact that they are poorer than whites, do not have access to the same kinds of decent schools as whites (because of segregation and relative poverty), and have less knowledge capital to pass on to their children (again because of historic discrimination).

This leaves D'Souza with one other possibility. D'Souza might be able to rescue his analysis of the internally generated intellectual infirmities of black culture if he could show that black parents, older members of extended families, black churches, social clubs, and community organizations, and other institutions of character formation in black communities actually told black children to turn away from academic achievement. The data on high school and college attainments of black adults over 25 since 1967 seem to contradict this sort of assertion, but Mr. D'Souza is quite an . . . artful fellow. Further, any claim of this sort would require detailed ethnographic studies that documented instances where black adults told black kids not to go to school, not to try in school, not to do well in school, and not to look forward to the rewards of school success (like a good job). D'Souza has no record of these sorts of actions by black adults because no one does these things. The best that he can do is present anecdotes of vicious songs and poses of black pop icons and hip-hop artists who say all sorts of horrible things about women, whites, Asians, the police, and schools (pages 499–514). This is an odd procedure, since judging a people by the low quality of market-directed youth culture is a silly exercise. Would anyone care to make sweeping generalizations of the intellectual abilities and morals of all white Americans based on the style of dress, music, manners, and movies currently fashionable among white teenagers and young adults?

There is something hilarious, in a creepy sort of way, about the popularity of these right-wing books about race. But there is something really dangerous about these volumes also. Both *The Bell Curve* and *The End of Racism* tell their frustrated conservative readers that there is no racial problem in America, but rather a problem with naturally stupid people or culturally stupid people who happen to be black. These books are popular and important because they lay the blame for America's racial problems on the "problem races." Whether blacks and Latinos are the chimps that Murray and Herrnstein claim or if blacks really are the loathsome trash that offend Mr. D'Souza's sensitive tastes is less important than the idea that race is a problem because THEY don't have what it takes to make a good life in modern society.

D'Souza's updated cultural excuse for racism is simply another variation on an old, and very tired, social Darwinist theme: the inherent superiority of certain cultures and races relative to others is revealed by the economic success of some groups over others. D'Souza insists that some "cultures" or ways of life are better than others and, more importantly, that "good" cultures also tend to be rich cultures. The problem with race in America, accordingly, is that some folks just can't seem to leave their bad ways and adopt better and more lucrative ways, either because they are terribly stubborn or, more likely, because they are ultimately the product of their genes, poor things.

One of the difficulties that writers like Murray, Herrnstein, and D'Souza pose for conservatives is that their positions undermine the legitimacy of free markets. These authors turn the market into a measuring rod that dispenses wealth or misery in ways that undermine social order, which is precisely what modern, market-obsessed conservatives want to avoid. The usual argument for free markets includes the claim that a well-ordered and peaceful society is the by-product of the choices of free, self-interested individuals. Private property, free competition for wealth and position, and a limited but effective government that prevents monopoly and the abuse of social power by elites, defends the nation's borders, and guarantees the safety and security of persons and property are, according to classical liberal lore, the foundation of prosperous and civilized societies. We have already seen that *The Bell Curve* advances the proposition that some people are too dumb to know their own interests or to make their way in a complex technological world, with the implication that the State must somehow arrange things so that they are relieved of the taxing responsibility of free choice. The implications of *The End of Racism* are even worse: racism is the rational response of white people to the chronic bad choices, bad morals, and bad culture of black people, who have shown themselves to be in the grip of psychotic subcultures that make them foul, incompetent, and dangerous people. If D'Souza is right, then black people don't want to choose better ways of living, so there is no reason for the rest of us to prevent them from suffering the full consequences of their lousy ways. Black incompetence should result in black suffering. Indeed, black people will only have incentives to improve themselves and dump their terrible folkways when they get tired of living like savages. This is the Marie Antoinette approach to conservative race policy: let the blacks eat dust and they'll figure it out, eventually.

Conservatives and the "Culture of Poverty"

Consider a more sophisticated, if problematic, conservative view of the link between culture, color, markets, and poverty presented forcefully in the work of Thomas Sowell. Sowell, like D'Souza, treats markets as devices that sift among the economic attributes of both individuals and racial and ethnic groups.[29] Those individuals who come from groups that emphasize hard work, initiative, socially sanctioned risk-taking, the value of education, competition, and other traits that markets value will earn high incomes and occupy positions of authority and prestige in the private sector. By contrast, those groups who consistently fail to teach these values to their children will find themselves with low incomes, occupying low-status positions in the job hierarchy, with limited chances for moving out of poverty. According to this view, markets are simply *registering* the economic efficacy of different, culturally induced attitudes and outlooks that guide individual behavior. It is as if the market were a vast, largely (though certainly not completely) impartial scale that records the economic "weight" of differing attitudes to work, schooling, family size and structure, and risk-taking among members of different groups. Those "cultures" that promote remunerative ways of being will be rewarded with a higher market score (income) than other, less economically viable cultures. In turn, groups that find themselves consistently impoverished are suffering because they have economically inappropriate values.[30]

Lawrence Harrison has developed an approach similar to Sowell's in order to explain the causes of economic success and failure among nations as well as ethnic and racial groups within the United States. In *Who Prospers? How Cultural Values Shape Economic and Political Success*, Harrison presents a straightforward argument that cultural values, in particular attitudes toward work, saving, effort, and merit, as well as culturally induced attitudes toward markets, schools, authority, the State, and other institutions outside a group's racial or ethnic orbit are the primary determinants of long-term developmental success for different nations and ethnic groups. Harrison stresses four primary determinants of economic success for ethnic and cultural groups (Harrison 1992, 1–26):

1. the extent to which a community or group identifies with larger social institutions and practices—markets, schools, the State— and the extent to which a community or group will consider the demands of institutions and officials outside the group to be legitimate demands on group members,
2. the role of religion and ethics in creating a strong sense of personal and social responsibility, including self-reliance and a concern for the well-being of the larger community,
3. the extent to which a community or ethnic group is both subjected to excessive authority by external agents and the extent to which a group is constrained by internal authoritarian attitudes that penalize risk-taking, initiative, or a willingness to experiment,
4. attitudes toward economic activity, including work, saving, profit, and innovation.

Harrison's argument is largely a reworking of Sowell's more subtle analysis. Nonetheless, both see culture as the source of values and attitudes that are then the basis for market success or failure.

There are two primary sources of bad economic attitudes that could plausibly be claimed to undermine the economic well-being of the black poor. One source of problems, which will be considered at greater length in the next chapter, is an outgrowth of the rapid black migration from the agricultural South to the urban industrial and post-industrial economy of all regions of the country from the 1940s through the 1960s. This migration, especially to the Northeast and the North Central states in the post–World War II period, created the typical problems of peasant agricultural workers adapting to life in a technologically and economically sophisticated modern society. Indeed, it is not too much to say that black Americans in this century, particularly after each of the World Wars, have had to leap the enormous divide between feudalism and capitalism. Sowell makes a point of noting that the shock of modernity has had a distinctly negative effect on the economic fortunes of blacks, whose low levels of education combined with little experience with the promise and perils of urban life left them ill-equipped to face the challenges of living in a dynamic, ever-changing market society.[31] Historian Jacqueline Jones has shown that both white and black migrants from the rural South to the industrial North in the aftermath of the decline in agricultural employment over the past fifty years had difficulty making the transition from rural to urban life, with the kinds of social "pathologies" associated with poor urban blacks showing up among first- and second-generation white Appalachian migrant families as well.[32]

A second, more controversial claim about the source economically dysfunctional attitudes among the black poor is that whatever adjustment difficulties black American peasant families have had in making the transition from rural to urban settings have been greatly worsened by the economic disincentives of welfare. Charles Murray, in his wildly successful, pre–Bell Curve work *Losing Ground*, has tried to claim that welfare allows the poor people to continue with the inappropriate, reckless, and ultimately disastrous attitudes and habits that delay or completely block their integration into the modern economy. As a result, welfare dependency can be seen as a reflection of the fact that the well-intentioned goals of the Great Society actually subsidized destructive, short-sighted, and slothful cultural traits that have to be eliminated in order for the black poor to begin to escape from their position as some of the poorest Americans.

Murray's thesis is not that the black poor are somehow different from the rest of us; indeed, in *Losing Ground* he goes to some lengths to argue that the black poor are exactly like everyone else to the degree that they respond to economic opportunities that provide them with income, goods, and services without the burden of work. Murray's major point, stripped of its tendency to mimic the worst Dickensian satire, is that poor urban blacks lack the skills, ambitions, and habits of thought and feeling that contribute to economic success. Poor relief actually makes poverty worse by encouraging generations of black children to emulate parental values that are simply inappropriate in a modern economy, rather than letting the brutalities of poverty in an urban setting force these people to adopt more appropriate values and habits. The famous example of Harold and Phyllis in *Losing Ground* is designed to show how the presence of welfare provides an incentive to avoid work, study, and marriage, thereby encouraging the very conditions that lead to child poverty, impoverished female-headed households, low educational attainment, and reckless youthful childbearing among poor urban blacks. By making poverty hurt less, welfare is assumed to blunt the ability of markets to mold the attitudes of poor urban blacks by punishing reckless behavior.

It is important to note that this unusual interpretation of Murray's argument has a number of implications that are actually perfectly consistent with *liberal and leftist* views of modern life. There is little question that the move from rural to urban areas involves a great deal of pain and culture shock for migrants who simply must adopt the language, outlook, and perspectives of modern science, technology, and cultural and social discourse if they are to survive and prosper in a technology-driven market system. For better or for worse, the attempt by rural folk to hold on to their gods, traditions, modes of raising children, patterns of gender domination and submission, and other very basic social institutions must fail in order for new, more appropriate and economically viable attitudes, ambitions, and outlooks to take hold among migrants. To be sure, the gradual loss of old habits and rituals is accompanied by pain, confusion, doubt, anger, and depression, which contribute to the usual high levels of martial discord, divorce, crime, extra-marital childbearing, and educational failure among many peasant immigrant populations to the modern, urban economy. The ability of markets to essentially destroy traditional culture in favor of a market-oriented (though certainly ethnically influenced) outlook is usually thought to be one of the great strengths of modern life, particularly since this process is essential if superstition is to be overcome. Nonetheless, this "modernizing" process is painful and is associated with great suffering.

The combined effect of Sowell's and Murray's pre–*Bell Curve* view of the role of culture and welfare in creating and sustaining black poverty significantly downplays the role of discrimination as a source of racial inequality and promotes the view that welfare policy is preventing blacks' adoption of a more appropriate modern market-based outlook. Given the inevitable pain that accompanies a peasant population's adaptation to the joys and sorrows of urban life, and given the additional realities of discrimination that will certainly reduce the availability of jobs, housing, education, and other essential goods for blacks, welfare has the pernicious, if unintended, effect of delaying the intellectual and cultural integration of the black poor into a dynamic modern economy. Only by eliminating welfare entirely, or, at a minimum, sharply reducing the extent to which the poor can depend on poor relief over their lives, can society force poor blacks to adopt more appropriate attitudes and outlooks that will facilitate economic success.

The conservative view of the race/culture/class nexus sketched above is analytically superior to sloppy, D'Souza-ish musing about culture for two reasons. First, the foregoing analysis treats "culture" as evolving systems of knowledge and meaning that change in response to economic and political forces, including but not limited to government policy. Welfare offers a life raft to people who are in economic trouble, to be sure, while also sustaining dysfunctional patterns of behavior. However, these currently dysfunctional values are themselves inherited from previous eras where they met a communal group's social, psychological, and spiritual needs. Community values and mores change slowly relative to the frenetic pace of change characteristic of capitalism's "creative destruction" of skills, technologies, and social values. The incessant change inherent in modern, technology-driven market societies means that many people, including black Americans, have found themselves stranded between the requirements of markets and technology on the one hand, and an increasingly inappropriate peasant culture on the other.

Second, the conservative view of the race/culture/class nexus we are sketching implies that the problem of racial inequality in American life is better seen as the reflection of different stages of adaptation to capitalist modernity among racial/cultural groups. One important conservative interpretation of black America's social predicament offered by Glenn Loury is that black social institutions have not fully adapted to the rigors of modern capitalism because segregation and misguided liberal racial policy interfered with the development of social capital in black communities. Loury's view of the sources of relative black economic backwardness, which we explore in detail in the next chapter, suggests that blacks must shoulder the burden of rebuilding their communities in order to successfully compete in the academy and in labor markets, because no one else can.

This conservative perspective is far more serious than D'Souza-like popular rants, though racist ranting has far more sway over public opinion and policy than clear and rigorous thinking. Our critique of rightist hate literature dressed up as social science is not a flat dismissal of all conservative thinking about the links between racial inequality and cultural practices. Indeed, the strain of conservative thought presented in the writings of Glenn Loury poses a powerful challenge both to racist-conservatives and to the broad American Left by asking us to consider the reciprocal relationship between markets and culture. To paraphrase Schumpeter's comment on why Marx is an important figure in modern thought: the possibility that some conservative thought about racial inequality admits of a leftist interpretation is a sign that it can be taken seriously.

Taking Society Seriously

Persistent poverty and racial inequality are produced by the interaction of four logically distinct institutions: families, communities, markets, and governments. Analytical distinctions between these institutions allow us to isolate the different functions of each arena as well as explore the links between them. However, social analysts make mistakes when they treat these institutions as actually separate, thereby downplaying or ignoring important ways that powerful social forces may shape or subvert the intentions of people in smaller, more vulnerable settings. Murray, Herrnstein, and D'Souza pretend that genes or "culture" are the primary determinants of the economic competence of blacks, with all other institutions playing, at most, subsidiary roles. Yet, a brief review of the analytical links between families, "cultures," and markets shows us why simple-minded genetic or cultural approaches are such sources of trouble.

Families are the primary institutions for the care and socialization of children, including their moral and political education. Parental investments of time, attention, and resources into their children's emotional and intellectual development are some of the most important determinants of children's well-being. In turn, "cultures," understood as thick textures of rituals, stories, family and ethnic customs, and religious beliefs that parents pass on to their children, literally create the personalities and life projects of the young on the substratum of the raw intellectual and physiological capabilities inherited from parents. In addition, parents pass their knowledge of the practical world to their children, including their (potentially limited) understanding of the world outside the boundaries of the family and the immediate community.

"Cultures" are not simply the accumulated folk wisdom of families and small tribes passed down through the generations: "cultures" are also widely shared systems of meaning and ritual that have been built up through time by the deliberate investment of energy, labor, and materials into objects, structures, schools, churches, business enterprises, and other organizations dedicated to preserving and transmitting meaning. The "culture" that families participate in is not only of their own making, but is instead the result of the ongoing actions of artists, writers, scholars, teachers, performers, cooks, and countless others trying to give life to particular ways of thinking, talking, and feeling. Ethnic and racial communities make collective investments to create cultural and social institutions that can protect and develop this social capital in order to maintain the integrity of particular ways of living and feeling.

The economists' idea of an externality, a resource or process that has effects on the material or social well-being of people who were not originally party to the exchange that created the goods, assets, or services in question, is a perfectly appropriate description for the economic function of social capital. Individuals, families, organizations, and governments invest in cultural and social capital in order to promote particular historical narratives, shape public consciousness of the nation's origins and the legitimacy of the national enterprise, preserve existing literary or intellectual canons or even initiate new ones, among other things. For example, bitter experience has taught us that consumer capitalism can be a powerful, and destructive, "cultural" force that shapes the desires of adults and children as part of the selling process, in that way promoting values that may be diametrically opposed to the religious, ethical, and tribal/ethnic verities that families, schools, churches, and community organizations seek to instill and protect.

Serious arguments about poverty and racial inequality are ultimately arguments about the relationship between families, communities, markets, and governments in shaping the way children grow and learn, the extent to which different groups of people have access to educational and economic opportunity, and the role of the state in redistributing opportunity and resources to overcome the unjust verdict of markets. There is little doubt that "culture" guides the choices that parents make in raising their children. Nor is there much doubt that some "cultures" may value learning or knowledge or academic ritual or market competition more than others. However, markets shape families through the distribution of income and wealth, the conditions of employment, and the array of products and services provided to buyers. Similarly, community institutions charged with building and maintaining cultural and social capital may thrive or decline depending on the economic fortunes of community members and on the relationship between community institutions and the larger state. Finally, the government plays a decisive role in the development of families and communities through its activities in providing income support, schools, police protection and law enforcement, protections of civil rights and liberties, and other public goods.

However, in a world where black people are playing economic catch-up after a long period of enforced backwardness, black "culture" is in a period of rapid change, making it difficult to claim that "culture" is an independent cause of black economic performance. The cultural capital that guides the actions of parents within families, workers in the economy, and citizens in the relationship with the State is an evolving set of rules, symbols, and interpretations that is constantly revised by the practices of a community's members and the pressures of the larger world. For example, the data on black educational developments since 1967 show black people taking schooling seriously since rising black high school and college completion means that black people willingly go to school, do the work, and graduate.

Does our critique of genetic and "culture"-based arguments for persistent black poverty and relatively low levels of economic well-being rule out genes and "culture" as important factors? No, the inheritance of physiological and cultural propensities clearly matters for how men and women from different social groups will fare in competitive capitalism. However, there is simply no good reason to believe that the abilities and values that markets reward at any point in time, particularly over the past thirty years—effort, ambition, practical intelligence as well as academic achievement and a good education—are in any simple way related to genes or distinct ethnic "culture." The remarkable speed with which black Americans have closed the knowledge gap with whites over the past thirty years, as well as the significant decline in relative black poverty over the same period, casts doubt on explanations for racial inequality that focus on the genetic or cultural infirmities of black people. We would all be better off if analysts would spend more time writing about the tangled connections between gender, families, markets, and government policy and less time on notions that ultimately pretend that society doesn't exist.

Next Steps

This chapter's brief review of the economic fortunes of black Americans between 1967 and 1996 leaves us with a complicated picture of the state of black economic well-being. There can be little doubt that the growth of a prosperous black middle class is a cause for celebration, not least because it is a sign that the nation is making room for talented and ambitious black people. This is the largest and richest collection of people of African descent in the world. One can imagine that a growing black middle class will have the material wealth to produce generations of intellectuals, artists, scholars, and statesmen and women whose arguments and actions can move America toward genuine racial equality.

Of course, the growth of a black middle class also means that there is a larger audience for a critical black perspective on American history, culture, and institutions. Indeed, white Americans will have to accept the fact that a richer black population is also a more intellectually assertive population that has less to fear when it challenges sacred myths of American grace that glide over the pain-filled record of black life in this country.

We have also seen that the gradual convergence of black poverty rates toward white poverty rates has apparently stopped, leading some writers to speculate about the existence of a permanent black underclass. If we rule out black intellectual inferiority or crude notions of cultural infirmity as explanations of persistent black poverty, we are left with the possibility that racial discrimination and American capitalism's "gale of creative destruction" have knocked black people off a relatively smooth path toward convergence with whites in matters of economic well-being. Discrimination is an ancient plague on the lives of black Americans that was diminished but not ended when the government discontinued support for segregation. Indeed, many writers now confidently assert that discrimination hardly matters as a cause of continuing racial inequality. Once the loose thinking of Bell Curve enthusiasts and other evasive writers is dispensed with, we must face the possibility of reduced social mobility out of the ranks of the poor, thereby creating the possibility of a permanent underclass for *economic* reasons. Other writers continue to hold that blacks are poorer than whites because of continuing anti-black discrimination in the face of all sorts of laws and regulations outlawing unfair treatment against blacks on the basis of race. We must now think about the connections between racial inequality and social class in a world with discrimination but without apartheid, without color-coded intellectual abilities, and where poverty and social disadvantage shape culture as well as the other way around.

In short, this book shows how racial conflict and free markets conspire to create racial inequality in a America. The poverty and violence, misery and death that follow from unrestricted free markets are the cause of the problem. After all, no one would care much about racial conflict if it only meant that race-mad crazies had an obnoxious desire to hang out together, with no poverty, unfairness, violence, or humiliation resulting therefrom. In such a world, the best policy would be for the saner members of society to discreetly separate themselves from their race-phobic neighbors in much the same way that the more stable among us are wary of drunken, deluded people who mutter curses and oaths in the air as they stumble along a city street.

TWO

Race and the Market

Capitalism and the Political Economy of Color

The deepening poverty and social distress among poorly educated and low-wage black populations that inspired Murray and D'Souza to write their tomes reflect larger economic forces that are reducing the living standards and life chances of all poorly educated people. The modern American problem of racial inequality in post-segregation America is that blacks are disproportionately trapped in the low-wage, low-skill sectors of the labor market at a time of fundamental economic and technological change, and, more importantly, in a nation that has largely abandoned attempts to promote economic equality. In addition, black middle-class men and women are trying to make their way in a merit-driven society where a belief in a single standard of merit for college admissions and employment trumps social justice arguments for race-conscious admissions and employment policies.

As a practical matter, therefore, black Americans must make their way in an aggressively capitalist society that eschews formal racial discrimination in government policy. Since the mid-1960s black people have been formally free to participate in a capitalist society dominated by the white majority, the sons and daughters of the former master race, under the protections of the Constitution. Modern America has abandoned its segregationist ways in favor of an open market setting where competition and class privilege determine the distribution of economic opportunities and rewards across color lines rather than government coercion or a government-sponsored culture of Negrophobia. The United States is a fundamentally conservative society in economic matters where the cultural commitment to free markets brings with it a high tolerance for inequality in incomes, living standards, and life chances, regardless of race. In turn, the fact that slavery, and especially segregation, left black Americans without important economic resources was not and is not, in and of itself, sufficient justification for a redistribution of income and opportunities from whites to blacks to compensate for the damage done by the previous authoritarian racial system. The commitment of Americans to property rights, individual liberty, and free markets effectively blunts any claims for the redistribution of income and opportunity in order to repair the damage of segregation.

One of the basic problems blacks now face is that the commitment to free markets has a profoundly brutal side: racial hatred, racial discrimination, and private efforts at racial exclusion, humiliation, and degradation are all consistent with the contours of American ideas of liberty, even if these actions and their underlying motives are deeply offensive to the traditional American sense of fair play. Yet, the persistence of racial inequality in the post-segregation era has given rise to an ongoing dispute between Left and Right about the limits of social policy in racial matters. This dispute, though usually cast as an argument between conservatives and liberals, is really a dispute between those who champion minimal government regulation of economic activity in the name of economic efficiency and those who, mindful of the threat that racial inequality and discrimination pose to the stability of a liberal democratic society, want to minimize the extent to which free markets can fan the flames of racial and social conflict.

On one side are those who claim that discrimination in a free market system is a perfectly legitimate, if regrettable, consequence of the free exercise of property rights. These champions of free markets, who mostly oppose all forms of government-sponsored racial oppression and segregation, nonetheless insist that social stability is enhanced if we can limit the role of racial politics in society by minimizing the need to resort to government policy to resolve racial disputes. By emphasizing market competition, and insisting on the need for government to promote market development in as many areas of life as possible, these (mostly conservative) market enthusiasts believe that whatever poverty and racial inequality that result from the dynamics of American capitalism are ultimately due to the talents (or lack thereof), ambition, and dedication of individuals who happen to be distributed across various racial groups.

Many thoughtful conservatives are all too aware of the role that white disdain for people of color has played in perpetuating black and Latino underdevelopment. Nonetheless, these conservatives see very little prospect for government policy, and particularly redistributive policies, to improve the lot of anyone, including blacks. According to these conservatives, government policy to regulate economic activity and redistribute economic opportunity usually runs afoul of the principles of merit and effort that are the driving forces behind the success of capitalism. For better or for worse, these rather more sophisticated and in many cases (though regrettably not nearly enough cases) strongly anti-racist conservatives see the market as the best answer to the problems of racial inequality, viewing black and Latino poverty as the result of people of color being excluded for too long from capitalist attitudes, opportunities, and institutions.

Advocates of free market approaches to racial reform are opposed by those who claim that a commitment to fair treatment across the color line requires the elimination of as many forms of racial discrimination in economic life as possible. These men and women—mainly though not exclusively liberals—who insist on the need for government regulation of markets in order to insure racial fairness are mindful of the way in which history *and* capitalism have combined to place blacks and Latinos in a condition of poverty and economic deprivation. Proponents of government involvement in racial matters are all too aware that the exclusion of blacks and Latinos by private agents, from realtor associations, through banks, labor unions, employers, and private schools, has played a central role in modern racial inequality.

But the regulation of markets in pursuit of racial fairness poses profound challenges for the American liberal Left. Can Americans create a society in which race plays little role in distributing economic opportunity across the color spectrum in a multiracial society? Can we take race out of the competitive struggle for education, wealth, and positions of prestige without paying a severe price in terms of economic efficiency and free choice? Does the attempt to create racial fairness require violation of the principle of merit, as some opponents of affirmative action claim? Does a principle of "merit" even exist in a society where discrimination is rife in the marketplace, and where past discrimination reduces the competitive prospects of current and future black and Latino populations?

The essential economic disputes between the Left and the anti-racist Right over the desirability and efficacy of racial policy center around three sets of questions.

First, what does the term "racial fairness" mean in a liberal capitalist society where the rights of free association and free markets are perfectly consistent with private racial discrimination that results in the unequal distribution of economic opportunity across color lines? What does the term "equal opportunity" mean in a capitalist society where racial groups are mutually antagonistic and where a significant plurality of the white majority is anxious to limit their contact with minorities? Why should the unequal distribution of income and opportunity across racial lines matter in a market society?

Second, how do we weigh the gains in "racial fairness," whatever that may mean, against the economic losses that may come from restricting the role of racial prerogatives in economic decisions? Is it even possible to restrict the role of racial prerogatives and racial hatred in economic life, or is the attempt to do so bound to make life worse for those members of despised groups we seek to help? How can we remove the barriers to the full participation of minorities in a market economy when those barriers are partially based on the social customs and preferences of the white majority, shaping the core institutions and relationships that are the foundation of American capitalism?

Third, suppose we are able to define what we mean by racial fairness and are able to construct a set of policies that a racially neutral observer thinks can achieve the proper balance between racial fairness and economic efficiency. How can we implement these policies in an actual market society compromised by racial hatred? How do we create genuine equal opportunity across racial lines when a sizable plurality, if not an outright majority, of white Americans harbor feelings of fear, anger, disgust, contempt, and resentment against minorities, especially blacks? How can policies be carried out, even policies that have no particular racial equity goals, when poverty and inequality have a racial cast, thereby reducing public support for any measures that promise the amelioration of poverty?

Our immediate task is to mine economic analysis for useful insights into the economic consequences of racial discrimination in a capitalist economy. We will for the most part limit our exploration of economists' writings on race and economics to a few well-known writers, including well-known conservatives, a couple of liberals, and a few radical analysts too. Our goal is to consider the logical links between racial discrimination and racial inequality in a world without apartheid. As we will see below, there are powerful reasons for believing that a competitive capitalist economy can greatly reduce the effect of discrimination on the well-being of social outcasts. There are equally powerful reasons for thinking that racial conflict in a competitive capitalist society can nonetheless result in the relative impoverishment of pariah groups.

Discrimination in Market Society: Insights from Economists

Racial discrimination in a free society, where men and women of various colors and ethnic groups are free to conduct their legal economic and personal affairs in whatever manner they choose, is simply the act of choosing against someone else on the basis of color. Discriminatory economic choices, like all choices, reflect the interests and attitudes of buyers and sellers in markets. For an anarcho-capitalist—a right-wing libertarian whose faith in private property and unregulated markets is absolute—discrimination is a necessary, even sacred part of individual liberty that may be deplored by other, less racially phobic people but should be left alone. The individual white man or woman who refuses to hire, live near, buy from, or in any other way associate with blacks out of feelings of vague or even extreme discomfort is simply exercising his or her right as a property owner who seeks to gain the maximum benefit from the unfettered use of his or her property. A right-libertarian may find this sort of racist belief distasteful, but he or she would also find free markets a perfect solution to the problem of organizing and coordinating the activities of millions of people in a racially diverse, and racially contentious, society. From a libertarian perspective, race discrimination in capitalist society may be insulting, demoralizing, or emotionally hurtful to the men and women who are objects of abuse and hatred, but it also safeguards both racists and their victims by severely limiting their interactions with each other, thereby promoting a cold but durable social peace. Landlords who are free to discriminate are denying a potential renter access to housing, but the discriminatory act also prevents conflicts by eliminating any contact between a hostile landlord and a despised tenant. Similarly, discrimination in employment and education can be seen as a device for minimizing social conflict and contributing to economic efficiency to the extent that racially phobic employers, fellow employees, teachers, students, parents, and other members of society can carry out their economic activities free from the need to engage in tainted social intercourse with despised people.

In turn, a right-libertarian's chief complaint against anti-discrimination laws and policies is that they interfere with the rights of property owners to the full use of their possessions.[1] First, anti-discrimination laws criminalize a certain subset of choices, in this case refusing to trade with racial undesirables, thereby reducing the autonomy and well-being of property owners with the threat of punishment. Second, the difficulty of proving that particular refusals to rent an apartment, hire, or admit blacks into a college or university is quite high, in large part because governments necessarily lack the relevant information for making these types of decisions.[2] The specific, local information about the qualities of applicants for housing, jobs, or schools is in the hands and heads of the buyers and sellers involved, whose experience in these sorts of transactions is based on more accurate information than are the judgments of third-party outside observers. An outside observer, like a government, can only see that a corporation has few black employees, or a school has few black students, but not whether these black students or job seekers are qualified for positions. Anti-discrimination laws are, accordingly, a source of economic inefficiency to the extent that they give individuals, enterprises, and other organizations (including other agencies of government) incentives to avoid the costs of punishment that might distort their decisions in favor of candidates who, based on merit, should not gain access to valuable resources or jobs. For example, firms that fear the costs of anti-discrimination law suits or penalties imposed by the State for violations of anti-discrimination regulations may hire blacks with lower grades and less talents than whites or Asians as a rational, profit-maximizing strategy, though the net result of these actions is to disrupt the market's ability to appropriately allocate jobs among the most talented individuals.

These claims against anti-discrimination laws are perfectly sound, and narrowly conceived applications of basic economic principles. While claims of this sort have a certain resonance in modern, conservative America, with its emphasis on competition, merit, and efficiency as well as widespread suspicion concerning affirmative action and so-called racial preferences, the economic analysis of discrimination extends far beyond the blinkered vision of right libertarianism. Most economic theory about racial discrimination is concerned with two kinds of questions: (1) what is the effect of discrimination on the distribution of economic well-being across racial groups in the short and long term and (2) what is the impact of racial discrimination, and proposed remedies to the inequities caused by discrimination, on the level of material prosperity (or economic efficiency) of the nation as a whole? Still, there are more than a few economists and social thinkers whose primary complaint about anti-discrimination policies is centered on violations of property rights rather than reductions in economic efficiency. Other writers support anti-discrimination policy because of the demands of equity and social justice, fully realizing that actions designed to promote racial equality may involve sacrifices in economic efficiency or even painful conflicts between important social justice claims. The potential problems that anti-discrimination policy poses for leftist economists will be considered later. Our current task is to briefly review economists' thinking about the impact of discrimination on the economic fortunes of despised castes, in this case blacks, in a modern, technology-driven economy.

Becker

Economists have developed a number of approaches to the problem of discrimination that can help us explore its effects on the economic well-being of blacks. One of the most famous, and in many ways controversial, analyses of the impact of discrimination on the economic well-being of minorities was developed by Nobel laureate Gary Becker of the University of Chicago in his famous 1957 book *The Economics of*

Discrimination. The basic insights of Becker's analysis are by now so well known that they have passed from being ideas debated among specialists in economics and law into the realm of general public knowledge. The following short summary of Becker's major points may strike many readers as close to common sense, which is a sign of the intellectual power of this line of reasoning.

Consider a job market where black and white workers compete for jobs offered by a large number of potential employers. These employers exhibit two types of racial "tastes" in terms of the color of their work force: rabid racists who refuse to hire blacks and racially neutral employers who only care about the competence of workers, not their color. This range of racial sentiments effectively creates two job markets in society, one for whites and one for blacks. If rabidly racist employers control a significant portion (say 99% for the sake of argument) of available jobs, then black workers will find themselves in a situation where there is a smaller demand for their labor than that for white workers. As a result, only a lucky few black workers will be able to find jobs if they are willing to accept very low wages relative to white workers, who have the good fortune of being in very high demand relative to their black counterparts.[3] If black workers insist on being paid the same wages as white workers, they will price themselves out of jobs because so few employers are willing to hire them.

However, this situation of unequal wages and job opportunities cannot last indefinitely. If black workers are as intelligent, honest, and hardworking as white workers, then firms that hire black labor will be more profitable than firms hiring white workers simply because black workers are relatively cheaper than white workers. In turn, the greater profitability of black workers will mean that racially neutral firms will grow much faster than racist enterprises, thereby increasing the availability of jobs for black workers. In addition, new firms will be overwhelmingly managed by racially neutral people who take advantage of the opportunities offered by hiring cheap, competent black labor. Over time, black employment prospects and black workers' wages rise as the racially neutral segment of the labor market grows relative to the racist segment of employers. In the long run (which could be a *very* long time) black workers' wages will be equal to white workers' wages (though there may be significant racial segregation in employment) because a subset of entrepreneurs was willing to pay more attention to the profit opportunities associated with hiring black workers than to racial etiquette. Becker's basic, and powerful point about racial discrimination in a capitalist economy is this: racial discrimination cannot lead to permanent wage inequality between black and white workers so long as

1. black workers and white workers are equally competent;
2. the market for labor is highly competitive, i.e. that there are a large number of firms competing for the services of an even larger number of independent workers, and where industries are open to the potential competition of new firms; and
3. governments do not regulate wages or employment in ways that prevent risk-taking entrepreneurs from taking advantage of low-wage black labor.

The idea that free markets can overturn the destructive effect of discriminatory customs on employment opportunities for blacks is very important, because it suggests that capitalism can be a progressive social force that undermines the practical consequences of racism on black economic well-being. Becker's conjecture has been subjected to ruthless criticism, largely because it rests on a rather special set of assumptions that are frequently absent from capitalism as it actually exists. We will shortly explore a number of these objections below. However, it is important that we see what Becker's simple analysis tells us about the economic effect of racism in modern society.

One implication of Becker's conjecture is that widespread disdain for blacks cannot lead to a permanent condition of low wages and restricted opportunities for blacks if competitive conditions prevail in job markets and in schools. Permanent black poverty and unemployment are only possible if competition is replaced by some form of monopoly, or if government power is used to close off competition in some other way.

Many writers have noticed that the Becker conjecture relies on the assumption that markets are perfectly competitive, that is, each market is comprised of such a large number of buyers and sellers that no one market participant or group of participants has any significant control of prices. In this kind of world, where the prices that buyers pay are independent of the actions of an individual firm, enterprises must pay particular attention to their production costs in order to earn the highest profits. In highly competitive markets, firms that let their production costs rise are putting themselves in danger of losing money because they cannot raise their prices in order to cover higher costs without losing the bulk of their customers. (Contrast this to a monopoly situation where a single firm has the power to pass on cost increases to customers in the form of higher prices without losing too many buyers because, frankly, they do not have anywhere else to go.) A discriminating manager in a competitive industry who chooses to hire expensive white workers instead of cheaper and equally productive black workers is very foolish since this will push the firm's costs up and profits down. In markets with razor-thin profit margins, racist managers would drive their firms out of business or would jeopardize their long-term employment prospects with the firm's owners.

The important logical point here is that ruthless competition in a capitalist economy will punish irrational actions that result in higher costs and lower profits. Racist managers would be eliminated from markets because they were stupid enough to let their business activity be influenced by their petty racist peeves. Alas, most markets are not perfectly competitive. Most types of goods and services, even in the same product category, differ in the eyes of buyers, as the virtually endless proliferation of deodorants, soft drinks, computer software, clothing styles, music CDs, automobiles, or many millions of consumer products makes plain. Firms use product quality, color, advertising and other sales promotion, service agreements and warranties, customer service, financing terms, and other devices to partially insulate themselves from the pressure of price competition.

This sort of product differentiation is a boon to consumers because it allows people to select from a vast roster of goods to satisfy their narrow needs, including the need to consume products and services that are consistent with their ethnic and racial identity. However, product differentiation also provides racist employers some shelter from the pressure of price competition. Consider the following example. The senior partners of several major law firms (firms with reputations for excellent work that handle a large volume of important cases) in a particular city may agree to limit black upward mobility by restricting the number of blacks they approve for promotion to full partnership.

These partners, though employed by competing law firms, are members of the same social circles—patronizing the same restaurants, country clubs, health clubs, and shops, living in the same exclusive communities and sending their children to the same schools—which makes it easy for them to share information and coordinate their hiring activities. The network of informal social contacts and relationships between senior partners in different law firms coordinates the embargo on black access to partnerships in law firms effectively and cheaply.

However, the ability of these firms to engage in this kind of *persistent* racial discrimination depends on these firms' ability to retain their market advantage. If the dominant law firms have a decisive quality advantage over other firms (due to specialized training or intellectual resources that are specific to the firms and that are not generally available) or if big customers tend to send their business to the same handful of firms out of habit or loyalty, then competition from other firms cannot push these enterprises to change their hiring practices.[4] Further, discriminating firms will be able to continue operations indefinitely so long as customers are willing to pay for perceived quality differences between firms. Even if other, less discriminatory firms offer excellent legal services at comparable prices, discriminatory firms will be able to carry on their practices without paying an economic price so long as they are shielded from the price and quality pressure of competitors. The situation we've sketched above, usually referred to as a monopolistically competitive situation, allows firms to discriminate, and even suffer higher costs of production (it may take dim lawyers a longer time to get something done, or dim lawyers make more mistakes that need to be corrected, etc.) without being driven out of business, so long as they have loyal customers who are willing to pay the price.

Monopolistic competition in the market for legal services may protect discriminating firms from extinction, but is not enough to limit black upward mobility by itself. If the large firms in question are partnerships, where the primary partners use the profits from their operations to finance expansion, then discriminating firms will not grow as quickly as nonracist firms. Over time, racist partners will have purchased racial good feeling at the price of growth, thereby reducing the enterprise's prominence in the community. More generally, if discriminating firms in any industry have race-neutral but profit-hungry stockholders, then racist managers will once again find themselves without jobs because they let their beliefs interfere with the "bottom line."

However, if discriminating law firms have access to specialized resources that make them the best law firms, then black lawyers will face long-term barriers to becoming partners. What type of specialized resources? Knowledge, particularly insights into the needs of clients, access to the talents and accumulated wisdom of senior partners, and the "institutional" knowledge embedded in an organization that is specific to the enterprise. Firms, including law firms, are collections of people who share special information with each other—"secrets" from the perspective of the outside world. This information is essential to the efficiency of the enterprise, but can only be elicited in networks of cooperation based on membership in the organization. Customers and stockholders pay for the efficiency generated by these specialized resources, which in turn gives the firm power to protect itself against the corrosive effects of external competition.

In turn, the only way dominant law firms can be overturned in the marketplace, and the noxious effect of their discriminatory habits reduced, is if other, less discriminatory firms possess an equally effective collection of specialized knowledge and competencies that customers find attractive. If it takes time to acquire and develop specialized abilities, and if the development of knowledge and productive ability is connected to experience (what economists call "learning-by-doing") then discriminatory firms may have long-term advantages in the market for legal services that cannot be overcome by other firms. Black lawyers will certainly have opportunities to work in less hostile firms if these firms can (1) find an appropriate market niche and (2) develop their own abilities through learning-by-doing. However, monopolistic competition and learning-by-doing blunt the power of free markets to break the link between color and well-being in a racially divided society.

The idea that free markets are a sure cure for the destructive effects of racial hostility on black well-being has a seductive quality in conservative times. This claim promises an easy road to virtue that will gradually replace racial inequality with equal opportunity and life chances for all people with equal ability. The almost mystical quality of the Becker conjecture is accompanied by a warning against government policies that interfere with free markets which may end up making black suffering even worse. For example, one implication of the Becker conjecture is that minimum wage laws may end up preventing capitalism from promoting racial equality by reducing the incentives that nondiscriminatory employers have to hire underpaid black workers. Minimum wage laws limit the extent to which black wages fall in response to discrimination, which in turn limits the incentives of profit-hungry capitalists to hire black workers. In the absence of minimum wage laws, wages may well fall to extremely low levels but firms will hire the great bulk of black workers at these low rates of pay. However, once minimum wage laws are introduced, firms will have less incentive to hire (relatively) high-cost black workers, which results in unemployment without wages for many people rather than employment at potentially dismally low wages.

This criticism of the potential effect of minimum wage laws on long-run black economic opportunity in capitalist society is an example of a more general line of reasoning that counsels against policies which displace market incentives in order to promote racial or social equality. The core complaint against government policy in this case is that it interferes with the market's capacity to enlist greed as a social acid that burns away the negative economic consequences of discrimination for blacks in the long run. Yet, a reasonable conservative stance in this matter might weigh the effects of free markets in matters of discrimination against that social pain and economic costs that discrimination imposes on despised groups and on society as a whole.

Race and Crime in Capitalism: A Complication

Our review of the Becker conjecture has the following nasty but realistic implication: despised social groups will, at least temporarily, find themselves pushed into the illegal sector of the economy as a result of discrimination. The widespread disdain of employers for blacks will push down black wages not only relative to white wages but also relative to the "wages" that can be earned from crime. If the wages from legal work are low enough, then black workers will opt for criminal activity. Romantic moralists like to cluck that genuine morality is impervious to the pressure of poverty, envy, anger, or humiliation. It may be true that the saintly among us, if faced with a lousy life of low wages, unemploy-ment, and as the object of widespread racial disdain, might nonetheless resist the lure of crime, particularly the easy money that can be made selling drugs or sex (so long as one can evade the pain and swift death that come with this type of work). However, most of us are morally ambitious but need to eat, get angry, feel depressed, and make mistakes. Our analysis in turn suggests that outcast groups will end up in the illegal sectors of the economy—stealing and robbing, selling drugs, guns, and sex, using lethal force to fight with each other for the control of these markets—if their legal opportunities are limited and if their wages are pushed down enough because of discrimination. Note that this outcome does not require that blacks or other outcasts be especially prone to crime because of some flaw in our "culture"; all that matters is that blacks face low wages and unemployment in legal labor markets in a society that has a thriving underground trade in stolen goods, drugs, commercial sex, and other bad things.

The Becker conjecture has a nasty, if unacknowledged, corollary that discrimination in legal job markets will push outcast groups into illegal activities, thereby leading to a situation where the criminal classes tend to be blacker than the rest of the population, which in turn feeds perceptions that blacks are criminals. Further, pushing blacks into the illegal sector through discrimination and then subjecting them to crim-inal sanctions is a fine way to destroy the possibility of social peace between blacks and the rest of society. The legitimacy of law and social rules created for and run by whites is deeply suspect among despised blacks who are forced to endure discrimination in the legal sector or commit crimes in order to make a living. There will be fewer reasons for blacks to support a regime that denies them opportunities on the whim of racists, even if capitalism might someday wipe the soiled social slate clean. Of course, the State could always use escalating force to keep disgruntled blacks in line, though at the cost of further increases in violence and, more importantly, the institutionalization of force as the primary means of maintaining "peace" across the color line, though crime is only likely to become a public problem in a racial regime of the type being considered if it spills beyond the boundaries of black com-munities.

A genuine conservative moralist interested in reconciling free markets with legitimate authority in a racially divided society would worry about this, and want to avoid this outcome, because it means that markets are creating a situation where a class of people is being pushed into criminality and alienation because of the whims and phobias of a discriminatory majority. As soon as we acknowledge the possibility that capitalist societies are composed of both legal and illegal sectors, and consider the effect of racial discrimination in legal employment on the incentives for crime among the despised castes, we have to face the prospect that free markets in racially divided societies may *create* a dual and colorized society of white lawfulness and black lawlessness. In other words, plain economic logic, rather than genes and "customs," can tell us why crime might be color coded. Capitalism à la Becker and the free market Right leaves a particularly brutal criminal "legacy" of discrimination. Other legacies are explored below.

Economic Logic and "Legacies"

The foregoing analysis has shown that extreme racial discrimination in a free market setting will not indefinitely reduce black incomes and life chances so long as the profit motive and perfect competition operate without restriction. However, the long transition from a situation of rampant discrimination and racial inequality to one where racial inequality disappears, even under conditions of perfect competition, is marked by a situation where white workers are paid more than black workers. This racial inequality could have a number of unexpected consequences that reduce the ability of free markets to eventually overcome the effect of customary racism on the economic well-being of blacks.

Suppose that black wages are so low that blacks are unable to afford the necessary food, housing, or medical care to work as efficiently as whites. This situation (which among development economists is described by the term "efficiency wages") would have to mean that black workers are generally less productive relative to whites because of their poverty. In turn, the declining productivity of black workers would make them less attractive to nonracist employers, who would have less incentive to pay black workers higher wages to secure their services. In time, black workers could be so much less productive than white workers that even nonracist employers would only hire blacks at lower wage levels, thereby locking in conditions of racial inequality into the indefinite future. In other words, the initial condition of wage inequality due to widespread racist sentiment against blacks becomes a self-fulfilling prophecy by creating lower levels of relative black labor productivity, thereby converting the initial social prejudice that blacks were undesirable workers into the social *fact* that blacks are unproductive workers. Worse, lower wages in this case would not be evidence that blacks were victims of discrimination because they are "objectively" less productive than white workers as a result of past conditions of social oppression and exclusion.

We can see that the Becker conjecture that capitalism can undermine the effects of anti-black sentiment on black well-being is potentially correct if inequality does not undermine the productivity of black workers. It is relatively simple to see how corrective government action—food and nutrition programs for adults and especially children, housing and health programs that create minimally decent living and health conditions for black workers, income support programs that boost the minimum incomes of poor people, among others—could reverse the damaging long-term effects of wage inequality on black well-being. The disastrous effects of low wages, poor nutrition, inadequate health care, and insufficient housing on the intellectual development of young children and the working ability of adults can be overcome relatively quickly (within a decade or two) so long as black adults and children are physically and intellectually similar to whites counterparts, contra *The Bell Curve*.

Life is more complicated when we add in the effects of unequal educational opportunity on the productive competence of blacks. Chapter 1 showed that black Americans have made great progress in closing the knowledge gap with whites in terms of high school and college completion rates. Gary Becker developed another very important idea in economics that has direct relevance to the issue of education and discrimination. In 1964, Becker published a theoretical analysis, *Human Capital*, that explored the economic relationship between investments in knowledge, labor productivity, and the distribution of income and economic well-being. The basic point behind the idea of human capital is quite straightforward: individual men and women spend money and time in school in order to acquire knowledge and skills which will then lead to higher future incomes. The act of expending current resources (tuition and the foregone wages associated with attending classes) in order to earn higher wages in the future is an act of investment that creates an asset (knowledge) that then yields a return. This knowledge-asset or human capital is embodied within the educated person. Any parent faced with the decision of whether and where to send a child to college is faced with the classic human capital problem: which college (if any) will provide the highest return (in terms of higher wages and a better quality of life) on the resources being poured into my child's education, given my child's aptitudes, ambition, and work habits (or lack thereof)?

One of the most important insights that comes out of the idea of human capital is that the effects of education are cumulative: the considerable skills and abilities of well-educated people are built upon a foundation of good-quality early schooling. In turn, people with poor-quality early schooling do not get as much out of later schooling than their more fortunate neighbors because they lack the knowledge and training to fully absorb more complex ideas. For example, it makes little sense to consider sending a child to Harvard at a cost of $35,000 per year (now in the spring of 1998) if the child has not completed junior high school, since (aside from the fact the Harvard will quietly dispose of your child's application) the child is simply unprepared to absorb the concepts and information through the lectures, readings, informal discussions and laboratory work at a leading university.

This commonsense point has a powerful implication when we consider the effect of racial discrimination on the long-term well-being of blacks. Return to an initial situation of racial discrimination that results in wage inequality between blacks and whites. Wage inequality, and especially black poverty, will mean that blacks will have less access to high-quality education than whites for two reasons. First, racial segregation in housing and schooling, combined with lower black incomes, will mean that black schools will be less well equipped than white schools, though this need not mean that black schools are radically worse than white schools in all aspects of basic education. Nonetheless, the material deprivation of blacks' schools will mean that black students will have less access to the updated materials than whites, which matters in a technology-driven society where knowledge is constantly being created and destroyed. Second, lower black incomes may lead to lower levels of black academic achievement if poverty is so severe that black children perform poorly in schools. If wages and living standards fall below a threshold level necessary for adequate intellectual functioning, then black academic success may suffer as a result of historic discrimination.

Third, the human capital that each generation of children can build up through schooling depends on the educational attainments of their parents and larger community as well as on the investments of effort, time, and money that parents and communities make in formal education. This simple observation has a powerful implication: historic discrimination can reduce the effectiveness of current educational investments in black children through its negative effect on the educational attainments of black adults. A great deal of recent work in economics, particularly in the area of economic growth, has shown that current levels of educational and economic performance depend on the extent and quality of past investments in schooling. Systematic underinvestment in black schooling in the past will reduce the amount of knowledge that black adults can pass on to their children, which in turn reduces the extent to which black children can absorb new knowledge relative to white children, thereby resulting in lower levels of black academic achievement. This idea that investments in education complement each other over time implies that the intergenerational transmission of class status from parent to child is strongly affected by historical forces that set boundaries on the ability of current and future governments, even those with radical egalitarian intentions, to improve the educational performance of historically abused people. (Readers who are not persuaded by this brief argument might want to explore a mathematical model linking historic discrimination to human capital presented in the appendix to this chapter.) In particular,

1. discrimination reduces the wages of black workers, thereby lowering the inflow of public and private resources available for schooling black children in a segregated society,
2. historic discrimination reduces current levels of black educational attainment relative to that of whites, which once again leads to

low relative black wages and recreating conditions of underfunded black schools,

3. black and white schooling outcomes differ because of the cumulative effect of historic underinvestment in black schools. Further, the relatively low level of black human capital, which is a by-product of historic racial discrimination in the labor market as well as in school funding, causes education spending on current generations of black children to be less effective than school spending on current populations of white children.

In the long run of the Becker conjecture, blacks are relatively less productive than whites because they have not been able to accumulate the same levels of human capital as whites. Once again, free markets fail to produce racial equality because historic inequality creates structural differences between whites and blacks. However, knowledge differences between blacks and whites are much harder to overcome than nutritional differences linked to low incomes because of the cumulative nature of human capital. Blacks must now invest heavily in human capital in order to catch up to the average level of knowledge attained among whites.

Our exploration of the Becker conjecture has shown us how historic discrimination can lead to persistent differences in current academic achievement and productivity between racial groups by subsidizing the accumulation of knowledge by dominant groups at the expense of despised groups. Discrimination can not only lock black people out of good jobs at high wages, it can also create long-term differences in the distribution of "abilities" across color lines for economic rather than biological or "cultural" reasons.

Uncertainty, Merit, and Discrimination[5]

There is a considerable range of variation in the talents, skills, ambitions, and capacities within each of these "racial" populations. Employers, lenders, private schools, and universities will all hire workers, finance investment projects, and admit students on the basis of imperfect forecasts about the skills and competencies of the people they are dealing with. This problem of imperfect information is endemic in market society; the wide variety of abilities within any potential population turns all employment, investment, and admissions decisions into lotteries. Decision makers will certainly have incentives to acquire information about potential clients or customers in order to reduce the uncertainty associated with hiring, lending, and admissions decisions, just as employees have incentives to signal their abilities to potential employers by acquiring the best education, maintaining satisfactory work histories, and acquiring impressive résumés. This type of uncertainty cannot be eliminated, no matter how many attempts firms make to reduce the possibility of mistakes.

The irreducible variety of motives, skills, and training among a population of workers, students, or potential borrowers obliges firms, schools, and lenders to make informed guesses about the outcome of important economic decisions. For example, hiring and training workers is usually a costly proposition. Firms faced with making hiring decisions have incentives to acquire as much information about potential job candidates as possible in order to reduce the costs of choosing the wrong person for the job. Résumés, letters of recommendation, test scores, and the academic reputation of a candidate's school(s) are important sources of information that help a firm assess a person's ability to perform job-related tasks. However, additional sources of information, including race and gender, are also used by firms to make predictions about a candidate's abilities. If managers believe that GPA and standardized tests scores are good predictors of a candidate's ability to perform on the job, and if blacks tend to have lower GPAs and test scores than candidates from other racial and ethnic groups, then a racially neutral hiring policy will tend to favor nonblacks. Further, blacks can still lose out in the competition for jobs, even if blacks have the same average scores and GPAs as nonblacks, if black grades and test scores display a wider range of variation than those nonblacks. This kind of discrimination, usually referred to as "statistical" or "rational" discrimination, is based on information and beliefs about the distribution of abilities of different populations of potential employees, or students, or borrowers. In each case, individual blacks may lose out in the struggle for jobs and income because blacks, as a group, have lower levels of achievement along with a wider range of relevant skills and abilities than members of other social groups in situations where accurate information about individuals is costly or unavailable. "Discrimination" in this case refers to the fact that individual blacks may lose opportunities because of the perceived characteristics of blacks as a group in a world where information is imperfect.

This sort of "discrimination," though unfair and harmful to individuals, cannot persist indefinitely unless blacks, on average, actually have lower and more widely varied levels of achievement than whites. However, widespread belief in black inferiority can become a self-fulfilling expectation. Think for a moment about the consequences of the widespread belief in black intellectual inferiority (as shown by the phenomenal popularity of *The Bell Curve*), held by employers, college admissions officers, and other key actors in the economy. A widely shared belief in black intellectual inferiority means, among other things, that any investments in black businesses, educations, skill development, or housing (via the mortgage market) are high-risk gambles when compared to similar investments in whites. Since investment in schools, technology, and businesses are the key to economic success in any country, region, or racial group, a belief in black inferiority necessarily means that free markets will invest fewer resources in black schooling or business development. A number of simple and terrible economic consequences follow from a widespread belief in black inferiority.

First, if whites believe that blacks are dumb and therefore incompetent as managers, business people, students, workers, or property owners, then whites expect blacks to fail more often than whites at whatever task they try. This does not have to mean that all blacks are expected to fail all the time and under all conditions; it only means that blacks, on average, are thought to be less successful than whites in their business endeavors, at school, at work, or as property owners. But if projects managed by blacks are high risk relative to projects managed by whites, then any rational, profit-maximizing lender (no matter their color) will *and should* offset the increased risk associated with dealing with blacks by discriminating against them, that is, by treating blacks differently from nonblacks.

One way for economically rational agents, *regardless of color*, to reduce the risk associated with lending to blacks is to simply refuse to lend to blacks because they will yield less profit than whites, which would be the outcome of laws that required lenders to offer loans at the same interest rates to blacks and whites. Alternatively, lenders may require that blacks pay higher interest rates than whites in order to offset the higher risk associated with black borrowing. Third, lenders may demand more information from blacks than they do from whites in order to reduce the chance of lending to a "bad" black. This last demand has the effect of increasing the cost of borrowing for blacks by forcing blacks to collect and present more information about themselves to potential lenders. Note that the belief that blacks are stupid relative to whites must lead to blacks being treated differently from whites since blacks are thought to be higher-risk applicants than whites. Any demand for equal treatment in lending across the color line will lead to lower bank profits and higher loan default rates if blacks are indeed less capable than whites.

Lending officers do not have to share personal beliefs about black stupidity in order to engage in rational discrimination; all that bank officers have to believe is that the societal belief in black stupidity reduces the chances of black success relative to white prospects. Hence, a bank is being perfectly rational when it denies loans to black home buyers on the belief that racial animosity toward blacks will reduce the resale values of houses owned by blacks. Similarly, a bank's refusal to lend to a black collegian is rational if there is reason to believe that a *societal* belief in black inferiority will limit the student's job prospects, or hurt the student's chances of doing well in a predominantly white school.

The idea that blacks are dumb by nature must lead to a low estimate of the chances of black success, thereby resulting in a rational reduction in the amount of capital invested in educating blacks, housing blacks, or black business projects. One consequence of the belief in black inferiority is that the restricted supply of capital to blacks leads to low levels of investment in black skills, restrictions on black access to technological advances (particularly those associated with higher education), lower levels of black home ownership, lower rates of black business formation and therefore less black business and technical experience in areas requiring significant amounts of capital. In other words, the widespread belief in black inferiority can become a self-fulfilling prophecy and that gradually creates the conditions of black underdevelopment that were attributed to nature.

The economic problem here is that racial beliefs are, for better or worse, part of the information that individuals and institutions use to allocate credit, capital, and technical knowledge. In particular, racial ideas play a powerful role in granting or denying black access to capital and schooling, the two most important economic resources for the development of blacks' competitive prowess. The lower level of investment in black skills and black entrepreneurs relative to whites must lead to a growing skills and experience gap between blacks and whites that justifies the low evaluation of blacks. But can an erroneous yet widespread belief in black stupidity persist indefinitely?

Once again, economic theory suggests that competition between firms run by misinformed or racially phobic managers and better informed firms will gradually cause job and investment opportunities for blacks to better reflect the "true" extent of black skills and ambitions. For example, ambitious and unconventional managers who do not share the conventional wisdom about black worker abilities (or the lack thereof) will take the initiative to develop better ways of discovering and evaluating talent in order to hire highly productive black workers at relatively low wages. In turn, other open-minded managers will imitate the mavericks, thereby encouraging the spread of more accurate views of blacks across the labor market. The idea that competition and free markets can force businesses, schools, and banks to revise their information about blacks under threat of economic losses may seem odd but is simply an extension of the logic of the Becker conjecture discussed earlier.

However, both the Becker conjecture and the idea of rational discrimination in competitive settings imply that persistent racial inequality in wages and employment opportunities reflect structural differences between blacks and whites rooted in learned skills, attitudes, or even basic aptitudes. Dinesh D'Souza's emphasis on the cultural basis for inferior black economic and academic performance is simply a hamhanded version of economic approaches to discrimination that view the market as revealing rather than creating persistent racial gaps. Similarly, Murray and Herrnstein's genetic explanation for perceived black underperformance in jobs and schools seems to be perfectly consistent with the economic theories of discrimination we have considered. Does economic theory provide intellectual cover for the slanders of D'Souza,

Murray, and Herrnstein by denying the possibility that differences in academic and economic achievement across racial and ethnic groups might be due to differences in social class—in terms of wealth, income, political power and organization, and the associated access to important goods and services—as well as "culture" and genes?

The data on black middle- and upper-class standardized test scores presented in chapter 1 are regularly used by enthusiasts of genetic and cultural determinism to show that race or culture are more powerful explanations for relative black "failure" than social class. Yet, our analysis shows why genetic and cultural explanations of black intellectual "failure" are vicious exercises in Sambo-bashing. The data in chapter 1 on black educational attainment and black poverty since 1967 present a picture of an impoverished people who had been denied income, opportunity, and knowledge in a capitalist society rife with a ritual "fear of the dark" in the North and State-organized discrimination in the South. The elimination of segregation in the South and the passage and enforcement of Civil Rights statutes throughout the nation since the mid-1960s gave blacks a chance to enter the American capitalist game on far fairer terms than ever before. But discrimination did a great deal of damage that left blacks in a state of economic and intellectual underdevelopment. As economic theory predicts, blacks have chosen to attend school at impressive rates because of the obvious income gains from schooling.

Yet, the cumulative nature of human capital means that history has left blacks with less experience in academic competition than whites, with the consequence that blacks are less likely to do as well as whites in the struggle for places in elite universities and for jobs. Discrimination has given whites an enormous head start on blacks that will persist for some time, especially in a technology-driven world economy where knowledge and academic achievement are ever more important sources of individual well-being. This interpretation of the evidence of black achievement and relative backwardness is perfectly consistent with economic theory and social reality, though it requires the analyst and citizen to admit that poverty does damage and that accumulation of knowledge within a racial or ethnic group is tightly linked to social class as well as to the practices of families and "cultures" across generations. It suggests that markets *both* reveal and create differences between racial groups in a society with a long history of racial subordination and persistent class disparities. Analysts who point to "culture" as an explanation of black performance are willingly ignoring the most basic insights of economic theory, that ability is as much a product of deliberate investments in skill and training over extended periods of time as it is the result of good folkways. Indeed, our analysis suggests that "folkways" are as much a product of the economic experience of racial groups as they are the expression of dubious racial authenticity.

Yet, the barriers to prosperity that confront the black poor are the same class barriers responsible for poverty and social stagnation everywhere: ignorance, illiteracy, structural unemployment, disease, crime, violence, fear, superstition, high birth rates, inadequate housing, lousy or nonexistent schools, and a deep, corrosive fatalism that is the inevitable counterpart of poverty. Some of these conditions can be blamed on the habits and morals of the poor only if one willfully and maliciously pretends that attitudes are somehow completely independent of opportunities and wealth. Poor people, like other people, do stupid, vicious, foolish, self-destructive things for all the same psychological and spiritual reasons that everyone else does. Because poor people are poor, they suffer the consequences of their folly or bad luck, whereas the middle class and the rich can afford to repair the damage caused by many of their self-inflicted wounds.

Some conservatives are much too eager to forget that *social class* hurts in this and other market societies, injuring the soul and spirit of men and women, leaving deep wounds that may fail to show up in any crude measures that might interest economists. Being poor hurts in a society where wealth and income are the key to status and esteem. The sting of poverty can be a powerful spur to work harder, study longer hours, and try even more ways to escape from the miseries of privation and low social esteem. But the pain of poverty can also lead to a desire to escape through drugs, through sex, or through the dangerous and exciting games of violence and gain that comprise the world of street gangs competing for the control of local narcotics markets. There is more than one response to poverty. One response is to "drop out" by becoming a junkie, a wino, or a street hustler, making oneself an object of use and abuse for others and a nullity in the eyes of the community. Another response is to reject the values and sanctions of the larger society, instead asserting oneself and one's ambition for wealth and power by participating in illegal markets. A third response is to do the best one can by following the rules, living frugally, and hoping that hard work and the joys of family life can someday pay off for oneself and one's children. The lives of many poor people combine these ways of being, just as many middle-class and upper-class people move through a life cycle that may feature youthful rage and rebellion, depression, self-destructive behavior, and finally an acceptance of the limits and joys of life. To be sure, the content of these life projects differs greatly between the middle class and the poor, but only because the middle class has more money and more opportunity.

Ethnographers, sociologists, and anthropologists have all documented how poor young men, particularly poor young black and Latino men in the current period, but including young white men in rural areas and in cities, will create and sustain status systems that put an emphasis on physical prowess, a capacity to inflict and withstand violence, and a premium on honor that can regularly result in death and injury for those who fail to show the proper "respect." All of this research points to the ubiquitous need on the part of the young to pursue ambitions of wealth, power, and status by whatever means, including status games that are dangerous and self-destructive. Conventional economists, and those who rely too much on the economist's view of the world, forget that human beings will do almost anything to avoid viewing themselves as failures, even at the risk of destroying themselves and their communities. For better or for worse, men and women in these communities deeply identify with the values of material success and power of the larger society, so much so that failing by those standards is so painful that other, plausible, and attainable standards are put in their place.[6]

Contrary to the assumption that the poor are somehow exempt from or immune to market values, the competition for status through sex, violence, and reputation among some (though not all) of the young urban poor are simply manifestations of market values. The primary difference between these forms of competition, and the conventionally sanctioned forms of market and sexual competition in middle-class areas is that the drive for status and gain is channeled into socially destructive activities among the young poor, rather than being directed toward uses that contribute to the economy by increasing skills, or acquiring knowledge, or making a marketable product.[7]

An honest approach to economic life also requires us to acknowledge that incentives shape behavior in the context of opportunities, most of which are the result of forces, both past and present, that are simply beyond an individual's or even a group's control. Once we acknowledge the fact that few people choose their circumstances, and that the choices people make are nonetheless guided by the complex interplay of incentives and their sense of self, we have to face up to the possibility that poor people make bad choices from a roster of even worse options. Unless we can somehow pin all of the blame for the poverty of the black and Latino urban poor on "bad" attitudes that set them apart from the rest of society, we will have to acknowledge that a person's attitudes toward work, family, and society's norms are as much a product of their opportunities and economic position as they are a cause of opportunities. If this all sounds a bit like the chicken and the egg, it should: opportunities create attitudes, which in turn create opportunities, in exactly the same way that chickens make eggs, which *later* make more chickens.[8]

An economic explanation of racial inequality that shows how historic discrimination can create persistent group differences in achievement because poverty hurts the poor, and because the damage inflicted on pariah castes takes a very long time to heal, does not automatically endorse any particular policy to overcome race-based disparities in life chances. Even if history and capitalism have conspired to wound black people in ways that take a long time to overcome, what about the effect of *current* discrimination on black people? Is it very important? If so, how? What is the relative importance of social class versus discrimination for modern racial inequality?

Overcoming Racial Inequality: The Conservative Stance

It is essential to understand that the conservative view does not necessarily imply that racial discrimination does not exist, as some right-wing hacks would have us believe, or that racial discrimination does not itself block the economic progress of blacks to some extent. What the conservative view presented in the preceding paragraphs does imply is that the gradual, if painful, integration of poor blacks into the culture of markets will eventually give blacks the cultural capital to compete successfully with members of other racial and ethnic groups, thereby diminishing the problem of racial inequality over time if barriers to participation in markets are removed. This view has powerful implications for the role of government policy in the matter of racial inequality. A conservative favoring minimal government regulation in economic matters is likely to resist most attempts of use public power to redress racial problems because of a general presumption that racial problems are the unfortunate by-product of individual liberty in a free society. Nonetheless, a serious conservative knows that many white men and women in a multiracial America will act on racist beliefs, thereby refusing to do business with people from despised racial and ethnic groups. Since this distaste for people from outcast groups is widespread, and since whites have significant control of the business and cultural institutions of society, racist beliefs inevitably result in the *temporary* impoverishment and unemployment of blacks and other despised groups.

However, the problem of black poverty and relative economic deprivation can be overcome in a free market society if blacks are willing and able to acquire education, work hard, and practice self-restraint in their personal lives. The serious conservative claims that white racial tastes hold power in a capitalist society by virtue of white technical and economic advantage in the competitive struggle. Assuming that government is neutral in the conflict between racial groups, there is no reason that willing blacks cannot gradually outcompete whites in schools, factories, and other areas, thereby gradually overturning white advantage and eliminating the ability of whites to create black poverty and underdevelopment as a by-product of white racial whims.

The key to reversing a situation of white racial domination and black humiliation in a free market context is for blacks to insist on government policies that bolster free markets and promote competition based on profit and merit. In a racially neutral setting, where government refrains from sponsoring any racial group preferences or phobias, those blacks who are willing to adopt an aggressive attitude in markets will be successful, since whites have no long-term monopoly on talent or economic ability (notwithstanding the claims of *The Bell Curve*). However, blacks who, for whatever cultural or historical reasons, eschew market competition or promote values that are inappropriate for economic success will continue to languish. In a free market society committed to racial neutrality in government policy, "racial" inequality will eventually be replaced by an inequality rooted in individual differences in attitude toward competition, hard work, and education. Inequality, per se, is not something conservatives worry about very much, largely because they assume that people in a free market society get paid in accordance with their ability, education, and willingness to work. Indeed, inequality in a capitalist society is assumed to be a good thing from a conservative perspective, precisely because it both reflects the distribution of skills and abilities in a population, and because it is an incentive to greater effort by those who are driven by a desire for wealth and power.

It is clear that this view of race in a free market setting relies on the Becker conjecture. If white racial anxiety cannot prevent blacks from succeeding in markets, then the best way to overcome black poverty is to find ways to change the dysfunctional attitudes and habits of the black poor. A vigorous government commitment to race neutrality in public policy is essential to promoting the power of markets to destroy racial barriers, since the historical white monopoly over public power was the essential weapon used to repress blacks politically and economically. Once the nation has assumed a permanent commitment to race neutrality that forever prevents the return of the tyranny of the white majority that caused slavery and segregation in the first place, there are no limits to black economic progress so long as blacks can complete the transition to a modernist, scientific cultural outlook.

There is no doubt that certain forms of discrimination that harm minorities are simply beyond the reach of government policy or free markets to eradicate. Glenn Loury notes that some types of discrimination—where to live, whom to live around, whom to date and marry, study with, work with and play with—may also perpetuate racial inequality by limiting black access to important economic resources.[9] Loury's argument anticipates much of the substance of the analysis of discrimination in a modern, technology-driven economy further developed in this book by suggesting that the freedom to choose which is at the core of American life and identity can effectively block black economic development if racial discrimination in housing, schooling, and employment also prevents blacks from becoming effective competitors in markets.[10] Loury notes that under these conditions, race-conscious government policy that tries to compensate for the negative consequences of whites' freedom to choose may be justified, at least from the perspective of a conservative economist interested in both economic efficiency and equity.

In an technologically static society that takes free markets seriously, there is little reason to believe that competition and individual liberty will not eventually destroy even racist social practices that can, for a time at least, perpetuate racial inequalities that are an echo from the periods of slavery and segregation. Though social and racial customs appear to be especially tenacious in the areas of romance, marriage, friendship, and living arrangements, there is little reason to believe that segregationist sentiment on the part of whites will overcome the power of modernism and markets to push racist ideology to the fringe of social life. The anarchic nature of human desire and the ongoing battle between secular, anti-racist thinking (which has the prestige and weight of science behind it) on the one hand and racial superstition on the other will almost certainly lead to the establishment of cross-racial contacts that can, over time, transmit important economic information, resources, and opportunities to pariah groups, especially if "white" and "nonwhite" cultural practices influence each other over time.

In the absence of ongoing economic change, especially in the form of technological development that destroys the economic relevance of the skills of backward groups, the usual solvents of desire, profit, and plain curiosity can be expected to whittle away at the ability of informal racist practices to result in black economic deprivation. The problem with discrimination in a modern, technology-driven economy is that it prevents the rapid dissemination of information, skills, and capital to pariah groups, thereby putting them in a position of permanent relative backwardness. The conservative interpretation of the critique of welfare dependency simply reinforces the point that poor relief can hinder the ability of poor blacks to "catch up" with whites by providing them with an alternative to participating in markets, thereby worsening an already serious problem of black economic and social underdevelopment.

But is welfare really a trap that limits black economic progress? Though popular sentiment, and now government policy, is based on the assumption that welfare is the cause of long-term poverty among the black poor, recent research on the impact of welfare on the behavior of the poor has not been kind to the welfare trap thesis. While extensive research has been done on many aspects of the impact of welfare on work incentives, family composition, and teenage motherhood, there is little overall consensus about the strength of these effects on the behavior of the poor. For example, there is no agreement about whether welfare increases the fertility of poor teenagers. The most that can be said for this part of the welfare trap thesis is that it is not supported by the evidence at this time (at least in the view of most researchers in this field), though later studies may reach a different conclusion. In general, most studies seem to support the following, rather weak, claims about the effect of welfare on the behavior of the poor:[11]

1. Welfare (primarily AFDC and Food Stamps) have statistically significant, but rather small, effects on the work incentives and family structure of the poor. Labor supply for women who are eligible for the AFDC program falls when benefits rise. In addition, increases in AFDC and Food Stamp benefits increase the number of persons who participate in these programs. However, the high unemployment rate among women who are also heading a household is not accounted for by welfare disincentives. As Robert Moffitt notes in his excellent survey of the economics literature in this area: "most AFDC women would, apparently, be poor even in the absence of the AFDC program."[12]

2. There is little agreement about the extent to which the children of mothers who receive welfare will themselves become welfare recipients later. To the extent that studies do support the thesis that welfare can become a way of life for succeeding generations of the poor, the evidence does not support the strong claims of some that welfare will trap large numbers of the poor into dependency over many generations.[13]

3. Welfare cannot account for the increasing number of families headed by women. Nor does welfare appear to be a very important factor in the long-term decline in marriage rates among poor women, especially since this decline has taken place over a period of time where the real value of welfare benefits has been falling.[14]

The most consistent finding of many studies is also the most difficult for conservatives to face: poverty, rather than welfare, seems to be the primary problem of the poor. Sheldon Danziger and Peter Gottschalk in *America Unequal,* an excellent summary of the extensive research on the causes of growing poverty and income inequality in the United States since the early 1970s, show that changes in the composition of families—that is, increases in the fraction of families headed by women—are an important source of the increase in poverty between 1973 and 1991.[15] However, Danziger and Gottschalk also show that the primary reasons for growing poverty were slow economic growth, particularly stagnant real wages for most of the working population (a subject we return to in the next chapter) and significant increases in the wage gap between skilled and unskilled workers that was noted in chapter 1.[16] Danziger and Gottschalk note that the primary causes of persistent poverty in this country are what they have always been: unemployment, bad schools, and low levels of academic and intellectual achievement among the parents of poor children. The failure of research to single out welfare as a major cause of declining marriage rates and the rising percentage of teenage births as a fraction of all live births (in the face of a *decline* in overall teenage fertility), means that we have to face the possibility that the problems of poverty and the underclass may be structural problems that go far beyond the issues of welfare, or even politics. Indeed, the problems of the urban poor may be rooted in the large-scale changes in the world economy and in the structure of family life and gender relations across the class spectrum that are destroying traditional social institutions with no obvious alternatives in sight. Singling out the black poor for their inability to negotiate this crisis of modernity is dishonest and unfair.

Beyond Race: Capitalism, Individualism, and Family Meltdown

The conservative view of the links between race, poverty, and black underdevelopment presented above can be summarized briefly by three statements:

1. Markets reward those individuals and groups who possess habits of thought and cultural practices that promote work, saving, risk-

taking, and education with high incomes and prestigious positions in the private sector.

2. The black poor are prevented from acquiring economically remunerative cultural traits by welfare, which blunts the effect of poverty on the integration of blacks into the full range of opportunities in the American economy. Welfare allows the black poor to hold on to dysfunctional ways of being by subsidizing self-destructive behavior, thereby preventing poor black youth from fully appreciating the need to study, work hard, and delay reproduction in order to achieve economic success.

3. If the black poor can be made to adopt more appropriate mores and outlooks, then a policy of race neutrality and vigorous free market competition will eventually eliminate the problem of racial inequality. Discrimination cannot lead to permanent and disproportionate group poverty among blacks so long as markets remain competitive and so long as blacks are ready and able to compete effectively.

Our doubts about the usefulness of the Becker conjecture make us skeptical of all conservative approaches to the question of racial inequality that ultimately rely on the easy virtues of free markets. Indeed, the recent tendency to bring black poverty into debates on racial conflict in this country, particularly in the form of debates about the role of welfare in creating and maintaining a black urban underclass, serves only to divert attention from the real problems of race and *class* in a complex, technology-driven economy. One surprising example of how talk about race, welfare, and the perverse consequences of kindness prevents us from thinking clearly about the role of class in racial matters is the debate over the meltdown of black families, particularly the problem of high rates of black teenage pregnancy.

We are all familiar with the wailing and moaning about the collapse, disappearance, or most dreadfully, conspiracy against the black family that accompanies the litany of statistics about high rates of black teenage childbearing. A brief look at recent data concerning black teenage childbearing will help focus our discussion and debunk a fair bit of useless (or worse) right-wing rhetoric in the process. The birth rate for black teenagers between 15 to 19 is the ratio of the number of live

Table 2.1 Birth Rates for Black and White Teenagers,
15–19 Years of Age, for Selected Years

Year	White	Black
1960	79.4	156.1
1965	60.6	144.6
1970	57.4	140.7
1975	46.4	111.8
1980	45.4	97.8
1985	43.3	95.5
1990	50.8	112.8
1995	50.1	96.1
1996	48.4	91.7

births per thousand teenage young black women in the age group. Table 2.1 shows the birth rate for white and black teenagers for selected years since 1960, while figures 2.1(a) and 2.1(b) show the evolution of annual black and white teenage birth rates between 1980 and 1996. The first thing that jumps out at the reader from Table 2.1 is that black teenage birth rates (the upper line in figure 2.1[a]) fell steadily between 1960 (the earliest year for which data is available) and 1985, then went up briefly in the late 1980s and early 1990s, before falling again through 1996. Second, the astute reader with an ear for political rhetoric cannot help but smile at the meaning of the fact that the black teenage birth rate in 1996 was the *lowest ever recorded*.

There are good economic reasons to worry about these trends, especially in times when unskilled workers find themselves with very limited wage and employment prospects. Teenage childbearing is an economic and social disaster for both mother and child. Teenage pregnancy and childbirth pose significant health risks to mother and child. Children born to teenagers tend to be low birthweight babies, which is in turn associated with long-term intellectual and emotional development problems. Further, teenage parents are ill-equipped to handle the demands of parenthood, which all too frequently result in high rates of child abuse and neglect among the children of pre-mature mothers that destroy the well-being of these children. Teenage mothers frequently drop out of school, or end their schooling earlier than is economically prudent, thereby reducing their already limited earning capacity and becoming trapped in low-skill, low-wage jobs.

Figure 2.1(a): Birth Rates for Black and White Teenagers. Ages 15–19,
1980–1996

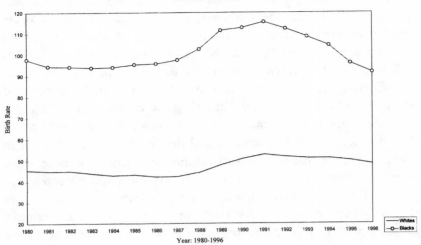

Figure 2.1(b): Ratio of Black to White Teenage Birth Rates,
1980–1996

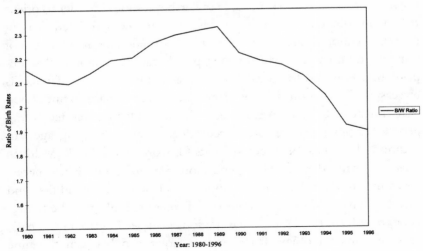

The question of teenage pregnancy and childbearing is exceedingly sensitive because it requires us to think about the sexual lives and attitudes of children, a very uncomfortable subject. We have already noted that there is little evidence that teenage childbearing resulted from welfare spending (specifically the now defunct Aid to Families with Dependent Children). In addition, data from the Center for Disease Control show that black teenagers have very similar patterns of sexual behavior to their white and Hispanic counterparts. Table 2.2 shows the distribution of black and white women by age at the time of their first act of sexual intercourse and the age of their first partner in 1995. It is clear that young black women are marginally more active than their white counterparts, who are in turn more sexually active that young Hispanic women. However, the differences in sexual activity shown in Table 2.2 are small enough for us to doubt that the primary cause of black teenage pregnancy and childbearing is that blacks have lots more sex at younger ages than whites. In the face of disturbing evidence about the consequences of teenage childbearing, social analysts have tried to understand why so many young women are bearing children at all instead of (1) using effective means of contraception, (2) terminating pregnancies via abortion, or (3) marrying the fathers of their children. Why are young black women choosing to bear children at higher rates than whites?

At this point, an unsentimental economist might make a couple of observations and then ask a couple of harsh questions in order to orient the discussion. One of the most basic and underappreciated facts of modern economic life is that the gap between the age of onset of puberty and the age at which young people can be economically independent agents able to provide for the material needs of their families is increasing. The reasons for this growing gap are not hard to find. Food is abundant and cheap in America, with the result that well-fed young people are physically capable of reproduction at very young ages. In addition, the educational requirements for work in a technology-driven society demand that children spend more time in school, which necessarily means that they are economically dependent on adults, and therefore unable to care for their own families (should they be foolish enough to form them) for longer periods of time. Logic and the basic facts of human biology dictate that a larger gap between the time

Table 2.2 Age of First Voluntary Intercourse for Women by Age of Woman and Age of Partner in the United States in 1995

| | | | Black Women | | | |
| | | | Men | | | |
	<16	17–18	19–20	20–22	23–24	>24
Women						
<16	26.0	41.1	21.6	5.7	1.7	4.0
16–19	0.5	23.8	39.1	24.2	5.2	7.2
≥20	0.2	0.3	3.9	31.0	18.7	46.0

| | | | White Women | | | |
| | | | Men | | | |
	<16	17–18	19–20	20–22	23–24	>24
Women						
<16	21.2	45.9	20.8	6.6	2.0	3.5
16–19	1.1	23.5	37.1	24.7	6.9	6.7
≥20	—	0.7	5.4	35.3	20.7	38.1

Source: National Center for Health Statistics
Updated: May 1, 1997

puberty sets in and the time required for economic maturity will lead to significant degrees of sexual activity between economically dependent young people.

For example, a nineteen-year-old male who had sex with his seventeen-year-old girlfriend in 1920 was expected to marry her and support his family while she was bound by custom and social pressure to devote herself to caring for the family. However, the same pair in 1920 could form this traditional family unit because a modestly educated man could find work that met his family's needs. Note that the social prejudice and discrimination that restricted her access to schooling and jobs also tied the couple together by backing stringent divorce laws and social disapproval of divorce, thereby assuring that husbands had to support their wives and children for life.

We all know that this family system was built on the radical restriction of women's freedom and is, for that reason, unacceptable. However, this system did channel the sexual desires of young people into socially acceptable *and economically viable* directions by tying sex to marriage and to a source of economic support. The problem with youthful sex in modern America is not that the young are having sex but rather that they are simply economically incompetent in a world where education is essential for long-term well-being. We might hope that young people delay their sexual lives until they are capable of assuming the economic responsibilities that go along with sex, but youth is blind, foolish, heedless, and above all reckless. The types of jobs that our young couple might have access to now are low-wage, low-skill jobs that offer very little in the way of training or career advancement. Both partners will have to work in order to make ends meet, which means that they will have to find some form of affordable child care unless they are able to rely on family or community help (though that requires some independent form of support for the provider of child care). Further, early marriages are notorious for being tumultuous and unstable unions that break apart for the simple reason that the people involved are still too unformed to make lifelong commitments to struggle through the considerable challenge of staying married.

In an odd way, modern economic life in the age of birth control has placed sexually active young people in an awkward position. Sexually active young men still resist using birth control, and even disease-preventing condoms, because they are reckless, stupid, and abusive of the young women they join with. There is evidence that many young, poor men engage in predatory sexual status games that are essentially tournaments where boys compete with each other to impregnate as many women as possible.[17] Yet, modern economic conditions make the traditional "shotgun" wedding impossible since the resulting marriage would be between two equally incompetent people who cannot support themselves. Shotgun weddings might have a better chance of success (at least in terms of economic viability) if the community commits itself (including through the public purse) to support young couples with children with income, housing, health care, and child care needs while they finish school (which, of course, would force society in invest heavily in schooling for poor children). The financial costs of supporting the couple and their children while they complete their schooling are likely to be high. Further, this sort of social support system might encourage large numbers of reckless young people to marry early, with little regard to the meaning of marriage aside from the initial sexual thrill and the fun of "playing house."

Finally, why would a young, poor, sexually active woman choose to bear a child? Why would a young, poor man engage in reproductive sex? Economics cannot shed much light on the reasons for a particular person's decision. However, a hard-nosed economic perspective requires us to see that the particular reasons a young person might make this choice are less important than the fact that he or she acts for personal reasons, without much concern for the social consequences of his or her actions. A young man has sex for pleasure, to impress his friends, to alleviate boredom, or to engage in one or another sadistic ritual of domination over women. A young woman may be just as shallow as her male counterpart, or may genuinely, but foolishly, want a baby, or want to impress her friends, or choose to take on adult roles without thinking, or just make a mistake that they cannot correct because of religious injunctions against abortion.

No matter their reasons, one thing is certain: these young people are acting on their own impulses, without any thought about how their actions will affect the lives of their own children, or their community. This is a classic example of a negative externality, which we earlier defined as an act that has negative consequences for third parties. Is the child who bears children, or her male partner who has sex without condoms, shortsighted, stupid, selfish, and vile? Of course. However, name calling is beside the point: these twits are having sex and making babies because they do not consider the effect of their behavior on the rest of us, or on their own futures. Economic logic and human nature suggest that we have to find ways of imposing effective penalties on these children that make them want to avoid reproductive sex in their own interests. This is a daunting problem, in part because we are not going to be able to impose penalties that encourage young people to avoid sex altogether until they are economically mature, nor should we. A commitment to individual liberty and social sanity should make us leery of creating government institutions that try to regulate the sexual behavior of young poor people. This sort of class-based regulatory scheme is obnoxious, and likely to be ineffective. A better way to proceed is to give poor young women something to lose if they have babies. If the nation would finally commit itself to providing high-quality schools to poor children, and if communities would also acknowledge the hard facts of the gap between economic and sexual maturity, then young women would see that they must put aside childbearing (and hopefully sex too) in order to focus on their education and their bright futures. However, unless they have bright futures, and the societal commitment to equal educational opportunity required for them to have any future at all, this nightmare will go on.

The idea that children can choose to become parents is an incredible absurdity that mocks the ideas of both parenthood and liberty. It is obvious that children in this situation are making foolish "choices," without much thought about the personal, ethical, or social consequences of their actions. The collective wisdom of the community's adult members embodied in edicts against irresponsible sexual behavior, stories of the pain and suffering that follows on the heels of early marriage and parenthood, and the nasty facts of life about the economic deprivation associated with early parenthood make no impression on these young people. Some D'Souza-esque writers who pretend that black folk "culture" fails to warn young people of the shameful and painful consequences of their actions conveniently forget that young people, especially teenagers, are foolish, fearless (in direct proportion to their ignorance), selfish, myopic, and nonrational. The black community's collective problem is that it must find ways to control the actions of young people in the face of weak incentives to forego early childbearing. The lousy economic prospects for young blacks from poor neighborhoods make the job of controlling poor black teenagers and young adults far harder than that faced by middle- and upper-income communities, whose children "behave" because their economic futures are bright so long as they refrain from selfish and destructive choices. Middle- and upper-class young people respond to the incentives to study, delay reproduction, and avoid destructive violence for lots of reasons, including the obvious reason that they will reap great economic and personal rewards if they obey the rules. In addition, middle- and upper-class families and communities have the income and wealth to buy therapies and other control devices in order to manage the behavior of their unruly children.

Poor black parents cannot credibly tell their children that their lives will be much better if they follow a conventional pattern of behavior because, in modern America, poorly educated people face a future of low real wages and lousy life chances. At best, black parents and communities tell their young that they can make life much worse for everyone else, and especially their own children, if they behave selfishly. In the absence of a significant improvement in the life chances of poor black children and young adults, black communities are faced with a truly daunting task: induce poor children and young adults to study, work, and delay child-bearing when schools are bad, wages are low, and the rewards from postponing reproduction accrue to the unborn child and the rest of the community in the distant future (at least from the perspective of a selfish and shortsighted teenager). Needless to say, this is a very difficult incentive problem.

Social Capital and Black Self-Help

One potential, but partial, answer to the multiple crises that are gripping poor black communities is found in the recent call to reconstruct moral and communal institutions among the black urban poor that can serve as effective counterweights to the destructive consequences of free markets. A black conservative view of black poverty emphasizes the need to change the attitudes and habits of the black poor in order to alleviate the distress and suffering that go with poverty. Glenn Loury's insistence on the positive role that bourgeois values can play in lessening black poverty is consistent with a free market approach to economic matters in a society committed to eliminating all vestiges of government-sponsored discrimination. Loury's stance on black poverty is not especially popular in certain circles, largely because of his conservative commitment to limited government intervention in markets. However, the approach of Loury, Sowell, and other black conservatives is perfectly sensible if markets really can whittle away arbitrary white racial advantage and if blacks can acquire the education, skills, and capital necessary to compete successfully without government help. Indeed, even if the problem of discrimination is a permanent barrier to black economic prospects in American life, Loury's argument about the role of conservative values in promoting black economic development is offered as the only viable strategy available to blacks in a time of fiscal retrenchment and anti-liberal and anti-black politics.

According to Loury, black poverty is best dealt with by the development of independent black cultural and economic institutions where the black middle and upper classes teach the black poor the values and skills necessary for economic success. This conservative call for black cultural and economic solidarity could be plausibly called a *progressive* and conservative program that requires the black middle and elite classes to put aside the universal disdain of the bourgeoisie for the poor in order to create a stronger and more unified black American community. In an article that criticizes the traditional black liberal interpretation of black poverty, Loury asks a series of rhetorical questions that highlight his belief in the responsibility of the black middle class for improving the plight of the black poor. In particular Loury asks:

> What, . . . should be the responsibility of the black middle class in allevi-
> ating the conditions of poor blacks, especially given the reduced involve-
> ment of the federal government [in the 1980s and 1990s]? To what
> extent is the current program of the civil rights community likely to have
> a beneficial impact on the conditions of the ghetto-dwelling underclass?
> What role do internal conditions and behaviors within the low-income
> black population—conditions and behaviors that middle-class blacks
> themselves strive to avoid—play in perpetuating the impoverished cir-
> cumstances of these communities? How, if at all, can a *genuine* [emphasis
> added] sense of nationalism and unity be forged among blacks, given the
> great disparity in our material conditions?[18]

Right after Loury raises these questions, he quotes Martin Luther King on the responsibility of the black middle class for the economic advancement of the black underclass. In this quote King says that

> It is time for the Negro haves to join hands with the Negro have nots
> and, with compassion, journey into the other country of hurt and denial.
> It is time for the Negro middle class to rise up from its stool of indiffer-
> ence, to retreat from its flight into unreality and bring its full resources—
> its heart, its mind and its checkbook—to the aid of the less fortunate
> brother [and sister].[19]

At its best, this stance asks prosperous blacks to form a multi-class coalition with the black poor for black economic development that mirrors the multi-class coalition that was the foundation of the Civil Rights movement. Given the limited appeal of income redistribution across the color line, a multi-class coalition of blacks for the purpose of group economic development has a certain plausibility if it creates viable and high-quality educational and cultural institutions that can do a better job than underfunded and dilapidated urban public schools. In addition, a multi-class economic coalition may be able to create cooperative labor-management relations between black capitalists and workers that might give black firms a competitive advantage in the marketplace, assuming that these firms can enter growing markets and that they have access to capital.

Nonetheless, two serious structural impediments stand in the way of Loury's progressive-conservative vision of a multi-class black coalition for economic and social development. First, a program of economic solidarity across class lines has little appeal to most members of the black middle-class because it is simply not in their economic interests. William Julius Wilson's analysis of the effect of black middle class flight from central city neighborhoods in his landmark work *The Truly Disadvantaged* points to the basic conflict of interests and attitudes between the black underclass and those blacks who have prospered in the aftermath of the Civil Rights victory.[20] Law-abiding, prosperous blacks want to avoid contact with those elements of the black poor—and especially the black criminal underclass in cities—for the same reason that everyone else does: middle-class blacks want to live as far away from the fear and hurt of poverty and crime as they possibly can. The class conflict between the black middle classes and the black underclass is a very real impediment to the creation of a conservative, nationalist black economic coalition. For better or for worse, the black middle class is likely to follow the lead of middle-class members of European ethnic groups in distancing itself from the behavior of its poorer relations. There is simply no reason to believe that blacks are immune to one of the major cultural imperatives of capitalism: middle- and elite-class disdain or even contempt for the lower classes because of the poor's lack of "bourgeois graces" (suitably adjusted to reflect black cultural traditions, no doubt).

Indeed, black middle-class men and women can be expected to resent being asked to take special care for the black poor. Ellis Cose quotes a black professional in his recent book, *The Rage of a Privileged Class*, on the anger and frustrations of being black and middle class in America:

Whites put entirely too much responsibility and burden on the black middle class for the structural and institutional racism we all inherited. It's not our responsibility. . . . It's the entire country's responsibility. Why should the onus be on . . . the [black] working couple who are just trying to make ends meet, who [themselves] are one step away from poverty.[21]

Indeed, Cose notes that any presumption of black middle-class responsibility for the economic fortunes of the black poor puts the middle-class blacks into a no-win situation:

What is it that the black middle class should do to eliminate poverty in black neighborhoods or stop young blacks from shooting each other? Getting black professionals to eschew success—in other words, to become one with the underclass—might eliminate the exasperation some people feel when they see the black middle class held up as an example to the underclass, but it would not improve anyone's condition. . . . Certainly black professionals can get involved in any number of ways in the lives of the less fortunate and can make a huge difference in individual cases. . . . But volunteer work among the disadvantaged is hardly the solution to deep-rooted problems that . . . are not the special province and sole preserve of America's black middle class.[22]

While Cose's point about the limits of charity is a good one, he fails to note how the attitude being expressed is itself part and parcel of the emergence of a black middle-class in America. There is absolutely no reason to expect black middle class people to be more socially aware, more socially responsible, or more active in the alleviation of the miseries of black poverty, or indeed anyone else's poverty, than any other Americans. While racial pride may lead the black middle class to favor charities that give to blacks, there is just no reason to think that blacks are any more willing to pay higher taxes, or to live among the black poor, or to sacrifice their time and money for the alleviation of someone else's suffering, than any other American. One bitter irony of the victory of the Civil Rights movement is this: middle-class black people are now free to ignore and flee from the black poor with as much right as everyone else. Isn't it the right of every member of the American middle class to feel superior to poor people?

Second, since no quasi-national economic institution with tax and transfer powers controlled by blacks exists at this time in the United States, it is unclear how the usual conflict between generosity and self-interest that cripples the ability of charity to address serious social problems could be overcome to provide the financial resources necessary for the kind of massive economic and social reconstruction Loury has in mind. In the absence of such an institution, which has the authority to redistribute income from consumption to investment purposes in order to provide high-quality education to the black poor and to provide capital to black entrepreneurs, it is difficult to see how the skills shortages and capital shortages that stand in the way of black economic development could be overcome.

The limitations of black self-help that are posed by the lack of black control of capital and central economic institutions are sharply demonstrated by the relative impotence of black mayors to change the economic fortunes of the black poor in a number of major cities. From Philadelphia to Detroit, Cleveland, Los Angeles, New York, Baltimore, New Orleans, Atlanta, and other cities, the fact of black control of city hall in recent decades has not led to declining unemployment for poor blacks, or a reduction in crime, or significant improvements in urban public schools. The fact that the black middle classes do not have significant control of capital in these cities has meant that mayors in the cities lack the tax base to mount serious reform programs of any type. While black political power has surely meant that the relations between the authorities and the black community are better than they might otherwise be, this has not and cannot lead to significant changes in the economic fortunes of the black poor. So long as blacks and those committed to improving the economic fortunes of the black poor lack significant impact on the national political agenda, any efforts to improve the lives of poor blacks will be hampered by the fact that public and private institutions currently controlled by blacks are simply too poor to tackle the task at hand.

Nevertheless, the fact that charity and black political control of cities cannot address the scale of the problems of the black poor is no reason to quit trying to create black economic solidarity across class lines, particularly in the creation of schools, hospitals, housing, and other essential infrastructure goods and institutions that can promote black development. The problem that the black poor face is that white racial phobias and hatreds have limited the extent to which the larger society will fund the education, medical care, and housing of the black poor. In the absence of government-sponsored redistribution that provides the same access to opportunity that was provided to European immigrants earlier in this century (through the auspices of the Democratic Party), blacks must somehow create new institutions to fund and guide black economic development in place of the welfare state. The creation of a series of nongovernmental economic and social institutions to coordinate and finance black economic and social development *independently* of the American government, and therefore beyond the reach of market-driven apartheid, is an unnerving political task. Yet, blacks are going to have to find ways to create more effective forms of teaching and learning as well as methods of influencing the reproductive choices of the young in ways that enhance the life chances of black children and the social condition of the whole community before free markets do us in.

About Dynamics and the Color of Political Economy

This chapter began with a series of questions about the difficult problems that modern, post-segregation America faces as it stumbles toward the future. We then asked if the insights of economists, particularly the fabled (and reviled) claims about capitalism's considerable power to overturn the consequences of racists' social customs might offer a way to think about modern American racial inequality. By reconsidering the Becker conjecture in light of new thinking about the nature of economic growth that has emerged in recent years, we have been able to see why free markets are not likely to offer an automatic path toward racial equality without the need to make difficult political choices that require the State to work against those customs and forces that continue to tie race and well-being together. Our reconsideration of the Becker conjecture has helped us see that "demand side" and "supply side" approaches to racism and its effects can be synthesized into a coherent account of the link between racist customs, free markets, and persistent racial inequality, once we understand how racism distorts the allocation of knowledge-creating assets and experiences across that color spectrum. Our discussion of labor market discrimination against blacks in economies where learning-by-doing matters in both work and schooling helps us focus on the most pressing, and most difficult, aspect of American racial history: historic racial exclusion can create systematic differences in economic and academic performance across color lines that cannot be easily or quickly reversed by capitalism or government policy.

This theoretical perspective allows us to throw "cultural" and "genetic" explanations of racial inequality into the intellectual dustbin with ease (and without the need to yell and scream a lot). When someone like D'Souza claims that blacks are intellectual and economic failures because of their degenerate "culture," we can reply that the links between discrimination, knowledge, and skill creation, and the transmission of poverty across generations in a class-based society, can account for relative black economic backwardness without resorting to cartoonish portraits of black folks. Poor black people are in trouble for the simple reason that they've been a neglected remnant whose lousy schools, lousy jobs, and poverty have left them with few valuable skills in a skill-driven world. Similarly, middle-class black people have a simple problem in a meritocratic order: their performance on standardized tests is rather poorer than that of whites and Asians, even after taking account of social class. Yet, an approach to racial inequality that pays attention to learning-by-doing allows us to see that the teaching and learning process at any point in time is the result of accumulated experience and investments over time. Black people, including middle-class blacks, have only recently been allowed into the modern, knowledge-driven sectors of the economy and larger society in the aftermath of segregation's demise. Though there have been superb black colleges and universities that have provided excellent schooling to generations of black professionals and scholars, the fact remains that these institutions, like blacks themselves, have also been on the margins of the process of research, innovation, and the dissemination of ideas that takes place in the university sector.

Blacks have a great deal of catching up to do. Blaming middle-class black people for not having vast experience in highly competitive academic settings, as *The Bell Curve* does with its claim that blacks are just dumb, is a cheap way of evading a nasty point: segregation, ordinary discrimination, and poverty have historically limited blacks' range of academic and work experiences, thereby also limiting blacks' ability to accumulate human capital. D'Souza and Murray/Herrnstein are just one more variation on an old, and rather disreputable, strain of American conservatism that wants to wish away the fact that the social pain inflicted on blacks has had cumulative economic consequences, in other words, that history really does matter.

Sadly, a dynamic approach to racism like the one we are advocating has the implication that current investments of money and time in black schooling will take a while to pay off since relatively little has been invested in the teaching and learning process in poor black communities. In an economy where technical change relentlessly creates and destroys skills and knowledge, black economic underdevelopment must be addressed by the creation of new, nongovernmental institutions that can bridge the gap between the demands of modern life and the beliefs and behavior of poor black people who have been left behind by capitalist development. The reconstruction of the teaching and learning process in black communities extends well beyond formal schooling to include the development of anti-natalist ideologies that can control the reproductive behavior of children in the face of the universal gap between physiological sexual maturity and social-sexual maturity. No government, least of all the American government, with its commitment to the needs and whims of a racially phobic white majority, can build social institutions that can meet the needs of a black population that feels routinely wounded by and rightly distrustful of whites in the United States. However, the American State can, and must, treat black Americans as full citizens whose basic well-being can be enhanced by developing coherent, and egalitarian, economic and social policies that can survive in a competitive global market economy. Nonetheless, black people are going to have to find ways to master the meritocratic game that makes sense in light of our history, that protects our dignity, and that lets us fight our enemies effectively. We face a long and difficult road ahead.

Appendix: Discrimination and Human Capital
in a Dynamic Becker Model

The Becker conjecture is a powerful piece of economic reasoning that pinpoints the power of competitive capitalism to gradually destroy the effects of labor market discrimination on the well-being of outcasts. The text notes that the Becker conjecture is valid if labor market discrimination is unrelated to systematic differences in the skills of black and white workers which might convert the discriminatory tastes of racially phobic majorities into structural differences between dominant and subordinate groups. This appendix presents a simple mathematical model that illustrates the logic of the Becker conjecture as well as its limitations. In particular, the model explored below shows why the link between discrimination and skill development can result in persistent racial differences in economic performance that are themselves the result of historic discrimination instead of nonmarket "cultural" differences between racial groups.

Imagine a simple one-commodity economy where firms produce and sell the composite good under conditions of perfect competition. The economy in question is a small open economy where capital is perfectly mobile and the world rate of return on capital is r^*. For simplicity, assume that the firms are small, owner-managed enterprises that use two inputs, labor (L) and capital (K), to produce output according to the production function

$$Y^j = \min[K^j, hE^j]$$

for firm j, where E^j is the level of employment offered by firm j and h is the efficiency of labor.

The society has just emerged out an era of apartheid. All firms in this economy are owned by whites, who are in turn divided into two camps: some white owners are colorblind employers who only care about profits, while other owners are rigid racists who will only hire and work with whites. If output is capacity-constrained (i.e., we are operating in a situation of labor surplus) and colorblind capitalists own $0 < \lambda < 1$ percent of the capital used in the economy, then they produce $Y^c = \lambda K$ units of output (where "c" stands for colorblind).

Racist and colorblind capitalists are willing to operate in the local economy if the rate of profit on local operations is at or above the world rate of return on capital. Given the real wage rate for white workers (ω), the rate of profit for racist capitalists is $r^w = r^w = 1 - \dfrac{\omega}{h^w}$ where h^w is the efficiency of white labor. Colorblind capitalists will distribute job offers to black and white workers so that the rate of profit from hiring black labor, $r^b = 1 - \dfrac{\beta}{h^b}$, is equal to that associated with hiring white labor (r^w), where β is the real wage earned by black workers and h^b is the efficiency of black labor.

Firms must pay workers efficiency wages in order to prevent workers from shirking. Borrowing from a version of the shirking model developed by Blanchflower and Oswald (1994), we assume that the utility of work is the difference between the level of real wages and the cost (in terms of utility) of work effort (assumed to be unity for simplicity). Hence, a white worker will provide maximum effort while at work if the net utility of labor, $\omega - 1$, is at least as great as the expected utility from shirking, which is in turn equal to the weighted sum of

1. the real wage earned by white workers (ω), multiplied by the probability of shirking remaining undetected ($1 - x$),
2. the real wage that white workers can earn if they can find another job, ($1 - e^w$) where $0 < e^w < 1$ is the employment rate for white workers, and where $0 < x < 1$ is the probability that shirking is detected by employers.

Therefore, white workers will not shirk if

$$\omega - 1 \geq (1 - x)\omega + x(1 - e^w)\omega$$

so that the real efficiency wage for white workers is $\omega = \dfrac{1}{x(1 - e^w)}$. A similar calculation shows that the real wage for black workers is $\beta = \dfrac{1}{x(1 - e^b)}$ where $0 < e^b < 1$ is the employment rate for black workers.

The employment rates for black and white workers depend on the distribution of capital between colorblind and racist capitalists (λ), the fraction of the work force that is black (b), and the racial composition of employment offered by colorblind capitalists (ϕ). This implies that black workers produce $\phi\lambda K = h^b e^b b L$ units of output so that the black employment rate is $0 \leq e^b = \dfrac{\phi\lambda\kappa}{bh^b} \leq 1$ where $\kappa = K/L$ is the aggregate capital-labor ratio. In addition, white workers produce $(1-\phi\lambda)K = h^w e^w(1-b)L$ units of output so that the white employment rate is $0 \leq e^w = \dfrac{(1-\phi\lambda)\kappa}{(1-b)h^w} \leq 1$.

The logic of the Becker conjecture is easily displayed in this toy model. There are two conditions for medium-term equilibrium in this model. First, colorblind capitalists will offer jobs to blacks (ϕ) in order to equate the returns from using each type of worker, i.e. $r^b = r^w$, which is referred to below as the internal arbitrage condition. Second, both racist and colorblind capitalists will move capital between the local and "world" economies until their respective rates of return are equal to the world rate of return (r^*) so that $r^b = r^w = r^*$, also called the external arbitrage condition. These two conditions can be written as

$$r^b = r^* \Leftrightarrow 1 - \frac{\beta}{h^b} = 1 - \frac{1}{xh^b(1-e^b)} = 1 - \frac{1}{xh^b\left(1 - \dfrac{\phi\lambda\kappa}{bh^b}\right)}$$

and

$$r^b = r^w \Leftrightarrow 1 - \frac{\beta}{h^b} = 1 - \frac{\omega}{h^w} \Leftrightarrow 1 - \frac{1}{xh^b\left(1 - \dfrac{\phi\lambda\kappa}{bh^b}\right)}$$

$$= 1 - \frac{1}{xh^w\left(1 - \dfrac{(1-\phi\lambda)\kappa}{(1-b)h^w}\right)}$$

We can solve these two arbitrage conditions for the equilibrium values of the capital-labor ratio (κ) and the racial composition of jobs offered by colorblind capitalists (ϕ):

$$\kappa = h^w + b(h^b - h^w) - \frac{1}{x(1-r^*)}$$

$$0 \leq \phi = \frac{b}{\lambda}\left[\frac{1 + (1 - r^*)xh^b}{1 + x(1 - r^*)[bh^b + (1 - b)h^w]}\right] \leq 1.$$

The interpretation of the expression for ϕ is quite straightforward: if black labor is as or more efficient than the economy-wide average degree of labor efficiency $(bh^b + (1-b)h^w)$ then the fraction of all jobs offered to black workers $(\phi\lambda)$ will be greater than or equal to the proportion of blacks in the labor force (b), and vice versa.

Learning-by-Doing and the Legacy of Discrimination

Our simple model of racial inequality in the labor market has assumed that black and white labor productivity is given by nature or "culture" or some other external circumstance. However, modern growth theory has taught us that labor efficiency is itself the result of on-the-job experience as well as deliberate investments in education and skill development. One way to incorporate the concept of learning-by-doing into our model is to assume that the growth rate of labor efficiency for workers in each racial group depends on the employment rate for the group according to

$$Dh^i = (\varepsilon e^i - \delta)h^i, \; i = b, w$$

where $D = d/dt$ is the differential operator, $0 < \delta < 1$ is the depreciation rate for labor skills (due, say, to the ongoing march of technological knowledge and the associated destruction of a portion of existing labor skills) and $\varepsilon > 0$ is the skill development or learning coefficient associated with employment.

Long-run equilibrium in this economy now requires that

1. the rates of return associated with employing blacks and whites are equal to the world rate of return,
2. the long-run levels of black and white labor efficiency are at their steady state values,
3. the steady state be locally (and hopefully globally) stable.

Note that the degree of labor efficiency for black and white workers is steady if $e^i = \delta/\varepsilon$. If black and white employment rates are equal, then the external arbitrage condition, $r^b = r^*$, implies that the long-run level of black labor efficiency is

$$h^b = \frac{1}{x(1 - r^*)\left(1 - \dfrac{\delta}{\varepsilon}\right)}$$

Finally, the internal arbitrage condition insures that white labor and black labor are equally efficient in the long run which also means that black and white wages are identical in the long run, seeming to confirm Becker's conjecture that competitive capitalism will eliminate the impact of racial discrimination on wage and employment prospects of pariah groups.

In order for the Becker conjecture to be correct, we must be sure that the long-run equilibrium configuration of equal employment rates and real wage rates across the color line can be reached from an initial situation where blacks are paid less than and are less skilled than whites. Specifically, the Becker conjecture is sensible only if the long-run equilibrium position is stable. In plain English, the Becker conjecture is useful if we have reason to believe that an initial situation of racial inequality in the aftermath of apartheid will *gradually* be eliminated by competitive capitalism. If the initial situation of racial disparity does not evolve toward one of racial equality, but instead veers off in the direction of greater racial disparity or meanders around in no particular pattern or direction, then the Becker conjecture is wrong, or at best rather less interesting.

The evolution of our model economy, whose resting state is one where blacks and whites face the same wages and employment prospects, is described by

1. the equations for the employment rates in the short run,
2. the expressions for the medium-term levels of the capital-labor ratio and the racial composition of employment for colorblind capitalists, and
3. the dynamic equations showing how the growth rate of labor efficiency is linked to employment.

This system is reproduced below for ease of exposition.

System I: Dynamics of Labor Efficiency in an Open, Racially Divided Economy

1. capital-labor ratio and racial composition of employment offered by colorblind capitalists:

$$\kappa = h^w + b(h^b - h^w) - \frac{1}{x(1 - r^*)}$$

$$0 \leq \phi = \frac{b}{\lambda}\left[\frac{1 + (1 - r^*)xh^b}{1 + x(1 - r^*)[bh^b + (1 - b)h^w]}\right]$$

2. employment rates for black and white workers:

$$\text{blacks: } 0 \leq e^b = \frac{\phi\lambda\kappa}{bh^b} \leq 1.$$

$$\text{whites: } 0 \leq e^w = \frac{(1 - \phi\lambda)\kappa}{(1 - b)h^w}$$

3. evolution of labor efficiency for black and white workers:

$$Dh^i = (\varepsilon e^i - \delta)h^i, \quad i = b, w$$

This set of equations can be reduced to a two-dimensional nonlinear system in labor efficiency units, i.e.

$$Dh^b = \varepsilon\left[bh^b + (1 - b)h^w - \frac{1}{x(1 - r^*)}\right]$$

$$\left[\frac{1 + x(1 - r^*)h^b}{1 + x(1 - r^*)[bh^b + (1 - b)h^w]}\right] - \delta h,^b$$

$$Dh^w = \varepsilon\left[\frac{1 - b\left(\frac{1 + x(1 - r^*)h^b}{1 + x(1 - r^*)[bh^b + (1 - b)h^w]}\right)}{1 - b}\right]$$

$$\left[bh^b + (1 - b)h^w - \frac{1}{x(1 - r^*)}\right] - \delta h^w$$

that can be studied using simple dynamical methods. The simplest way to study the properties of this model is to explore a numerical version

Table A2.1 Base Parameters Used to Study
System I

$r = 0.03$, $\varepsilon = 0.05$, $\delta = 0.05$, $b = 0.15$, $\lambda = 0.5$, $x = 0.5$.

of the system. The base parameters used to study System I's properties are listed in Table A2.1.

We already know that black and white workers are equally efficient, i.e., $h^b = h^w = 5.498$ in this case. However, the characteristic roots of the Jacobian associated with System I (when evaluated at the steady state) are -0.014 and 0.03, respectively, so that the steady state of System I is a saddlepoint. This means that if black workers are not initially as productive as white workers, perhaps because of the considerable depredations of segregation or widespread racial discrimination in employment and schooling in the past, then competitive capitalism is not likely to create equal employment and wages rates across the color line. Instead, any initial disparities between white and black employment rates and labor skills will grow steadily over time as white workers acquire greater experience than blacks, which only reinforces the initial racial disparities between the two groups. Colorblind capitalists actually worsen the initial skill differences between black and white workers by shifting jobs away from blacks and toward whites whose initial skill advantage was due to the legacy of organized racism.

A skeptical reader may wonder whether the saddlepoint configuration is not due to the particular parameter values used to study the stability properties of System I. That is a valid concern that is simply addressed. Figures A2.1 and A2.2 are plots of the larger characteristic root of the Jacobian of System I for various values of the skill development coefficient (ε) and the depreciation rate (δ). (A similar numerical analysis, not presented here, showed that there is no relationship between the probability that shirking is detected [x] and the characteristic roots of System I). Figure A2.1 shows that a larger skill development coefficient is associated with a larger positive root, which suggests that a stronger link between experience and skill growth will only increase the productivity gap between blacks and whites. By contrast, Figure A2.2 shows that the skill depreciation rate is a bifurcating parameter: "low" to "moderate" rates of skill depreciation are associated with system instability, while higher depreciation rates transform the steady

Figure A2.1: Impact of Changes in Skill Development Coefficient on Largest Characteristic Root

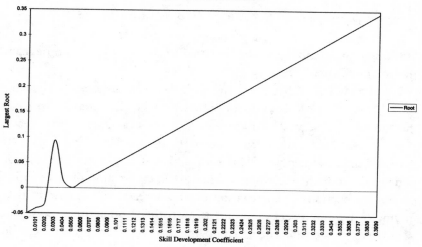

Figure A2.2: Impact of Skill Depreciation Rate on Largest Characteristic Root

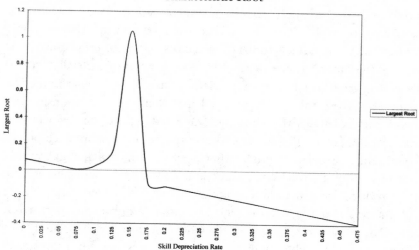

state from a saddlepoint into a stable node, as shown by the switch from positive to negative roots as δ rises in the figure. The economic meaning of bifurcation in this case is very plain: high skill depreciation rates mean that technological change destroys the benefits of learning-by-doing at a sufficient rate to undermine whatever accumulated advantage segregation and the culture of racial hatred may have conferred on whites. This suggests that blacks are better off in any economy with very rapid technical change, or at least one where the benefits of learning evaporate quickly over time.

The lesson of this toy model is simple enough: if discrimination gives white workers more work experience than black workers, and if work experience matters for the development of labor skills, then competitive capitalism may not eliminate the consequences of discrimination on wage inequality. Though the egalitarian steady state that Becker has identified also exists in our model, a capitalist society comprised of a mix of racist and colorblind entrepreneurs is unlikely to find itself rushing toward bliss if it has emerged from segregation. Easy virtue is, alas, unlikely virtue. Evidently, capitalism and colorblindness are not enough to guarantee equality across color lines in a post-segregation society where the distribution of economic outcomes affects the development of labor skills.

| THREE |

Confusion and Woe

Race, Capitalism, and the Retreat from
Social Justice in America

Race and Macroeconomics

It may at first seem odd to tie race and macroeconomics together. Macroeconomics—the study of the evolution of employment, unemployment, prices, wages, interest rates, and wealth of national economies—is usually divorced from questions of race, in part because the subject is difficult enough without also having to consider the diverse fortunes of opposing racial and ethnic groups. Yet, the fortunes of black Americans have been strongly affected by the overall state of economic activity and the course of economic policy throughout American history, especially in the past thirty years. In chapter 1 we saw that black family poverty rates in the late 1990s are lower than they have ever been, in part because of the remarkable run of economic good luck throughout the decade of the 1990s. Further, some blacks have managed to acquire high levels of schooling, thereby benefiting from the shift in the composition of employment toward jobs that require significant degrees of literacy, numeracy, and scientific or technical knowledge. The overall change in the skill requirements of the American economy, driven by the spread of modern computer technology, telecommunications, and seemingly limitless innovations in the once declining but now revived manufacturing sector, has reshaped the nature of work throughout the system as well as tilted the distribution of income and economic rewards away from unskilled workers as we saw in chapter 1.

Black people have been pushed along by these deep changes in employment and wages just like everyone else. However, blacks are in a peculiar economic position in this time of change, largely because the political and social environment in which they live is one in which the United States is enmeshed in a hyper-competitive world economy that dissolves national boundaries, thereby creating one vast job market and consumer society that ruthlessly punishes those who lack skills with poverty, low wages, and the usual invisibility of the poor. We have already noted that the emergence of a high-technology economy has been accompanied by the development of a type of meritocratic capitalism that rewards education while simultaneously blocking poor people's access to good schools. However, the combination of ruthless domestic competition across color and class lines for places in good schools and for high-wage jobs with equally vigorous competition between global corporations for customers, cheap unskilled workers, and competent skilled labor has largely undermined the movement toward racial equality.

All of these changes have occurred at a time when the US has been forced to deal with daunting economic problems (particularly low rates of economic growth as explained below) that have threatened to weaken the nation's long-term economic health, and when the solutions to these problems seemed to require the nation to pull back from its commitment to equality, including racial equality, in order to safeguard the economic futures of the social classes that matter in America: the rich and the white suburban majority. In order to understand why macroeconomic events have blocked the road toward racial equality, and how the economic policy choices of conservative governments since 1980 have made these problems much worse than necessary, we need to first explore the long-term problems of the American economy.

Productivity

Productivity is a rather dry and confusing idea that is at first hard to get across to noneconomists (and even some economists). Yet, it is fair to say that there is no more important source of a nation's economic well-being than the ability of its workers to produce output with the minimum amount of effort and waste. We will therefore spend a page or two making sure that the reader understands what productivity is and why it matters in general, before we then see why productivity problems have been a barrier to the quest for racial justice in the U.S. in recent years.

We all confront the basic issue of productivity every day when we ask the question: how can I get more done for each hour of time I spend at my tasks? Students facing the inevitable crunch of exams, where fond memories of parties and play are pushed aside by the dread that comes from the fear of failure, want to study "productively," meaning that they want to get the most test-taking benefit from each precious hour of time put into each subject. Employers worry about productivity for a very simple reason: a highly productive worker produces a great deal of output relative to his or her wage, which in turn means that the firm can sell goods and services for low prices, even if the absolute level of the wage is high. The arithmetic of productivity is quite compelling. Suppose that a grocer employs two cashiers at eight dollars an hour each. One cashier can process twenty customers an hour while the other can only handle fifteen customers in the same time period, with the result that the first cashier costs the firm 40 cents per customer ($8.00/ 20 customers) while the second costs 60 cents per customer.

This very simple inverse relationship between productivity and cost is important for two reasons. First, simple arithmetic tells us that higher levels of productivity mean that goods and services will cost less, which makes these goods and services more affordable. The genius of American capitalism in this century is founded on mass production, which is the idea that huge factories that pour out vast streams of goods and services can nonetheless produce these items at a low cost per unit, which in turn lets firms sell these goods cheaply, making them available to a large number of people, including people with low and moderate incomes. Mass production ultimately works because high production volume is associated with high labor productivity and low cost, which in turn allow for low prices and high profits. One consequence of higher labor productivity is that the purchasing power of wages, also called the real wage, rises even if the money wage paid to workers does not change. Hence, if labor productivity in the US were to miraculously double overnight then production costs would be cut in half, which would in turn lead prices to fall by roughly one-half as well. Even if the dollar value of the average worker's pay packet doesn't change at all, the doubling of labor productivity will result in a doubling of each worker's standard of living by doubling the amount of goods and services that can be bought with a given amount of money.

A useful way of thinking about the central role of productivity in economic life is to imagine that the total amount of goods and services in society can be represented by the size of a pie. The pie is produced by the nation's workers, each of whom contributes an amount of brains and brawn to making the pie. The level of productivity is simply equal to the size of the average slice of the pie, which is the total volume of the pie divided by the number of workers. An increase in the number of workers, with no change in the level of productivity, will result in a larger pie with an increased number of thin slices. Note that the size of the slices in the new pie are exactly the same as those in the old pie, but the new pie is bigger because we have more people making it. By contrast, higher productivity can be represented by a larger pie that has larger slices for each person (if the same number of people make the pie) or that has both larger slices for each person and more people in the kitchen.

Second, the ultimate source of American workers' high standard of living is the high level of American worker productivity. A highly productive work force can feed, clothe, house, and care for itself by each person working a moderate number of hours per week, thereby providing itself with the option of taking some time off for family life, religion, study, sports, or other things. The steady decline in the length of the workweek all over the world as well as the steady growth in the number of people in school (whether as students or teachers) is due to the growing productivity of labor over time. Increases in labor productivity mean that a smaller work force is required to produce the same amount of output or that the same number of workers can generate a larger volume of output, or any combination of these two things. If a society wants to both increase the real wages of its workers as well as reduce the length of the workweek or increase the fraction of a growing population that is exempted from work (children, students, young parents with children, or the elderly) it must boost productivity accordingly.

A highly productive society has the luxury of reducing the number of people who need to work while supporting a larger nonworking population in valuable pursuits. Equally important, a highly productive society can afford to promote social and economic equality because it is able to redistribute a portion of the nation's output from middle- and upper-income classes to the poor through the tax system while simultaneously increasing the incomes of the working population. Though taxes reduce the amount that income earners ultimately take home, higher levels of productivity allow employers to pay higher wages without causing higher prices, thereby resulting in a situation where wage earners see higher take-home pay while government receives higher tax revenues that can then be used to improve the health, education, housing, and employment prospects of the poor. In a very real sense, social justice in modern society is made possible by growing productivity, which increases the size of the economic pie enough so that the poor can be helped without requiring anyone else to make sacrifices on their behalf. The redistribution of the *extra* income and output generated by increasing productivity helps racially and ethnically diverse societies avoid divisive battles over the distribution of income and opportunities by providing all classes with more of everything.

One branch of economic theory, usually referred to as growth theory, is devoted to the seemingly simple task of explaining how labor productivity grows over time. While economists know a bit about why productivity grows, there is still a great deal to learn about the relationship between labor and wealth. Nonetheless, we do know a few things about the sources of productivity growth.

First, improvements in technology, typically in the form of new types of machines and production facilities (also called physical capital) boost the amount of output associated with a given amount of labor input. For example, the replacement of the typical typewriter by a personal computer has led to a rise in the amount of paperwork that can be processed by the average office worker (after an initial period of training and learning). Old machines are replaced with new machines because firms can thereby lower their costs of production, expand their productive capacity, and boost their profits. Of course, the replacement of old machines with new machines frequently requires workers with very different skills from those associated with now obsolete equipment, though it is sometimes cheaper for firms to retrain their existing labor force rather than recruit an entirely new one, especially if the new machines are not too different from the old ones.

However, more radical changes in technology may require very different skills from those embodied in the current work force, so that investment in new machines may displace and destroy a portion of the existing skill base of a nation's labor force in favor of a new matrix of talent. This process of "creative destruction" in the skill base of the work force, that in turn reflects the tendency for technological change to consume old techniques in favor of new ones, has been the primary reason for the shift in the fortunes of skilled and unskilled workers in the past two decades that we considered in chapter 1. "Skilled" workers are not only workers with high levels of training on particular machines (for example, machinists) but those whose technical education allows them to adjust quickly to new forms of machinery and, in the computer age, software, thereby making the absorption of new technologies into firms and sectors of the economy a less costly process. Sadly, "unskilled" workers are not only those men and women who lack any marketable skills that can command high wages, but also people whose skills are tied to particular types of machines and production processes, making them vulnerable to the whirlwind of changing methods of production that are characteristic of modern capitalism.

Investment in new types of physical capital are usually financed by savings—either from a firm's own accumulated profits or via loans from banks or people who buy a firm's bonds or stocks. A bond is simply a promise by the borrower (in this case a corporation) to pay the lender a fixed sum of money (interest) each year for as long as the loan is outstanding. At the end of the loan period, the borrower promises to refund the full amount of the loan to the lender, thus ending their relationship. Stocks, on the other hand, are certificates of ownership that entitle the owner to a portion of the firm's profit, should there be any. The difference between stocks and bonds should be plain: a bond is a less risky asset than stock, since the bondholder must be paid a fixed sum of money and must receive the principal at the end of the loan, while a stockholder gets a portion of the uncertain, but potentially very substantial, profits that the corporation may earn. Savings, by individuals or corporations, are simply the total purchases of new assets—increases in checking and savings accounts or purchases of new bonds and stocks—in order to increase a person's or corporation's wealth. Of course, companies and other borrowers, most notably governments in times of deficit spending, will offer savers incentives, including interest or high potential returns, in order to induce them to lend. At times where the demand for borrowed funds is very high relative to the amount of available savings, borrowers will vigorously compete with each other by offering higher interest rates and financial returns to savers, squeezing out those weaker enterprises who cannot afford to offer high returns to lenders without undermining the profitability of their investment projects.

Though this set of connections between savings, investment, interest rates, and productivity may seem a bit obscure and far removed from the issue of racial equality, it is of the utmost importance. Societies with large pools of savings, most notably those nations whose citizens tend to save large fractions of their incomes, are able to support a wide variety of investment projects in new technologies, thereby improving the productivity of the nation's work force and the profitability of its enterprises. Of course, increases in productivity from this source require businesses to have sensible projects in the first place, which in turn depends on a host of factors that are beyond the scope of this book. Nonetheless, a nation with a large pool of savings can, under certain conditions, create conditions for rapid productivity growth. We will shortly explore what these special conditions are, what happens when they are not met, and why slow productivity growth has a nasty racial dimension.

Productivity increases for other reasons as well. Workers and managers may find better ways of using existing technology to produce more output over time as a result of experience, thereby boosting the level of output per worker without any need to add new machines. We have already noted that the link between experience and increased worker productivity undermines the easy faith in the racially progressive character of free market capitalism, since historic discrimination against blacks in employment and education also shuts blacks out of the opportunity to improve their work and academic skills through experience, thereby putting them at a significant disadvantage vis-à-vis whites in the race to acquire experience-related human capital. In addition, workers can upgrade their skills and knowledge as a result of investments in formal education.

Human capital is an especially important source for productivity growth that has important implications for racial inequality in this country. A highly educated work force that has extensive experience with rapidly changing technologies, and that can pass on knowledge of how to succeed in academic competition to its children, will be able to improve its ability to work over time, quite apart form any investments in new types of machines and production methods. The spread of knowledge over an existing population will gradually boost the productivity of labor, even if the particular outfit of tools and physical capital doesn't change, by spreading better ways of using capital efficiently, thereby replacing less efficient ways of working with better ones. Further, the process of teaching and learning over the generations will lead to teaching innovations which improve the ability of instructors to communicate complex ideas to students, thereby reducing the portion of each generation of students who fail to acquire knowledge because of flaws in the teaching process rather than any inherent limitations in the minds of students. These improvements in the work ability of the labor force and the teaching capacity of the schooling system make every investment in businesses more valuable, thereby improving the incentive to invest and further promoting the growth of productivity. The link between investments in human capital and physical capital are a classic example of a "virtuous circle," which is a situation of positive feedback where two or more activities or processes add to each other's growth, thereby causing more and more growth after an initial period of development.

Racial and class groups who have been historically excluded from this virtuous circle of development, or who are excluded by virtue of their poverty and lack of education, are in danger of being left behind by the rest of society. One of the central problems with poverty in modern America is that the poor are also the badly schooled, which means that the ongoing march of technology and knowledge in society puts them at an increasing disadvantage in the race for skills and jobs. The virtuous circle noted above happens because each generation of children in decent schools staffed by knowledgeable and innovative teachers in neighborhoods where academic success is valued because its rewards have actually been experienced, receives the wisdom embodied in the lessons of the past as well as the new information and ideas that have developed as a result of scientific and technological development. Poor children, in lousy schools and in neighborhoods where the rewards of study are more myth than reality, are not likely to be swept up into the virtuous circle because they are simply too far behind the rest of the nation, which has moved so far along the path of technological development as to be another country with a separate language and set of customs.

Consider this simple example: the higher wages of "skilled workers" in this country reflect the growing importance of eighth-grade algebra and science in various types of jobs.[1] One cannot achieve this level of proficiency without first learning most of the lessons from the previous seven levels of study, which in turn requires that (1) teachers are collectively competent to guide students through the curriculum to reach this point and (2) students come from families which value knowledge, or at least know enough about the world to know that eighth grade math and science are worth knowing in order to get a high-paying job. Poor children have little chance of achieving this level of schooling for three simple, *economic* reasons:

1. these students come from homes and communities that have relatively little human capital to pass on to their children, which gives teachers a much lower base level of knowledge on which to build,
2. teachers of poor children generally work in schools that are themselves badly equipped, with poor working conditions that prevent them from pursuing innovative approaches,
3. teachers of poor children are themselves poorly paid because the districts they work in have limited funds, while teachers in wealthier districts have higher pay, better working conditions, better prepared children, and incentives to pursue innovative approaches to their craft.

Current unequal access to resources across class and color lines, combined with the considerable legacy of historic underinvestment in the human capital of blacks, lock poor black children out of the virtuous circle of growth that economists have identified as the primary source of growing productivity. Even a radical program of redistribution that led to absolute equality in education funding across color and class lines cannot quickly overcome the near fatal hold that America's nasty racial history has on the minds of poor black young people.

Productivity Arithmetic

Productivity in the United States has grown at about 2.5% per year since World War II. Unfortunately, productivity growth has slowed down a lot since 1970 (to a little under 1.5% per year), so much so that the nation now faces a number of severe social problems that the economic boom of the late 1990s can mask but cannot ultimately solve. Table 3.1 shows the average rate of productivity growth for each decade since 1950, as well as the average for the years 1990–1997. Table 3.1 shows a disturbing pattern: productivity growth has gradually slowed down so much that the average growth rate during the 1990s is just one-fourth the rate of the 1950s.

In order to understand what this means in practical terms, the reader should know a basic fact about the principle of compound interest which also applies to economic growth and a nation's overall well-being. Imagine that you put $1,000 in the bank at an interest rate of 3% and will leave your money with the bank until the sum doubles to $2,000 (we will ignore the complications that inflation introduces into this calculation for the moment). How long will you have to wait? This is a fairly straightforward question that usually requires a bit of messy arithmetic and a calculator, except for the fact that there is a convenient rule of thumb, called the "rule of 70," that helps you make this calculation quickly (those who want to know where the rule of 70 comes from should consult the appendix to this chapter). The "rule of 70" can be stated simply: divide the value of the interest rate into 70 to get the number of years that must pass before the quantity of money placed in a bank doubles. In our example, the rule of 70 tells us that our $1,000 deposit will double in 70/3 or approximately twenty-three and one-third years (or twenty-three years and four months). However, the remarkable thing about compounding is that a small rise in interest rates has enormous consequences for the size of one's bank account. For example, if the interest rate were 5% rather than 3%, then, according to the rule of 70, we would only have to wait 70/5 or fourteen years for our money to double. Alternatively, if we waited twenty-three years to withdraw money from an account that earned 5% per year, we would have over $3,121 instead of the $2,000 that we would have had if the interest rate had been 3%.

Table 3.1 Average Rate of Productivity Growth by Decade, 1950–1990, and Average for 1990–1997

Year	Productivity Growth Rate
1950–1959	3.48
1960–1969	3.19
1970–1979	2.04
1980–1989	1.22
1990–1997	0.875

Business Sector Output Per Worker, Series ID PRS84006092
Source: Bureau of Labor Statistics, 1998 Department of Labor

Why are we interested in the amount of time it takes something to double in size? One useful way to think about productivity growth is to ask this question: given the speed with which productivity grows, how long will it take for the standard of living of an average person to double? We know that the standard of living, measured by the purchasing power of wages, is directly related to productivity. Therefore, this question of the "doubling time" for the standard of living is quite useful. According to the rule of 70, if an average rate of growth of productivity is 3%, then the level of productivity will double in a little over twenty-three years, thereby causing the buying power of wages to double as well. However, if productivity growth sinks to 1% per year, then it takes *seventy years* for the standard of living to double, whereas if productivity growth rises to 5% per year then living standards can double every fourteen years.

It should now be clear why low productivity *growth* is a major social problem in the US: one of the central social themes of American life is that each succeeding generation of adults will be better off than their parents. In order for that to happen, productivity must grow reasonably quickly, and certainly faster than 1% per year. Further, any program for promoting social equality that requires that resources be transferred from well-off to poor workers will be opposed by earners in situations where productivity growth is low, since redistribution in that case requires middle-class workers to accept possible reductions in their after-tax incomes in order to finance the improvements in education, housing, health care, and other vital goods and services that the poor need. There is no way around this social arithmetic: the promotion of social justice requires growing productivity in order to avoid potentially destructive conflicts between the badly off and the better off. In turn, slow productivity growth means that the standard of living of the average worker grows slowly (or in many cases actually declines for reasons we explore below), which will in turn cause many nonpoor workers to resist taxes to finance egalitarian policies aimed at improving the lot of their less fortunate neighbors on the grounds that they cannot afford to be generous when their own living standards are threatened.

The decline in American productivity growth since the early 1970s has largely halted the drive toward racial and social equality by reducing the willingness of the public to accept the higher taxes necessary to finance fairness. The end of apartheid in the 1960s not only meant that black Americans were granted the same civil rights as whites, but that the needs of the black poor were treated with the same legitimacy and urgency as those of the white poor. However, the 1960s was a period of relatively rapid productivity growth that created economic room for greater spending on the poor, and greater spending on the Vietnam War, without requiring the white working and middle classes to sacrifice their own living standards in order to promote equality.

The Economics of Liberal Racial Reform

The now denigrated welfare, education, and job training programs of the Great Society during the 1960s that were intended to ease the transition of black migrants and their children into the industrial labor force were financed out of the expanding economic resources made possible by the steady economic growth of the period. Unfortunately, the now two-decade-long slowdown in American productivity growth has destroyed the economic conditions that made the liberal program of racial reform possible. In hindsight, it is obvious that American economic and political dominance in world affairs after the Second World War was a critical factor that not only shaped the economic fortunes of blacks, but that also had a profound effect on the strategy of liberal racial reform. The prosperity of the American economy between 1946 and 1973 was largely due to a constellation of domestic and worldwide economic conditions that are not likely to appear again. The fact that the United States emerged from the war with its industrial base intact, with the most productive economy in world history, and with little international competition meant that there were few constraints on the extent to which employment, output, and living standards could grow. American workers earned high and rapidly growing wages because of low rates of unemployment and moderate rates of productivity growth. In addition, American workers were, and by many measures still are, the most productive workers in the world, meaning that they were and are so efficient relative to workers from other countries that the cost of goods and services produced in the United States is low relative to those of other workers, even in the face of high wages.[2]

Liberals in the 1960s hoped that growth could take care of the problem of offering economic opportunity for blacks without requiring any significant sacrifice from whites, by creating more than enough opportunity to go around. One of the most succinct and thoughtful presentations of the intellectual foundations of liberal thinking on the incorporation of blacks into the American economy was by Nobel laureate James Tobin in "On Improving the Economic Status of the Negro."[3] In this 1965 article, as well as in a subsequent analysis of liberal ideas about poverty relief entitled "Raising the Incomes of the Poor," Tobin lays out a comprehensive strategy for bringing black Americans into the economic mainstream. A brief review of the economic assumptions that lay behind liberal strategies regarding black economic development will go some way to explaining why the liberal program was sensible, sober, timely, and right for its time. Only after fully appreciating the goals and logic of mainstream liberal thinking on this matter will we be in a position to appreciate the brilliance of the liberal plan to dodge American racism as well as why the program was defeated by subsequent economic events.

Tobin's analysis in "On Improving the Economic Status of the Negro" makes three important claims. First, Tobin notes that black poverty in the 1950s and 1960s was primarily due to high levels of persistent unemployment, which was in turn the result of sluggish overall economic performance. Tobin notes that black unemployment, which was (and is) much higher than white unemployment because of discrimination and the relative underdevelopment of blacks' labor skills, could be greatly improved if national economic policy were focused on creating and maintaining a full-employment economy. By taking this approach, Tobin is making a fundamental Keynesian claim that has been part of liberal racial reform strategy since Myrdal's *American Dilemma*: blacks, who suffer more in periods of high unemployment and recession, can be most effectively helped into the economic mainstream by increasing the labor demand through a policy that boosts the overall demand for goods and services in the economy.[4] An expansionary government macroeconomic policy that cuts taxes, increases government spending on public projects, or entices businesses and consumers to spend more by reducing the cost of credit, will raise the level of overall buying in society.[5] In turn, a general rise in the demand for goods and services will lead to more jobs for all workers, thereby reducing the need for and the effect of discrimination on job opportunities for blacks and raising the incentives for employers to hire blacks for open positions.[6]

Second, once the general demand for labor is increased to a high and sustainable level, social policy should aim at increasing the skills of blacks, thereby giving them the chance to enter high-paying professions.[7] Tobin notes that while the problem of unemployment due to low levels of overall spending certainly hurts blacks most, blacks' relative lack of job skills and education keeps them trapped in low-paying jobs, thereby limiting their chances for upward mobility in even the best of times.[8] While educational policies and job training policies can only be expected to work over the long term, there is every reason to think that a gradual rise in the number of blacks with adequate qualifications will greatly improve overall black economic achievement.

Finally, welfare policy must aim at providing effective and generous assistance to those blacks who cannot find work in a high-employment economy and who are unable to improve their job skills.[9] Tobin is careful to point out the potential pitfalls that any anti-poverty policy must contend with: effective anti-poverty policy must try to deliver income and services to the "truly needy" without encouraging people to leave the labor force or engage in the kind of behavior that created the problem of low skill levels in the first place.[10] Tobin worried that guarantees of income support might distort the incentives of poor adults to work, and poor teenagers to succeed in school, thereby creating a welfare trap that locks already marginal people into permanent underclass status. Tobin proposes a form of the famous "negative income tax," originally proposed by Nobel laureate Milton Friedman in *Capitalism and Freedom*, as an alternative to bureaucratically run welfare systems in order to avoid welfare traps.[11] The negative income tax, which is the precursor to a successful modern program (the Earned Income Tax Credit explored in the last chapter) would have required the government to pay low-income workers the difference between their wages and an adequate minimum income. A key virtue of this sort of scheme was (and is) that it requires the recipient to work for wages in order to qualify for the payment. The particulars of Tobin's proposal are less important than the tenor of his remarks about liberal approaches to providing welfare, which are thoroughly consistent with the recent, so-called "conservative" emphasis on minimizing the work disincentives associated with poor support.

Tobin's proposed strategy for incorporating blacks into the American economy in 1965 is relevant to present-day concerns about black poverty and underdevelopment for two reasons. First, despite the obvious differences between Tobin's liberal Keynesianism and the current dominant mood of fiscal retrenchment and general economic timidity, both approaches share a common belief that rapid economic expansion is the best way to improve black economic fortunes. The saying "a rising tides lifts all boats" is perfectly compatible with any economic vision that puts rapid economic expansion, and especially high levels of employment, at the top of the economic policy agenda. Second, Tobin's strategy repeats a claim made by present-day liberals and conservatives alike: blacks must enter more highly paid professions and labor markets by acquiring better educations and job skills. No one would disagree with the claim that black people must be ready to seize opportunities when they arise, which means that they must be well educated and acquire whatever specialized training they need to compete.

American liberals like Tobin and others committed to reducing the role of inequality in American life were willing to use the increased tax revenues generated by high growth and employment to fund programs that would improve the lives and employment prospects of the poor, including the black poor. This form of the welfare state, the American version of the Keynesian welfare state that had been developed in Europe in the period during and especially after the Second World War, departed from European practice by avoiding high rates of redistributive taxation and generous social expenditure across wide segments of the middle and working classes (with the notable exceptions of Social Security and Medicare) in favor of an approach that targeted spending to the working classes and the poor. So long as the economic pie was growing, especially when steady increases in productivity allowed workers' wages to increase in a situation of growing overall demand and stable or falling unemployment rates, room could be made for minority workers without any negative effect on the rising living standards of white workers.

The scheme for the incorporation of blacks into mainstream American economic life rested squarely on the ability of the government to create a full employment economy by maintaining high levels of aggregate demand. Tobin's article notes that there are two possible obstacles to the success of this program. First, high levels of demand, and the associated low levels of unemployment, may be accompanied by inflation. Tobin recognized that though higher prices are certainly a problem, the economic difficulties associated with inflation are small when compared to the considerable problems faced by the unemployed.[12] Second, inflation may present problems for the US in international economic affairs by increasing the country's balance of payments deficit.[13] Tobin claims that the economic problems that can be expected to follow from the complications of international economic affairs are once again small compared to the cost of unemployment.

Clearly, the liberal program for the use of full employment policy as the primary weapon against black poverty and unemployment requires the US to be in a position to endure the economic costs of whatever inflation and related trade and balance of payments difficulties result. It is perfectly obvious that economists and citizens who have a different judgement about the costs of inflation would object to the use of full employment policy to bring blacks into the economic mainstream. Indeed, the concern with inflation following the two OPEC oil shocks of the 1970s did lead to a willingness on the part of the authorities and the general public to tolerate very high levels of unemployment in the battle against rising prices. To the extent that the anti-inflation strategy of conservative governments has required high levels of unemployment, one cost of that strategy is clearly the restriction of black economic advancement, which depends on reducing white unemployment rates in order to make room for black workers.

A clear weakness of the liberal program of economic reform, quite apart from the barrier to black economic progress posed by the use of unemployment as a weapon against inflation, is that any impediments to the use of aggregate demand to maintain full employment will block black economic progress. Recall the logic of Tobin's argument. Black economic progress is promoted in three linked stages:

1. increase the overall demand for labor, thereby increasing black employment by reducing white unemployment,
2. use the extra tax revenue from a full employment economy to improve the education and skills of black workers over the longer term,
3. use poor relief for that (hopefully) small segment of the black population that cannot work due to infirmity or an irremediable lack of skills.

If productivity growth slows or if long-term white unemployment is high, then any program aimed at improving the skills of black workers will have to involve increased taxation of white labor to improve the skills of black labor. As a practical matter, this means asking white labor to tax itself to improve the skills of blacks to compete with whites for jobs. Further, if the program is successful in improving the job skills of blacks, then whites would have to suffer a reduction in wages as well as a higher tax burden as part of a program that aims at improving the economic status of blacks.

But why would white workers consent to improve the lot of black workers at their own expense in terms of either taxes or future job prospects? Liberals believed that they could use fiscal and monetary policy to get around a white veto of black economic development by running a full employment economy. If liberals had been successful, they could have used full employment to convert a harsh battle between black and white workers for jobs and wages into solid support for the extension of the New Deal to blacks, through the Great Society programs, with no negative effect on whites. However, there were a number of political impediments to extending the New Deal to blacks, not the least of which were battles between blacks and whites over the control of education and the public sector at the local level.

Race and the Breakdown of the New Deal

Growth was not able to overcome all of the obstacles to the incorporation of blacks into the modern industrial and post-industrial sector of the economy. First, while the means for funding black education, housing, and job training might come from the proceeds of economic growth, racial conflict between working-class blacks and whites demonstrated the limits of liberal racial reform. So long as the economic prospects and social mobility of whites were not in any way threatened by the redistribution of income and resources toward blacks, and so long as white demands for segregation in housing, schooling, and employment were not dramatically affected by government policy, a program that touted economic fairness to all Americans was broadly acceptable. Racial competition between urban blacks and working-class whites for the control of the public sector in major urban areas, particularly over the issues of school desegregation, school funding, and discrimination in the employment of blacks as policemen, firemen, teachers, and public employees more generally, eventually undermined the cross-racial alliance that backed liberal reform.

From an economic perspective, the battles over busing, voting rights, and public-sector job discrimination in major Northern cities in the 1970s and early 1980s were a struggle between those whites who could not afford to separate themselves from blacks by living in suburban areas and black migrants seeking greater access to job markets and education by demanding a more equitable distribution of resources across the color line. Black demands for equal provision of public services, for equal access to public education, and for a redress of past discrimination in public-sector employment and promotion decisions meant the loss of white jobs and a drastic diminution of the status of working-class whites. The presidential campaigns of George Wallace in 1968 and 1972 were largely fueled by white working-class resentment of liberal reform policy that reallocated resources from urban whites to blacks as part of a program of creating formal equality of racial opportunity or compensating blacks for the harm done by previous discrimination. This resentment, most dramatically expressed by the violent reaction of working-class whites in Boston to court-ordered school busing and to affirmative action programs in public-sector employment since the middle 1970s, has been a direct response to the fact that scarce public-sector resources are being stretched to cover a large and economically backward black population at perceived white expense.[14]

Of course, the growing needs of cities—the site where the economic incorporation of blacks into the modern economy has been occurring—could have been addressed by drastically increasing funding for urban schooling, housing, police and public safety needs, and infrastructure beyond the considerable rise in expenditure on urban areas that did take place during the 1960s and 1970s. To the extent that the battle between working-class whites and blacks for the control of the public sector in urban areas was (and is) primarily a racial clash, one might doubt whether even more funding would have made much difference. However, any strategy of increasing funding to urban areas in order to offset the racial battles between working-class whites and blacks would have required a much more explicit redistribution of income across both class and color lines. Such a drastic rise in the burden of taxation as part of a program of racial reform—particularly in the midst of the Vietnam War effort during the middle and late 1960s—was, and still is in America in the 1990s politically impossible.

Budget Deficits and Racial Reform

Tobin's economic strategy for liberal racial reform, which still guides liberal thinking, is obviously expensive. We have already seen that black economic incorporation into the American mainstream by liberal means, by redistributing resources across the color line, threatened (and still threatens) to undermine white demands for economic and social distance from blacks. One possible solution to the problem of raising money for financing the incorporation of blacks into the modern economy without asking middle-class whites to share in the economic burden of racial reform was to run budget deficits. American worldwide economic dominance during the 1960s allowed the U.S. government to run budget deficits without any serious economic consequences. The small budget deficits run in the 1960s through the early 1970s were not due to any explicit policy to give blacks the economic resources they needed. These earlier deficits were, like the rather larger budget deficits the country faced throughout the 1980s, the result of a combination of economic and political forces that had little to do with black incorporation. Nonetheless, it is fair to say that the ability of the U.S. government to run budget deficits made it easier to extend the social safety net across the color line for a time in the 1960s and 1970s.

A full appreciation of the economic tightrope that liberals tried to walk as they moved to incorporate blacks into the American middle class requires us to spend a few pages reviewing the seemingly arcane subject of budget deficits. Though deficit talk in modern times is everywhere—and is as boring as it is ubiquitous—deficits nonetheless play a crucial role in the just attempt and brilliant failure of the liberal program to overcome the burden of segregation in America. Our first task is to understand what deficits are and why they matter in any economy. After that we will see why current worries about the deficit in the new world economy have undermined the economics of liberal racial reform, and set the stage for a rather nasty racial conflict under the aegis of conservative economic policy.

Budget Deficits: A Primer

In these days of relief over budget surpluses after more than fifteen years of gloom and doom about deficits, it is worthwhile remembering that a budget deficit is, in and of itself, neither a good thing nor a bad thing. There are plenty of reasons a society might choose to spend more public money than it collects in the form of taxes. For example, a society might choose to build airports, cure cancer, or provide a previously excluded racial or caste group with better-quality houses, schools, and public facilities. In each of these cases, the decision to borrow in order to finance these projects in excess of tax receipts is perfectly sensible, because each of these projects promises to improve the long-term well-being of society. If a society must borrow to pay for these kinds of projects, it is certainly appropriate to do so as long as the benefits of these kinds of investments, including the additional tax receipts that come from an increase in the nation's productive ability, exceed the associated costs. Even if the benefits of public spending cannot be unambiguously evaluated in money terms it is still economically sensible for a society to run a budget deficit, and therefore borrow, so long as the perceived benefits of doing so outweigh the costs.

The problem with deficits in modern times is that the costs of borrowing in order to spend for public purposes are assumed to vastly outweigh the benefits. There is more than a bit of hysteria in some calls for the government to balance its budget, especially by people who propose that the government automatically balance its budget every year, regardless of economic circumstances or the needs of the country. This sort of clamor, which fuels recurrent calls to pass a balanced budget amendment to the Constitution, is economically foolish once we remember that borrowing is only a problem if we use borrowed funds for silly and unproductive purposes. For example, a suburban family is more than a bit silly if it takes out a second mortgage on the house to finance a lavish trip to Paris, complete with glorious hotels, swank shops, fabulous meals, and beautiful vistas along that great city's boulevards. Needless to say, it is perfectly possible, if more than a bit doubtful, that the family members will be so invigorated by the trip that they are more than willing to work two or three extra jobs to pay off the additional debt they incurred from taking the trip. A more likely outcome in this case is that the family must tighten its belt a bit further as it pays a higher fraction of its income to reduce its indebtedness and cover its interest bill. However, the family is still behaving rationally if it is willing to sacrifice future consumption (by suffering through higher debt repayments) in order to enjoy an increase in its current consumption. After all, who is to say whether or not a Paris vacation financed by a second mortgage is a waste if it saves a dying marriage by reinvigorating a sagging love life and providing a wealth of new experiences to be shared over a lifetime?

We would all feel better if the family took out a second mortgage in order to add an extra couple of rooms onto the house or finance a college education. In these latter cases it is perfectly clear that borrowing is economically justified, in the sense of being an act where the money benefits of borrowing outweigh the money costs, because the increased value of the house or the increased lifetime income of one's child is greater than the cost of borrowing. Asking a family badly in need of a marriage-saving vacation, or of an extra room, or of funds to send a child to college to finance its spending out of current income is both punitive and, from an economic standpoint, questionable.

Nonetheless, there can be significant economic costs associated with budget deficits. The process by which a government borrows money in order to carry out its spending plans is rather simple (if tedious), despite the tendency of economists and other "experts" to cloud the issue by speaking in gooey "economese." If a government wants to spend more than it expects to receive in taxes, it does what everybody else does when they spend more money than they have on hand: it borrows the difference. Of course, a private individual who spends more than he or she has in his or her bank accounts usually uses a credit card to make a purchase, thereby borrowing money from the bank or group of banks that issued the card. A government that wants to borrow in order to spend doesn't use a credit card in the same way. Instead, a government borrows money by selling bonds to potential lenders.

Governments, whether local, state, or national governments, sell these bonds to people who want to earn interest income by buying assets that promise high returns at reasonably low risk.[15] The fact that the US government sells bonds in order to finance its spending poses a potential problem for businesses that want to raise money in order to finance potentially profitable projects. If the US government needs to raise a lot of money because of a large budget deficit, then it may have to be willing to pay higher interest rates in order to attract potential lenders. The government is in a position to do just this, given the fact that it has future taxes as a sure source of revenue from which to pay interest. However, companies seeking to raise money may be forced to promise higher returns than governments in order to induce potential lenders and stockholders to provide capital. These higher promised returns to lenders and stockholders are a cost to firms since these returns must inevitably come out of firm profits. Some firms may choose to abandon potential new projects, including new buildings, factories, or factory upgrades, because the cost of borrowing the money has risen as a result of the government's need to finance its deficit. In that case, certain potentially lucrative and economically important activities may be delayed or completely dismissed because of high interest costs.

Whether the effect of government borrowing is economically damaging or not depends largely on whether the projects pursued by the government are of greater or lesser economic benefit than the projects pursued by the business sector. Despite the tendency in modern times to assume that nothing the government does is ever as economically valuable as any scheme hatched in the private sector, there is no reason to think that deficits are economically damaging per se. However, the possibility that interest rates may rise as a result of budget deficits does mean that there is a potentially significant cost to deficits, even if the benefits of the deficits exceed the costs. This is especially true in modern times when, for whatever reason, Americans simply don't save very much of their income, with the result that there is an insufficient source of potential funds for either private or public purposes. In a situation where there is not much in the way of potential savings from which firms and governments can borrow, the competition for funds between the public and private sector can result in a more severe financial crunch for the private sector. In that case, budget deficits can result in what economists call "crowding out," that is, the high interest rates the governments can pay in order to attract lenders simply push out a large volume of private investment, thereby causing business to cancel or postpone many otherwise lucrative projects.[16] In turn, lower levels of business investment may well lead to slower productivity growth, thereby reducing the rate at which the productive capacity of the economy grows and jeopardizing the system's ability to provide resources for both public and private purposes.

Deficits and Exchange Rates

Of course, the problem of crowding out can be reduced considerably if Americans would increase their savings, for then the pool of resources available for private and public investment purposes would be much larger. However, an economically strong nation has a second source of potential savings that can be used to finance a budget deficit. This second source of funds is none other than foreign savings. If foreign nationals want to buy US government bonds in large numbers—perhaps because US government assets are considered a safe place to park one's money, or because these bonds offer a high return compared to government bonds in other countries—then the US government can sell lots of bonds without having to promise high interest rates. This makes it possible for the government to engage in deficit spending without causing a large volume of domestic investment to be crowded out. Of course, this second source of savings is always liable to dry up in the event that foreign nationals change their minds about the attractiveness of US government bonds. Nonetheless, this kind of deficit finance is certainly within the ability of an economically powerful nation to sustain for a while, especially if the budget deficits in question are small relative to the size of the economy as a whole.

Unfortunately, a society that relies on foreign savings to finance its budget deficits pays a price for the privilege, quite apart from whatever interest is necessary to attract lenders. A society dependent on foreign savings must be sure to keep its own interest rates above the rates of interest available to lenders in other countries in order to attract the necessary volume of loans.[17] The problem with keeping American interest rates higher than foreign interest rates is that the need to attract foreign savers must eventually hurt the nation's capacity to compete in the international marketplace by making US goods more expensive relative to those of rival nations. Since foreign savers usually buy US government bonds in dollars, they first convert their marks, liras, yen, pesos, and francs into dollars by buying dollars in the foreign exchange market. The price of dollars in terms of other currencies is simply the exchange rate, which is determined by the forces of supply and demand in financial markets worldwide.[18] Hence, a demand for dollars will rise when foreign nationals want to buy US government bonds, or cars, or other goods, services, or assets that can only be purchased with dollars.

But a high value of the dollar inevitably means that US goods are more expensive abroad. By definition, a high value for the dollar means that the dollar is worth a large number of marks, yen, pesos, or francs. Hence, a rise in the value of the dollar will mean that the dollar buys a greater number of units of another currency. Unfortunately, this also means that goods produced in the US, which are priced in dollars, are now more expensive for foreign nationals to buy. For example, a 1500 yen radio produced in Japan will be priced at $15 if the dollar is worth 100 yen on the foreign exchange market. If the value of the dollar were to rise to, say, 150 yen per dollar, then the dollar price of the radio falls to $10. In general, the prices of imported goods fall as the dollar becomes more valuable in terms of foreign currency, making imports cheaper and more attractive to American buyers. Similarly, a $10 software CD produced in the US will have a yen price of 1000 yen if the yen/dollar exchange rate is 100 yen per dollar, but will rise to 1500 yen if the value of the exchange rate becomes 150 yen per dollar.

The economic cost of a strong dollar is now perfectly clear. American exports are more expensive when the dollar is strong, which leads to a smaller level of export sales, lower export profits, and fewer jobs for Americans in export industries. Even more, a strong dollar makes imports cheaper, thereby encouraging Americans to buy fewer American-made goods and more foreign goods. The end result of Americans switching from domestic goods to foreign goods is once again fewer jobs for domestic workers and reduced profits for American firms.

Deficits, Globalism, and the End of Racial Reform

What does all this mean for racial reform?

Reliance on foreign savings pushes the value of the dollar up, making American goods less competitive on world markets and contributing to unemployment and low sales in those parts of the American economy that are vulnerable to international competition. This problem is not particularly important for an economy that is so productive that it can continue to produce cheap, high-quality, profitable goods even with a strong currency. Nor is it important in an economy that is experiencing very low rates of unemployment because of a vast consumer binge combined with vigorous business investment spending and low interest rates, as in the miraculous late 1990s. If the United States were still the economic colossus it was immediately after the Second World War, with the ability to produce cheap, superior-quality goods that simply could not be produced anywhere else in a war-shattered world, then changes in the value of the dollar just would not matter much. The rest of the world, hungry for American goods, would simply pay whatever price needed to be paid to acquire them. In the late 1990s, where the US is once again the pre-eminent economic performer in a world economy plagued by high unemployment in Europe (for reasons that matter for understanding American racial reform which we will explore shortly) and a financial disaster in Asia, the value of the dollar has relatively little effect on the economic fortunes of the nation for short periods, though economic conditions have a way of changing quite suddenly in nasty ways.

However, over the long term the value of the dollar is a problem for the United States, when it is no longer the economic behemoth of the modern world, and when its trading partners in Europe and Asia are free of serious economic distress. The technological advantages of the United States have largely disappeared with the reconstruction of Europe and Japan from the rubble of war, as well as the miraculous spread of markets and modern technology to many nations in East Asia, South Asia, and Latin America. This widespread availability of technology, particularly in mass production industries like autos, steel, consumer electronics, and chemicals, means that nations will have to compete on the basis of cost and prices rather than presuming that they can rely on retaining any technological advantage over their rivals. In turn, American workers in industries exposed to rigorous international competition through free trade will face foreign managers who are as good as US managers and foreign workers who are as well educated as US workers, and *willing to work for lower wages than American workers*. American producers may well be able to retain their competitive edge by a thin margin, but only by continually improving their production techniques and lowering their costs. In turn, the relentless drive by American producers to raise worker productivity and cut costs has meant that firms will replace workers with machines and streamline other aspects of their operations.

In this kind of hyper-competitive economic environment, the value of the dollar could be the difference between American firms winning and losing in the struggle to survive. A strong dollar makes U.S. goods expensive, thereby threatening the jobs and profits of those caught up in the ruthless battle for position in international markets. While there is certainly no guarantee that a weak dollar will give U.S. firms an edge in markets where foreign firms are equally obsessed with improving productivity and cutting costs, a strong dollar can only make life worse.

Old-style liberal racial reform is simply not possible in a competitive global economy. Traditional full-employment policies, particularly those financed by budget deficits, cannot be pursued without worsening trade deficits and increasing interest rates. Worse, liberals can no longer get around the veto power of whites by running budget deficits to finance education, housing, and health care for blacks who are excluded from these things by free markets catering to the phobias of middle- and upper-class whites. Blocked by the new realities of international competition, liberals have only one alternative: use redistributive taxation to finance the economic advancement of the poor, particularly the black poor. But since high taxes and blacks (aside from basketball players) are rather unpopular with whites these days, liberals are left without many economic tools to pursue racial reform in modern America.

Race, Welfare, and the "Modern Class Conflict"

The belief that sustained budget deficits undermine the long-term economic prospects of the nation has been the primary explanation given for the obsession with curbing public spending. In view of the distaste that the American middle class has always had for welfare in general, and for those programs (like AFDC) that have become synonymous with black poverty, failure, and "profligacy" in particular, it is not surprising that cuts in poor relief and welfare spending receive broad support from middle-class whites. Despite the evidence presented in chapter 2 about the complicated and uncertain effects of welfare on the work habits, family structure, and life chances of the poor, particularly the black poor, most political debate and public policy begins with the simple assumption that welfare rather than technological unemployment, international competition, and the resulting long-term decline in the demand for modestly educated workers is at the root of most of our important social problems. Even though anti-poverty spending has never been a particularly large portion of overall government spending— despite the endless lies told by politicians and talk show hosts—the feverish drive to reduce deficits has made welfare an irresistible target for the budget ax.

We have noted that the problems of unemployment, poor schools, crime, and the mind-bending social difficulties that the transition from patriarchal to more egalitarian gender relations pose for this society are sure to survive the end of "welfare as we know it." Whether poor men and women are forced to work for income support does not change the fact that these men and women are poor because they are an economi-cally marginal population that has little access to education, training, technology, or capital. The forces that have led to the long-term decline in marriage rates among the black poor and working classes, or the increase in prevalence of black single mothers, and single motherhood generally, or the rise in the poverty rate for black children, are not strongly affected by poor support policy or by the extent to which the larger society punishes poor people for behaving badly.

Nonetheless, the black poor are caught in the middle of economic storms that have inspired the demand to slash and burn those parts of the welfare state that they have depended on for their livelihood. In truth, the welfare state is simply not designed to help a chronically undereducated and technologically backward population make the tran-sition from being an industrial work force to a highly flexible post-industrial labor pool. Indeed, the welfare state is nothing so much as a gigantic insurance policy that workers collectively grant to themselves in order to insure that they can survive the vicissitudes of capitalist life. The taxes and contributions that workers pay for unemployment insur-ance, health care, disability insurance, and social security are all part of a scheme where a working population contributes to a common fund that each of its members can then draw from in the event that they are jobless, hurt, sick, or old. By forcing everyone who works to contribute to these schemes, the hope is that the risks of job loss, sickness, injury, and old age can be spread over a large population that can support the needs of the smaller group of beneficiaries.[19] In turn, beneficiaries earn their right to these benefits by working and paying into the system, thereby preventing the problem of dependency where workers are per-manently subsidizing the consumption and care of nonworkers. It is obvious that the underclass is in no position to contribute to any social insurance system. This makes whatever claims they have to public sup-port weaker precisely because they cannot be expected to pay taxes into the public till while they also rely on public support for their health care, housing, food, and other essentials.

A basic problem with redistribution from the working classes of society to an underclass, quite apart from the usual arguments about whether and how redistribution undermines work incentives and family stability, is that the dependency of the underclass is inconsistent with the ethic of economic independence and responsibility that Americans hold dear. Political philosopher Judith Shklar has noted that American social values place a premium on economic self-sufficiency, in part because the ideal of the good citizen includes the principle of self-reliance as the basis for social respect and political standing.[20] The presence of a large dependent population threatens to undermine self-reliance and self-determination by tying those who are capable of producing to a class of people who cannot be self-sufficient because they lack the material preconditions for independent judgement and action. The problem is not primarily that the underclass is in need of assistance from the rest of us: social solidarity between those who have high incomes and those who are poor does not undermine a commitment to either self-reliance or independent judgement. Rather, the problem with the underclass is that its members are not in a position to act independently, thereby undermining the assumption of independence that is, paradoxically, the foundation for American ideas of social solidarity.

Though conservative politicians make a great show of getting the underclass off the dole by requiring workfare and by imposing punitive sanctions in an effort to reform the presumed bad character of the poor, the harsh reality is that the presence of a technologically unemployed and unemployable underclass forces the rest of society to pay for the damage done by poverty. Whether the society chooses to pay for the underclass by building prisons, hiring police, and funding a massive supervisory bureaucracy to make sure that the poor follow the rules or instead chooses to fund some kind of welfare state is really beside the point: under modern conditions, those who work and pay taxes are forced to assume responsibility for the underclass whether they want to or not. Shklar has noted that both liberals and conservatives, Democrats and Republicans, share a profound belief in the need for all citizens to be independent, self-supporting members of society in a thriving market democracy:

> Both parties [Democrats and Republicans] deeply believe in self-discipline, in independence, in work as the primary source of all value and all dignity, and in the ideal of a society of self-supporting democratic citizens. Each one [each party] sees the other as a threat to democracy and to the values of work and independence that they profoundly share.[21]

Shklar notes that this shared commitment to the dignity and necessity of work for effective citizenship and social standing in America is a survival of the historic American antipathy to both aristocrats and to slaves and slavery that developed during Jacksonian times.[22] Indeed, Shklar notes that these beliefs have especially important implications for the social standing of the dependent poor:

> To those who want to see workfare made compulsory, the idle poor are no longer citizens. They have forfeited their claim to civic equality and are well on their way to behaving like unemployed slaves, kept consumers who do not produce. It is not claimed by either side [liberals or conservatives] that the work to be performed is likely to be socially useful or personally satisfying or well-paid. *Workfare has nothing to do with economics.* It is about citizenship, and whether able-bodied adults who do not earn anything can be regarded as full citizens. If they are not, may they not, as is now often the case, be treated with that mixture of paternalism and contempt that has always been reserved for dependent classes? . . . Unlike the unemployed, they [the underclass] are not trying to reestablish their standing, for they generally had none to lose in the first place. What workfare is expected to achieve is to get them to maintain acceptable standards of civic conduct.[23]

Members of the underclass lose their social standing for many reasons, not the least of these being, for the black poor, the fact that they are black. Nonetheless, racism is not the only reason that the underclass loses the respect of the middle classes in America. The unemployment and economic marginality of members of the underclass undermine the respect of employed Americans for their poorer, unemployable neighbors, precisely because it is a signal that the adult poor have failed to behave in a responsible, disciplined, and self-reliant fashion.

Of course, there is a large dose of self-righteousness and self-deception in this view of the underclass as a collection of shiftless, lazy, and irresponsible adults. Middle classes have always viewed unemployment, poverty, and want as the result of individual folly and have similarly been reluctant to see broader economic forces as the cause of individual deprivation. It took the Great Depression to convince a majority of Americans that unemployment could be caused by forces that were simply beyond the control of the unemployed, though many politicians, pundits, professional loudmouths, and narrow-minded citizens still cling to the idea that the unemployed are always the cause of their own misery.

The underclass poses an even more severe challenge to the faith of middle-class Americans in the worth and virtues of free markets, competition, and technology than do the traditional capitalist problems of recession, depression, unemployment, and inflation. As Shklar noted, the unemployed can be seen as victims of the vagaries of a market economy that has destroyed their jobs and lives as part of capitalism's metabolism. Though unemployed men and women may call on their neighbors for support and employment, there is no reason to believe that they will become a permanent dependent class that will never be able to fend for itself. Once the particular economic problem has been solved, there is every reason to expect that the unemployed will take their place as productive citizens who themselves contribute to the economy and to the system of social insurance. The underclass, by contrast, is very different. They represent that nightmare vision of capitalist life: a class of people who have been permanently rendered useless by competition, technology, and free markets. Though the employed public can certainly invest in retraining, housing, and caring for the members of the underclass, the kind of expenditures required are so large and involve such a time commitment that they permanently connect the winners in meritocratic and economic competition to the losers.

Merit and Social Regard

In a skill-driven, meritocratic society like that in the United States, the widespread belief in merit has an underside, namely, that failure due to lack of merit (intelligence, good grades, or a past record of achievement) is seen as a proper penalty for doing poorly in school, bearing a child while young, and failing to stay alert to the changes in technology that are reshaping the world economy. This harsh new outlook is an exaggeration of the notion that earning is an essential ingredient of citizenship and social respect that Shklar described above. In particular, the emphasis on merit as the basis for both economic success and social support effectively excludes those who lack credentials or other symbols of merit from serious claims to public support, by dividing society into a hierarchy of knowledge or skill classes.

This hierarchy is a far cry from the idea that workers are a class that is collectively threatened by the specter of unemployment and the economic contradictions of capitalism. In a merit-based system the risks of unemployment, low income, and poverty are now concentrated at the lower end of the educational and occupational spectrum, thereby shattering the possibility of a social contract that binds workers to support each other through the welfare state. Since the unemployment and poverty associated with rapid technological change and vigorous competition are so skewed toward the unskilled and the less educated, any program of social solidarity would inevitably involve massive transfers of money and resources from the "successful" knowledge classes to the "unsuccessful," badly schooled underclasses.

But this kind of redistribution not only violates the idea that the smart and well-schooled should reap the benefits of their hard work, it also asks the technologically secure to subsidize people who have been labeled as permanent failures. Social support for the underclass is simply not going to benefit the skilled and schooled economically in any significant way. At best, those who have succeeded "on the merits" may be willing to finance special efforts to educate the children of the poor in the hope that the intellectual and educational deficits of poverty can be overcome through public efforts. Even then the goal of this sort of policy will be to give the children of the poor a chance to compete in the struggle for good grades and places in good schools, not to overturn meritocracy or its inevitable division of a population into the skilled and the damned.

However, the skilled and the schooled have no intention of exposing their children to the risks of failure in the race for schools and skills when they have a much more effective way of guaranteeing their children's success. Unlike the welfare state, which spreads the risk of unemployment and poverty due to unemployment across a vast, vulnerable population, the unequal vulnerability of American workers to the risks of technological unemployment, international competition, and poverty only threatens to destroy the lives and futures of those who cannot afford to invest in knowledge and technology. But since those who possess good educations and valuable skills are in the best position to pass these skills and knowledge on to their children, there is simply no economic reason for the skilled and schooled to invest in other people's children, especially if those children are the presumed miscreant spawn of an inferior race.

Absent the sense that the disasters that can come from life under capitalism are a threat to everyone, and that workers as a whole must therefore unite to create and sustain a system of social supports that can see them through hard times, there is very little that the welfare state can do to eliminate the underclass. It is certainly true that the consumption of the underclass can be subsidized, at the cost of intense supervision of the personal lives and mores of the poor by a nosy, censorious bureaucracy. As Shklar noted above, workfare is imposed on the assumption that the underclass is simply too dumb, incompetent, or undisciplined to find steady work for itself, thereby relinquishing its claim to social respect. While some claim that it is possible for workfare programs to train the underclass for economic independence, this prospect is very doubtful given the failure of public schools to provide the requisite training for such a large number of people over a long time. Further, the process of technological change and economic competition will continue to create new categories of marginally employable and unemployable poor people, thereby broadening the pool of economically superfluous people and adding to the problem of social division between the "successful" and the "failures." Once the risk of poverty, unemployment, and limited prospects is no longer shared across the population, there is simply no continuing justification for the traditional welfare state in the eyes of the middle classes.

The division of society into the technologically able and the technologically incompetent strikes at the very core of liberal racial reform in America. As long as blacks were prevented from taking the blue-collar road to the middle class by government policy, there was every reason to hope that the elimination of segregation would simply extend the promise of opportunity to include everyone. The key assumption underlying liberal racial reform was that blacks are every bit as qualified as whites to be part of the American middle class; the only impediment to black progress, according to this view, was the legacy of backwardness and segregation bequeathed to blacks as well as the ever present problem of current discrimination.

The closure of the blue-collar road to the middle class has been well documented in chapter 1, though it cannot hurt to reemphasize the differences between the economic circumstances of the 1990s and the middle 1960s. Sheldon Danziger of the University of Wisconsin and Peter Gottschalk of Boston College, in their comprehensive summary of the causes of income inequality in the United States since 1973, *America Unequal,* have shown that the inflation-adjusted wages of young high school graduates (both male and female) in 1992 were 18% *lower* than they were in 1963. Further, the gap between the wages of college-trained workers and those without college degrees has exploded since the mid-1970s. First, the inflation-adjusted wages of male college-trained workers have risen by 8%, while those for male high school graduates (across the age spectrum) have fallen by 40% since 1973. This latter result follows directly from the simple and terrible (if one is a modestly educated worker) law of supply and demand: the wages of the college-trained rose because the demand for their services exceeded their numbers; just the opposite for the less well educated occurred. Second, the wage premium associated with a college degree, that is, the percentage difference between the wages of young college-trained workers and young high school graduates, has risen from 23% in 1979 to 43% in 1989.

The conclusion we draw from the evidence in chapter 1 and the impact of merit and technological change on the logic of the welfare state is that the road from poverty to the middle class is now far longer and much less reliable than it was a generation ago. We have seen that blacks were relatively more vulnerable to the closure of the blue-collar route to the middle class than whites, even though millions of white working-class men and women have been similarly locked out of the middle class. White workers, the primary financial and political foundation of the welfare state, are now divided into those who are well prepared to thrive in the modern world and those who are facing the prospect of stagnant living standards for themselves and their children. This division has crippled the prospects of the welfare state for the reasons already discussed: the technology-driven division of the working population undermines the possibility of social solidarity based on shared vulnerability to economic misfortune. Race worsens the situation by giving the technological division of society a distinctly racial flavor:

the knowledge classes are disproportionately white while the vulnerable groups are far "too dark."

In this setting, the drive to dismantle the welfare state is hardly surprising. What is surprising, and sobering, is that the conservative strategy intended to replace the welfare state, and to re-ignite economic growth in this country, has almost no chance of improving the lives of poor people. As we will see below, the almost certain failure of conservative economic policy—the second such failure in a generation—threatens to turn the white retreat from the welfare state into open social and racial war.

Race and Markets Kill Social Decency: A Restatement

We are now in a position to review the economic basis for the end of Civil Rights, as well as to understand the horrendous racial consequences of conservative economic policy. The economic demise of the Civil Rights rebellion has three parts. First, legal segregation was replaced by informal, market driven segregation as middle-class whites used their high incomes to demand economic and social distance from blacks. This free market racism has proven to be an effective barrier to the incorporation of blacks into an ever more technologically sophisticated economy by limiting black access to schools, training, capital, and technology.

Second, the fact that the United States is now one of many countries competing in a skills-based, technology-driven international economy has led to drastic changes in the demand for unskilled, modestly educated labor, thereby destroying the blue-collar road to the middle class. In addition, the U.S. is no longer in a position to use Keynesian fiscal policy to boost employment, nor can the country use persistent budget deficits to finance various projects, including racial reform to help blacks move into the middle class. But the inability to use budget deficits to finance racial reform means that government-sponsored racial reform is dead, since whites have consistently refused to tax themselves to eliminate the barriers that past discrimination and free market racism place in the path of blacks.

Third, modern technological change and international competition have driven a wedge between highly educated workers in economically vibrant sectors and more modestly educated labor exposed to the ruthlessness of world capitalism. These different groups of workers have different, frequently antagonistic interests that largely destroy support for the welfare state. A black economic underclass is simply a burden to the secure, well-educated technological classes, while being an economic threat as well as a despicable insult to struggling white workers. The welfare state was never designed to finance the transition from segregation to freedom in an economy where white workers are themselves threatened by the same economic forces that account for black poverty.

These developments sound the death knell of mid-twentieth century American racial liberalism. The end of American economic dominance, coupled with the technological dynamism and "creative destruction" of capitalism, have foreclosed the possibility of incorporating blacks into the middle class without radically challenging white demands for continued racial separation in economic and political life. Unless there is some way to make the welfare state viable in the new, hyper-competitive international economy without asking whites to finance black economic development, then the liberal gambit to sidestep middle-class white separatism has failed, and market segregation has won.

Conservatives and the American Dilemma

The dynamics of the knowledge society, where the working population can be divided into an economically vibrant skilled class and a fearful, declining, undereducated, unskilled class has radically altered the nature of America's racial "dilemma." The apparent victory of free market racism over liberalism poses severe racial problems for American conservatives. The decisions by the governing conservative coalition in political and economic affairs to dismantle the welfare state over the last decade is most certainly depriving the poor, especially the black poor, of what little access they may have had to important economic and educational resources. Yet, the conservative enthusiasm for gutting the welfare state is largely beside the point: since the poverty, economic isolation, crime, and social suffering of the black poor cannot be laid solely, or even primarily, at the door of the welfare state, cutting the welfare state will not eliminate these problems. The almost laughable conservative mantra that most of the country's social ills can be laid at the feet of liberals and lazy, lousy, stupid blacks can't long hide the fact that international competition and technological change are destroying the prospects for lower-middle-class whites with legendary capitalist efficiency. Indeed, one of the great ironies of the decisive victory of free market racism is that white conservative politicians are now robbed of their favorite bogeyman, the undeserving, welfare-cheating, quota-loving black (though the echo of the lazy, dumb, and violent darkie will resonate with elements of the nonblack voting public for a while longer). The fundamental changes in economic life that blocked liberal racial reform are now threatening those working-class whites—the fabled Reagan Democrats—who deserted liberals because of their attempt to change the racial system that delivered jobs and prestige to whites. Now these same working whites must place their trust in the wisdom and foresight of anti-labor, small government, pro-market conservatives who generally favor the kind of market forces that ruin the lives of white working people.

This puts conservatives in an awkward position. The country is facing difficult economic choices in the wake of the loss of its favored position in the world economy, choices that will either go a long way to reconstructing the economic vitality of the nation or further weaken the ability of the society to provide a prosperous standard of living for all its citizens. A conservative program of cutting taxes on consumption, cutting poor relief, and ending the redistribution of income to the poor on the pretext that redistribution is the cause of poverty is likely to repeat the mistakes made in the Reagan era, where government policy fostered greater poverty, inequality, and social misery among the underclass without offering viable economic alternatives to the poor. But the endorsement of free market solutions to the country's economic and social problems, including a renewed endorsement of free market racism, is a cheap rhetorical gambit by conservative politicians in both major parties that may win white votes but will not absolve conservatives of the need to formulate credible policies. Ultimately, conservatives are going to have to decide how to use government power to address the outstanding economic problem for both blacks and whites: the decline in living standards and life prospects for a significant number of low- and moderate-income American workers. Conservatives can take little comfort in the fact that blacks suffer disproportionately from poverty, unemployment, and the dislocations of technical change and global capitalism. In time, the majority of displaced and distressed workers in the American economy, who are white, will demand action on their behalf.

Race and the Strategy of Inequality

The conservative case against liberal economic policy since the 1960s has rested on a combination of strong ideological claims about the relationship between free markets and individual liberty on the one hand and a specific analysis of how the welfare state reduces economic growth on the other. Ideological conservative economic policy is based on three fundamental propositions. First, free markets in a stable, law-abiding society are the most powerful engines of growth and prosperity for the great majority of people in America. Second, government should promote free markets, specifically rigorous competition, wherever possible. Third, governments should specifically refrain from redistribution, either to ameliorate or to abolish poverty or to provide essential goods and services to the largest number of people, or even to prevent severe social or environmental damage done by free markets. This view insists that while there may be compelling evidence that free markets cause enormous social injury, the costs of supplanting markets with government power are usually as large, or even worse, than the damage caused by unregulated capitalism. Finally, the free use of private property, according to this argument, is the basic safeguard of personal liberty, which is in turn the foundation for political democracy. Regulation by government, no matter how noble, morally correct, popular, or even economically effective, is nonetheless unjust because it inevitably interferes with the rights of property owners to pursue their own interests.

The astute reader will note that this summary of the basic tenets of conservative economic policy is a summary of Nobel laureate Milton Friedman's classic 1960 statement of libertarian capitalist principles, *Capitalism and Freedom,* as well as Nobel laureate Friedrich Hayek's more extended and nuanced treatment in *The Constitution of Liberty.* Indeed, Friedman's *Capitalism and Freedom,* with its proposals for school vouchers, monetarism, the abolition of social security, minimum wages, legislation favoring unions, and licensing procedures, as well as the elimination of bureaucratic forms of welfare provision, could be fairly considered the blueprint for the current conservative drive to dismantle the welfare state. The libertarianism of Friedman, like the Becker conjecture in the last chapter, sees free markets as both the best protector of individual liberty and the greatest possible long-term solvent of economic inequality due to racial discrimination. Like Becker, Friedman believes that only free markets can, given time, destroy the brutal and unethical disparities that racists may impose on pariah groups, especially blacks.

Trouble for White Labor

It is worth noting that a conservative commitment to free markets means a commitment to the free mobility of capital. This means that owners may move their capital, whether in the form of stocks, bonds, and other financial instruments, or even physical capital like factories, in order to earn the highest return. When a commitment to capital mobility is combined with a commitment to free trade, unskilled workers—who are disproportionately black and brown in America but who are nonetheless overwhelmingly white in absolute numbers—are threatened with potential impoverishment. American firms are always on the lookout for workers who are both efficient and cheap. If American workers become too expensive, either because of a general labor shortage or because of the welfare state, free capital mobility means that firms can seek out cheaper labor abroad. In a world with free trade and the unfettered movement of capital, the ruthless logic of markets puts American workers in a bind: if the wages of unskilled and low-skilled workers are too high, either American consumers will switch to substitute goods made by cheaper foreign workers, or American capital will flow abroad in search of cheaper labor. Blaming US consumers for not "buying American" or US firms for pursuing cheap labor is beside the point: global capitalism means that expensive labor is unemployed, period.

The logic of global free markets also means that a policy of restricting immigration must fail to raise the wages of unskilled workers. Suppose that the American people can be frightened into approving brutally harsh anti-immigration laws through their representatives in the Congress, far worse than the already nasty pieces of legislation that have become law since the early 1990s. There is little reason to think that these kinds of laws could really stem the tide of immigration: given the economic benefits of coming to the US for so many of the world's people, restrictions on legal immigration would greatly increase the problem of illegal immigration in much the same way that drug laws help create a vast, profitable, and deadly market for drugs. Do we really want a new, extensive, international illegal market for entry into the US that resembles the market for illegal drugs?

But suppose that the tough immigration policy were successful in reducing both legal and illegal immigration into the US. Then the supply of labor in the US would gradually shrink relative to the number of jobs available. This would in turn boost wages for all workers, including unskilled workers. However, if US labor is more expensive, then US goods are less competitive. Increased US wages will lead to both less demand for US goods and the flight of firms from the US to places with cheaper labor. In the end, whatever benefits US labor receives from tough immigration laws would be temporary, at the cost of permanent job losses.

Do migration, capital mobility, and free markets always mean that US labor, particularly unskilled and low-skilled labor without specialized and scarce skills, is vulnerable to competition from low-wage foreign competition? Probably, unless the US government enters into agreements with other governments to either manage trade or, hopefully, to improve economic and social conditions abroad so that the wages of foreign workers rise. In a world of free trade, migration, and capital mobility, skilled and unskilled workers alike are left to fend for themselves. Skilled workers are in a better position to thrive in the global economy because they have a competitive edge on potential rivals in other nations. However, unskilled workers, and especially blue-collar, middle-class workers, face the prospect of stagnant or declining living standards and unemployment as they are forced to compete with foreign workers who are just as efficient as they are and who are willing to work for less. As time passes, the gap between the living standards of well-educated and modestly educated workers will increase. Even worse for the white proletariat, well-educated whites will have little incentive to help pay for better schools for badly schooled white workers who are vulnerable to the whirlwind of international competition and technological change, for the reasons noted above.

While a conservative approach to economic policy favors free markets and free trade, thereby exposing unskilled workers to the harsh gale of international competition in trade-sensitive sectors of the economy, conservatives, like liberals, have been trying to find a way to increase economic growth without igniting inflation. However, the conservative indictment of liberal economic policy, and the related prescription for restoring the nation's economic health, emphasizes the need to restore profits as a precursor to rapid economic growth. Conservative economic policy is based on the insight that rapid productivity growth is the most important source of economic well-being over the long term. Since private enterprise is the primary source of jobs and technology in a modern capitalist society, the best way to foster widespread prosperity is to create conditions favorable to high rates of investment in new technologies and production facilities by encouraging high profits. In turn, governments can encourage high profits by reducing the costs of government regulations and social programs, and, of course, by lowering taxes on profits. The key to economic prosperity, according to conservatives, is to let free markets guide the allocation of labor, capital, and other resources to their most profitable uses, with minimum distortions from government.

A key part of the conservative critique of liberal economic policy is the observation that generous social welfare policies, including welfare (Aid to Families with Dependent Children), public housing, child nutrition subsidies, and other programs grant low-income workers, who are also usually people with few marketable skills, access to goods and services without requiring them to work. Further, taxing middle- and upper-income workers to pay for social benefits to poor workers (and nonworkers) reduces the take-home pay of the nation's more productive citizens, thereby reducing their incentive to work as well as encouraging ambitious people to evade taxes in various ways. These types of policies effectively reduce work incentives, which lead to a reduction in the number of people willing to work, and must therefore put upward pressure on wages, though the higher wages will not offset the bite of taxes on disposable income. Higher wages for both skilled and unskilled workers will lead to lower profits which in turn reduce the incentives of firms to hire workers. In addition, the higher labor costs that result from the welfare state's tendency to subsidize less productive workers by taxing more productive labor and capital will encourage firms to find production technologies that reduce labor costs by shedding workers, thereby contributing to the problem of skills-based unemployment. The conservative critique of welfare as the cause of the underclass presented in chapter 2 is simply an extension of this more fundamental analysis, which sees progressive social welfare policy as a barrier to economic growth because its taxing and spending policies reduce work incentives and profits, thereby undermining the economy's ability to expand.

The conservative prescription for economic growth in a post-liberal era is well known to any adult over the age of 25: low taxes, less regulation, and cuts in certain types of social welfare benefits in order to encourage work and investment. While the conservative diagnosis of slow economic growth (which includes calls for the abolition of corporate income taxes and capital gains taxes as fetters on the profitability of investment) does *not* logically require the abolition of the welfare state, or even require free market societies to be indifferent to the problems of poverty and income inequality, the American conservative program has favored promoting economic growth at the expense of equality. It is perfectly possible for conservatives to insist that poor people work and that business activity be as free of regulation and taxation as possible, while also pursuing equality through an aggressive program that guarantees high-quality schooling, health care, and access to housing for all citizens, no matter their class or color. This kind of conservative egalitarianism would champion free and fair competition in all markets, and allow the winners in the competitive struggle to keep a large portion of their earnings, while at the same time financing schools, hospitals, and other essential social goods by taxes that have as small an effect on work incentives as possible (which is one goal of the various proposals for a flat tax). One of the mysteries of modern American conservatism is that it has pursued an extreme free market agenda that not only opposes work exemptions for the poor but also completely ignores the problem of poverty. It is one thing to see inequality as a necessary part of capitalism's incentive system, and quite another to actively oppose efforts to reduce poverty as an excuse for promoting growth.

One of the profound ironies of the extreme American conservative commitment to free markets and high profits is that it is destroying the historic compromise between the white rich and the white working class on the role of race in economic life. Michael Lind notes in *The Next American Nation* that American nationalist ideology, and therefore American public policy, has historically been based on the belief that the United States is a "white nation" that celebrates both free markets and the self-determination of the common, white citizen.[24] An essential part of American *Herrenvolk* (white people's) democracy has been a compromise between white capital and white labor that effectively protected white workers from competition with nonwhite labor. Though American labor history has shown that white workers and white capital have frequently clashed over the use of nonwhite workers as strikebreakers, these battles were continually resolved in ways that prevented nonwhites from having the same access to jobs, education, housing, health care, or the right to participate in politics on the same terms as white workers. The liberals' successful destruction of legal segregation in the 1950s through the 1970s undercut the political foundation of white workers' influence over both labor markets and the public sector. Once blacks could vote without fear of intimidation or reprisal, and once blacks could, at least theoretically, compete for jobs and education on the same formal terms as whites, white workers inevitably lost the economic benefits that went along with segregation. However, so long as white workers have had effective control of the labor market by virtue of their numbers in an industrial economy, they could still benefit from their racial status.

Conservative economic policy represents a final, irrevocable breakdown of the compromise between white economic elites and the white working class. In a word, the white working class has been fired in favor of a worldwide labor force that is as efficient but cheaper than white American labor. The creation of a vigorous global capitalist system means that both American workers and American business are forced to re-examine every aspect of their relationship, including the compact between unskilled white labor and capital to maintain a white republic.

The harsh realities of modern world capitalism mean that American elites simply get no benefits from supporting modestly schooled white labor's demand for social and political privileges over nonwhite labor. White labor cannot use strikes to regain its political and social dominance over nonwhites in an era where immigration and free trade have created a vast pool of cheap labor. White elites are not fussy about the color of workers in other countries, especially since they don't have to share space or control of the state with foreign labor.

Politics and the Strategy of Inequality

There is a second, critical difference between the black underclass and the emerging white underclass that promises to make life exceedingly difficult for conservatives who favor the strategy of inequality. Since there are far more whites than blacks, the emergence of a white underclass displaced by global competition and technological change will presumably lead to vigorous demands for government action of its behalf. Though one of the Left's favorite daydreams is that the impoverishment of a significant portion of the white electorate will fuel the formation of a progressive multiracial political coalition, there is little reason to think that whites, shamed by their underclass status, will want to band together with "colored" people they have despised for generations. The rhetoric of class solidarity is empty compared to the powerful appeal of race and nationalism in this country, particularly in a situation where white workers find themselves sharing the benighted class status of blacks in the world economy. Members of the white underclass are not likely to respond well to the destruction of their livelihoods by vigorous global competition and technological change. They are even less likely to be comfortable with sharing space, public resources, and political power with blacks whom they see as morally inferior and dangerous. While there is little doubt that white nationalist politicians (Patrick Buchanan, for example) will make the case that globalism has robbed whites of the means to live apart from blacks, there is also little reason to suppose that these same whites will be in any mood to band together with despised blacks.

White nationalist voices urging the "cleansing" of America's cultural institutions of the influence of minorities and the recreation of opportunity for whites have been steadily gaining favor in various parts of the country, as the political success of race-baiting candidates attests. The fact that the interests of a displaced, angry, and racially hostile white proletariat will be represented in the halls of government may well mean that demands for the restoration of white racial status will become as important as demands to do something about long-term white unemployment. Global capitalism and technological change mean that many whites will lose their ability to use the market to satisfy their demands for racial distance, thereby leading many to turn to the government to resurrect various forms of state-sponsored racial segregation.

Of course, so long as the white underclass represents a minority of the white population, and so long as the economically secure white population can govern effectively without the support of the white underclass, then demands for the recreation of segregation are likely to fall on deaf ears. Further, even if economically secure whites must make concessions to the white underclass in order to retain control of the state, there is very little reason to think that full-blown segregation is likely to return to America. Conservatives will be limited to harsh, racially charged symbolic politics because globalism constrains their ability to use government to recreate separatism. Just as liberals cannot use budget deficits to finance the incorporation of the blacks into the modern, technology driven economy, conservatives will not be able to use fiscal policy to finance the development of a racist regime that relies on the police power of the state to physically separate racial groups or to re-impose a world of "separate but equal." Whites who can afford to be apart from blacks will continue to do so. Well-off whites may even have considerable sympathy for the plight of poorer whites who are forced to live near blacks or share a decaying public sector with them. Nonetheless, economically secure whites are unlikely to support financially the recreation of grand segregation, especially since the ideology of meritocracy strongly suggests that working-class and underclass whites are poor because they are as stupid as blacks.

The recent demise of affirmative action in American life is a good example of how conservative politics will fail to address the underlying economic forces that promise to worsen American racial conflict. There has always been great ambivalence about the legitimacy of affirmative action in the minds of even the most progressive, anti-racist forces precisely because it seems to make race a primary criterion for the distribution of economic rewards. Yet, the elimination of affirmative action on the belief that it has contributed to the economic decline of the white working class is a conservative political sop to a frustrated white working class. There is no evidence that whites, as a class, have suffered significant job or income loss because of affirmative action. Nor is there any reason to believe that white employment prospects or living standards will be enhanced by the elimination of race-based affirmative action programs. While conservatives can continue their recent practice of basing political campaigns and public pronouncements on increasingly virulent anti-black themes, their commitment to free markets in modern times means that they are essentially committed to a racial version of "bread and circuses," where the occasional sacrifice of racial scapegoats temporarily appeases an angry and disillusioned white working class.

The death of affirmative action points to another problem for both conservatives and liberals in the modern economy. Even in a knowledge-driven economy, not all of the dirty, dangerous, or nasty jobs of society can be done abroad and supplied to the knowledge and managerial classes through free trade. Someone will have to collect the garbage, cook the meals, sweep the streets, clean the toilets, drive the cabs, buses, and trucks, and wipe the noses and bottoms of the children of the managerial classes. In addition, growing poverty and inequality will require more policemen, more courts, more jails, parole officers, social workers, and other personnel to run the internal security and law enforcement apparatus. One of the primary consequences of affirmative action has been that minorities, and especially blacks, have used the policy to increase their share of employment in the government sector, including the public safety and law enforcement areas. This has meant that middle-class blacks employed in the public sector have played a larger and larger role in managing poor blacks.

The end of affirmative action in an economy where the white working class is being squeezed by global capitalism and technological change means that whites will once again try to claim the lion's share of internal security jobs as one way of avoiding the dirtiest, least respected jobs in this society.

There are two serious problems for the managerial class that follow from this situation. First, the prospect of whites once again managing the black poor in cities will create a situation where the white proletariat is employed to watch, jail, prosecute, and execute the black proletariat. This will only worsen racial conflict in this country by converting the downward mobility of the white working class into a racial war between the black working class and underclass and the State. Police brutality, periodic riots, and the general coarsening of daily life in this country are only likely to accelerate under these conditions.

Second, the conservative strategy of inequality combined with the end of affirmative action means that a large portion of the black population will be effectively closed out of the educational system of this country, again. By killing affirmative action, and more importantly, by refusing to create an equitable system of high-quality schooling in this country, a conservative strategy of inequality is directly telling large numbers of young black people that they have no choice but to accept their fate as a poor, trapped class that is genetically incapable of rising above its lowly station. A merit-driven society is characterized by an ideology of desserts, based on intellectual superiority and academic achievement that is reminiscent of the musings in *The Bell Curve*. The experience of the past two decades has shown, among other things, that poor blacks will not accept the judgement of the rest of society that they should simply shut up and accept their fate as servants and social trash. If the larger society refuses to fund education and social services for the poor *and* kills affirmative action, it has cut the last links between itself and a large black pariah class. Black American alienation from the world the conservatives have made seems destined to grow.

The conservative strategy of inequality promises to create more social conflict and more racial division in a country that has seen its share of both. The inevitable result of policies that slavishly respect market outcomes is the growing need for police and internal security forces to quell the inevitable increases in crime and violence that must follow the hardening of class and caste barriers implicit in modern, knowledge-driven capitalism. The central failure of conservative economic and social policy is that it tries to recreate the conditions of aggressive free market capitalism where those ideas simply cannot apply. Though modern conservatives hail meritocratic capitalism as the most effective system for creating wealth in world history, they refuse to acknowledge that the hierarchies created by modern educational systems and re-flected in the increasing inequality between the skilled and the unskilled must lead to ever greater social warfare between knowledge and income classes and racial groups. The breakdown of the welfare state means, as a practical matter, that there is no effective social contract between the various classes of society. American national identity is not strong enough to overcome the racial divisions that have split this country into the mutually hostile racial reservations which have arisen in our cities and suburbs. In a society where the ideology of merit means that the skilled absolve themselves of the need to contribute to the well-being of their unskilled and therefore "inferior" neighbors, each class has an incentive to pursue its own interests, by whatever means it can get away with.

This must inevitably lead to a situation where the American political economy fragments into largely separate spheres that are more tightly linked to their respective counterparts in the world economy than they are to each other. For example, the suburban communities of Boston, filled with the professional classes trained in the elite universities for which that city is famous, have much more in common with profession-als in Chicago, Los Angeles, and Paris then they do with their "neigh-bors" down the street. Over time, the spread of meritocracy around the globe will mean that American professionals will compete for jobs, pay, and education for their children with similarly placed professionals in other countries. These men and women will be focused on succeeding in their part of the world economy, which just happens to be located in the United States. Their needs for good schools, good roads, and public services in general will either be satisfied through their own taxes, or in national coalitions with other well-educated people through the auspi-ces of one of the current political parties or a new party.

Without the welfare state, in a society badly divided by race and now divided into disparate knowledge castes, conservative worship of free markets promises to create a new kind of caste system. Any attempt by right-wing politicians to use white nationalism as a glue to hold this badly fractured social order together may work for a time, especially if these politicians are successful at finding a series of plausible scapegoats (like immigrants, blacks, Latinos, and other "enemies") who can oc-cupy the attention of the white underclass and working class. Yet, scapegoating will not make American labor more productive in the world market, nor can it overcome the basic economic fact that threatens the livelihoods of millions of Americans: the rest of the world has caught up to the Americans in technology and hundreds of millions of people in other lands want to do the same work as modestly educated Americans for far less money.

In the end, the return of unregulated capitalism to America means that conservatives are willing to abandon huge segments of the white population to the same forces of technological change and hyper-capitalism that have thwarted the incorporation of blacks into the modern economy. This gradual bifurcation of American society will probably proceed slowly, so slowly that most of the white majority will only gradually see that their country is slipping into a condition of social strife and division that is usually associated with the so-called Third World. Nonetheless, it is important to note that an America split into a number of mutually murderous, chronically poor, undereducated, economically marginal, racially divided proletariats and an economically comfortable, predominantly white majority is perfectly possible and, if the policies of conservatives are pursued to their logical conclusions, quite likely. There is nothing in the economic logic of a market economy that precludes this possibility, especially if the American middle class is willing to use whatever force is necessary to shield its itself from the social costs of market-driven inequality and racial segregation.

The advent of meritocracy in a competitive global economy does not have to lead to the abandonment of social decency and the escalation of racial warfare between economically insecure and marginal black and white workers. The return of the market can be made consistent with racial peace and the final integration of black Americans into the modern economy as well as the successful modernization of the economy for white workers if the country is willing to move beyond the limitations of the traditional welfare state. It is one thing to respect the limits that the world market imposes on the various devices for rebuilding the American economy in a way that promotes social and racial justice, and quite another to pretend that markets are forever incompatible with all attempts to promote fairness, compassion, and equality. The drive by modern conservatives to return, thoughtlessly, almost mindlessly to raw capitalism means that the movement for racial equality is gravely wounded in America. For many conservatives, bitter racial conflict is tolerable so long as it does not interfere with the prerogatives of the educated middle classes, the rich, and those who are, at least for the moment, a fair distance from the world capitalist maelstrom. Unless conservatives are prepared to return to the days when the racial status of poor and lower-class whites over blacks was backed by the power of the State, then their drive for unlimited capitalism is likely to produce slow-motion civil war. This brings us to the final irony of the conservative strategy of inequality and the politics of race in America: even though conservative economic policy promises to worsen the lot of millions of white workers for exactly the same reason that black workers are stymied, insecure white workers prefer to blame blacks for their troubles rather than confront the mind-bending complexities of modern, skill-driven global capitalism. Like the long intellectual hangover that the Civil Rights victories have inflicted on blacks and liberals, one marvels at how the slow death of the memory of white privilege is making it hard for working-class whites to accept the fact that they live in a bitter and harsh new world that has no place for them.

Appendix: The "Rule of 70"

Our discussion of productivity growth mentioned the "rule of 70" as a convenient rule of thumb for calculating the time it would take for a bank account or the average person's living standard to double. This rule is a very general convention that can be applied to any situation where growth is occurring. This appendix presents a brief review of the mathematics of growth and compounding that are the basis for the "rule of 70."

For simplicity, let's return to the example developed in the text, where a person wants to know how long he or she must wait before a $1,000 deposit in a bank becomes $2,000 through the magic of compound interest. If the interest rate on bank deposits is 3% (not a very good rate, to be sure), then after one year the account would be $1,000 × 1.03 = $1,030. Please note that the number 1.03 is the interest factor that tells us how much $1 today will be worth one year from now. If the interest rate were 5%, the interest factor would be 1.05, while if the interest rate were 0%, then the interest factor would be 1.00

(and the problem would be intensely uninteresting). If we wanted to know how large the account would be after two years, we would simply multiply the initial $1,000 by the interest factor twice, so that we would have $1,000 × 1.03 × 1.03 = $1,000 × 1.03^2 = $1,069. In general, if we want to hold the funds in the account for T years, we can find out how much the account is worth at the end of that period by calculating the product $1,000 × 1.03^T.

We are now in a position to note the miracle of compounding that is the secret to financial success, economic growth, and every other process of steady expansion. In the example where we want to hold the account in the bank for two periods, please note that the calculation can be rewritten as follows: $1,000 × 1.03 × 1.03 = $1,030 × 1.03 = ($1,000 × 1.03) + ($30 × 1.03) = $1,030 + $30.90 = $1,069. When we leave the funds in the account for a second year, the bank applies the interest factor to the initial $1,000 and to the $30 earned in the first year. Compounding refers to the fact that the account will earn interest on interest with the result that money seems to grow on itself, as shown by the fact that the interest in the second year is $0.90 greater than that received in the first year, which is 3% of the $30 in interest earned in the first year. If one keeps the account in the bank for a longer period of time, the impact of compounding increases accordingly. For example, if we keep the account in the bank for ten years, the dollar values of the account would be $1,000 × 1.03^{10} = $1,344.

We are now ready for the "rule of 70." To continue with our example, suppose we wanted to calculate the amount of time it would take for the $1,000 to double if the interest rate is 3%. That means that we want to find the number of years (T) it takes for the account to go from $1,000 to $2,000, which is equivalent to solving the following equation for T: $2,000 = 1.03^T × 1000. This looks very complicated, but it's really very simple if we remember the point of natural logarithms. First divide both side of the equation by $1,000, which converts it into a general expression for determining how long it will take any process of expansion to double: $2 = 1.03^T. We must now solve for T. For those of you who don't remember this idea (or who never encountered it at all), consult your nearest encyclopedia for a brief discussion of this important piece of mathematics. In any case, a simple way to find T is to take the natural log of both sides, which converts our ugly equation into another ugly thing that is easy to work with: $\ln(2) = T$ $\ln(1.03)$ or $T = \dfrac{\ln(2)}{\ln(1.03)}$. Though this looks awful at this moment, it is about to become quite lovely. Please note that the $\ln(2)$ is approximately 0.7 (which you can verify by using any calculator). In addition, the natural logarithm of any number $1 + x$ is approximately equal to x for small values of x (certainly for values of x less than 0.2). Hence we can see that $T = \dfrac{\ln(2)}{\ln(1.03)} = \dfrac{0.7}{0.03} = \dfrac{70}{3} \cong 23.333$ or twenty-three and one-third years. The name "rule of 70" comes from the fact that we multiplied the numerator and denominator of our fraction by 100, which converts the numerator to 70 and the natural logarithm of the interest factor to a whole number that is 100 times the interest rate or, more generally, the growth rate.

Uninitiated readers should now feel confident in their ability to calculate the doubling time of all sorts of things, including the standard of living for the average citizen of a nation. In the case of productivity, readers should know that when they hear a new report that "American labor productivity has risen by 1.3% on an annual basis" (typically read by a beautifully coifed man or woman who hasn't a clue about the meaning of what he or she has just said), they can see that this is not good news, since it would mean that the typical American's standard of living would double in 70/1.3 or approximately 53.9 years. If the news reader instead says that productivity is growing at an annual rate of 2.4% a year, then the standard of living doubles in about 29.1 years, which is much better.

The general formula for the "rule of 70" should now be clear. If we have a process that grows at an average annual rate of $z\%$ then the doubling time can be exactly calculated by the formula

$$T = \frac{\ln(2)}{\ln(1+z)}$$

which can be approximated by

$$T \cong \frac{70}{100z}.$$

FOUR

The Political Economy of Hope and Fear

The Predicament

Must markets and merit stitch race and well-being together forever in America? No, but we must acknowledge (though not accept) the fact that the combination of free markets and meritocracy is likely to hurt low-income people, especially poor and working-class black people, for a long time to come. Our predicament, as a nation, and especially for blacks, can be stated simply enough: *the twin commitments to individual liberty and private property that are the pillars of American capitalism are perfectly consistent with long-term racial inequality, so long as racial disparities occur without the support of government power and do not obviously violate anti-discrimination law*. The bitterness of this compatibility between the tenets of liberty and private racial hatred has led some observers to conclude that racism is a permanent feature of American life that blacks, especially, must acknowledge and then somehow confront. A recent, and profoundly disturbing, statement of this thesis has been presented by Derrick Bell in his book *Faces at the Bottom of the Well: The Permanence of Racism*:

> Black people will never gain full equality in this country. Even those herculean efforts we hail as successful [anti-discrimination laws, affirmative action, occasional glimpses of genuine racial openness] will produce no more than temporary "peaks of progress," short-lived victories that slide into irrelevance as racial patterns adapt in ways that maintain white dominance. This is a hard-to-accept fact that all history verifies. We must

acknowledge it, not as a sign of submission, but as an act of ultimate defiance.[1]

The problem that Bell points to is fundamental: the racial preferences of the white majority will continue to be beyond the reach of the law, even if the procedures of government are formally neutral in racial matters. There is simply no way that law can make whites associate with blacks on the basis of mutual respect or equality. As a result, the routines of daily life will continue to be affected by the racial phobias and whims of the white majority, thereby restricting the life chances and quality of life for blacks so long as markets are allowed to allocate access to schooling, health care, and housing, with no concern for the way that unregulated capitalism reinforces blacks' bitter historical legacy of under-development.

But Bell's indictment of American society as irredeemably racist is, if anything, too mild, precisely because it fails to explain how a liberal, capitalist society that has specifically broken with its segregationist past nonetheless ties blackness and poverty together. It is important to understand that racism alone is not the primary problem that black people face, even though racism, especially the sort of sly anti-black appeals popular with right-wing politicians and their public, does immense damage to black well-being. The problem black people now face is that a terrible new synthesis of racism, free markets, and meritocracy has replaced the old system of organized Negrophobia that has been our nemesis for three hundred years. Black people have been abused for so long and in so many different ways that is it sometimes hard to realize when old enemies have surrendered and newer, subtler barriers to our collective well-being have emerged. "Racism," as the application of State power (in the form of the police, the courts, and the executioner) to support a sadistic social system of dominance and submission based on color is gone (forever, we hope, but do not quite believe). The old system simply used the courts, cudgel, and lynch mob to push black people out of jobs and opportunities for which they were eminently qualified. Throughout most of American history, when a young agrarian country rapidly changed into an expanding industrial power whose hunger for labor brought millions of African slaves and European peasant immigrants to its shores, there was no real difference between black and white workers, except that whites owned the state and used it to keep blacks down. The blue-collar road to the middle class would have been open to blacks except for rampant discrimination that only abated in times of labor shortages brought on by national crises—particularly the two World Wars in this century—prior to the victory of the Civil Rights rebellion.

It is misleading to say that "black people," as a single, undifferentiated mass, face a single set of economic problems, because the real successes of the Civil Rights rebellion have created two black Americas from an economic perspective. Technology-driven, meritocratic, hyper-capitalist America presents very different problems to poor and working-class black people, on the one hand, and middle-class blacks on the other.

Poor and working-class black Americans are an under-educated, low-wage population whose adults are caught in an economic squeeze between a growing domestic supply of unskilled labor due to immigration, increasing competition with unskilled workers abroad via free trade, and a declining demand for their skills as a consequence of technological change. These men and women live in segregated areas that have limited fiscal resources, or in metropolitan areas where residential segregation, combined with the political power of middle-class and upper-class white majorities (usually in suburban areas), denies blacks access to important public goods, particularly decent schools. Black children are subjected to inferior education in modern America because black adults are at a competitive disadvantage vis-à-vis whites and Asians in job markets and housing markets, which in turn creates growing black disadvantages in education, health care, and employment in the future. Poor white adults and children are in the same economic position, though poor white populations are more evenly distributed between urban and rural settings than poor blacks. As the literacy, numeracy, and intellectual demands of work increase with the development and spread of new technologies, poor and working-class blacks will find it increasingly difficult to succeed in a meritocratic society unless they can convince the middle- and upper-class majority to invest in schooling, across class and color lines. Sadly, poor and working-class whites and blacks are not able, and appear unwilling, to form a viable coalition that can join with middle-class liberals to create more egalitarian economic and educational policies.

Black and Blue and Very Scared

Some blacks, especially college-educated blacks, have successfully entered the meritocratic sectors of the economy, though their place in elite colleges and professions is being challenged because many have gained access to these positions as a result of affirmative action. Yet, middle-class blacks live in highly segregated communities (like poor blacks).[2] Chapter 1 presented data that show that middle- and upper-class black families have lower incomes than their white counterparts, which, combined with continuing residential segregation, means that well-off blacks are crowded into black suburbs and sending their children to black schools.

The relatively low standardized test scores of middle-class black children pose a severe problem for the black bourgeoisie. On the one hand, middle-class blacks have escaped the poverty, deprivation, and abuse that have been the historic lot of blacks in America. However, well-off blacks are seen as failing in the competition for positions in elite colleges and professions to the extent that they have acquired these positions through affirmative action.

The debate over affirmative action is, among other things, a battle between blacks and whites over the legitimacy of race as a criterion for selection in college admissions and employment in light of the nation's history of racial oppression, continuing racial segregation, and the legitimate fears that blacks have about whites' lack of commitment to genuine racial equality. The issue that middle-class black people face is whether or not they will be able to redefine merit to include proper consideration of the realities of racial conflict and the need for racial representation in the selection of elites. If they are blocked from bringing questions of minority status into the definition of merit, then middle-class blacks are likely to be blocked from elite educational institutions and professions until they master the meritocratic game.

Opponents of affirmative action like to claim that colorblind "merit" should be the only principle for distributing positions of prestige, power, and high earnings in a diverse society. The idea that effort and achievement should be rewarded without regard to race is treated as a direct extension of the economic principle of efficiency and as an equally straightforward moral principle that directly follows from the claim that race, gender, religion, sexual orientation, or (as far as possible) physical impairment should be an irrelevant consideration in assessing a person's fitness for a position. While this claim is very appealing in the abstract, it fails to address an essential problem of hierarchy and power in a bitterly divided society like the United States. For better or worse, university education is a gateway to authority in a complex, hierarchical, technology-driven society that distributes power and prestige on the basis of achievement. College graduates, who later become lawyers, politicians, doctors, engineers, teachers, scientists, entrepreneurs, writers, artists, and managers of the vast machinery of persuasion and propaganda called the Media, direct the allocation of human and material resources from their positions of authority and expertise, in light of their understanding of their particular jobs and the needs of the larger society. While an economic point of view tends to emphasize the need for selection procedures for jobs and colleges that place the most able persons in these positions of authority regardless of race, there are nonetheless vital political and social reasons for paying attention to the racial composition of the nation's leadership cadre in public and private life. Many of the institutions that are directed by and staffed by college- and university-educated people, particularly the courts, the police, and the legal profession, are directly responsible for the use of coercive force in order to enforce the law in society. Government bureaus, law firms, and the management of most small and large corporations are comprised of college-trained persons. Not only are the most highly paid positions occupied by college-trained people, but most of the important decisions about employment, pay, the flow of information, the allocation of people, talent, capital, and materials, and the use of power are made by men and women who have been selected for their positions by virtue of their academic credentials, not their sensitivity to the exercise of private power in racially divided societies. Most of these people are employed by private enterprises. Most of the decisions made by managers are beyond the scope of government regulation, and even the control of the stockholders of major corporations, much less the voices of despised social groups.

One of the most powerful arguments in favor of "merit" as a criterion for access to wealth, power, and prestige is that it can be an effective counterweight to the oligarchic tendencies of capitalist elites, who use their economic power to promote their own narrow interests. Open competition for jobs and education allows a society to distribute its rewards on the basis of talent as well as encouraging the poor and social outcasts to develop their skills in the hope that they too might succeed under certain conditions. Competitive mobilization of a nation's intellectual resources in a merit-based system gives middle-class people an independent source of economic rewards, thereby liberating this portion of the population from any degrading dependence on selfish economic elites.

However, "merit" in a racially divided society is a potential trap for a despised social group that is blocked from access to key resources, particularly high-quality schools, by virtue of widespread race hatred and economic inequality. Black people, as the nation's historic pariah caste, can ill afford to trust in the fairness and goodwill of a racially phobic white majority that uses "colorblind" merit to select the police, judges, and lawyers in a society where racial hatred influences the allocation of schools, housing, and other critical resources. Blacks have well-founded reasons not to believe that the police, the courts, or the legal profession will treat them fairly. Black distrust of a white monopoly on power in criminal justice and politics is quite legitimate, in light of American history and the white majority's sorry inability of abandon its belief in black inferiority.

Black middle-class men and women support affirmative action for many reasons, among them issues of principle and naked self-interest. However, beneath the debate about the legitimacy of affirmative action is another, more basic question: when should race be a consideration in hiring and employment, given the fact that college-trained elites exercise enormous, and largely unaccountable, power over the lives of black citizens, who remain the nation's most visible pariah caste? At a minimum, race has to play a role in hiring a police force and in the composition of the judiciary, the prosecutors, and the jailers, all of whom exercise considerable power over the daily lives of despised blacks, particularly poor blacks. An insistence on colorblind "merit" in staffing the machinery of criminal justice, and therefore in law school admissions and the recruitment of police officers, is either based on the preposterous assumption that the State enforces the law and uses force in a colorblind manner, or that the victimization of blacks in this way is unimportant (a rather compact definition of racial oppression). Rigid advocates of colorblind "merit" in hiring and school admissions are willing to overlook the fact that high achievers in positions of power will exercise their racial prerogatives in ways that are to the detriment of blacks. At a minimum, the debate over affirmative action needs to make a sharp distinction between those areas where race does not matter, like graduate training in architecture or biochemistry, and those where race does matter, like the law or the military.

This type of distinction implies that there can be no simple, comprehensive criteria for merit in allocating college training or for hiring and promotion. Some jobs, like prosecutor, policeman, criminal lawyer, social worker, nurse, doctor, or teacher, require people to exercise authority and practice their craft along the fault lines of racial division. Trust between citizens and these representatives of the State is essential if a regime is going to deliver important goods and services to all citizens on an equal basis. In turn, workers who deliver public goods to citizens, or represent their interests in disputes with the State (like lawyers) must deliver these services without racial bias or disdain. The State cannot know if its staff of workers is free from racial animus, nor can it seek to discover the racial beliefs of its workers without violating their fundamental liberties. A government must therefore weigh the efficiency benefits associated with colorblind forms of merit against the gains that racial diversity can bring in terms of service delivery to the citizenry.

This justification for affirmative action ultimately rests on the claim that the State is the sole provider of important goods and services to citizens across the color and ethnic spectrum *and* that pure "merit" for staffing government positions system cannot provide adequate protections for despised groups. An anarcho-capitalist would suggest that there are few legitimate public goods—aside from national defense, the courts, the police, the monetary system, and perhaps publicly financed schooling (though schooling itself should be privately provided)—so that affirmative action ought to disappear. However, even an anarcho-capitalist must wonder about whether race hatred can result in the unequal provision of public goods and services to despised groups, and therefore whether a racially diverse work force is necessary to offset the effect of racism on the activities of the public sector.

This argument is unlikely to appeal to many because it assumes that racism is permanent and bound to affect the behavior of public-sector employees at every level of government. This sort of fundamental pessimism, which is a necessary part of being black in America, is likely to be opposed by Americans who do not wish to see the nation as fundamentally warped by race hatred. If it comes down to a contest of visions about the place of racism in American life, blacks must lose, which means they must be prepared to live and struggle without affirmative action in a much nastier world.

Adversity and Opportunity

Black middle-class fears that whites will use "merit" to limit black upward mobility make sense in a nation where *The Bell Curve* is a best seller. Yet, it would be a mistake for middle-class blacks to conclude that widespread anti-black animus among whites is as potent a force for harm now as is was in the past. Derrick Bell's claim about the permanence of racism is fair warning for those blacks foolish enough to think that the majority of whites will ever accept them as genuine equals. The hard evidence of everyday black life in schools, on the job, searching for an apartment to rent or a home to buy, or as parents and voters shows that blacks are just not welcome in this country. The end of affirmative action in favor of "colorblind" policies in hiring, promotion, school admissions, and government contracting will certainly reduce black access to the best schools, the most lucrative jobs, and a host of profitable activities financed by public money.

Middle-class black people are not in the same position as their parents and grandparents, whose valiant efforts to live dignified lives and to educate their children were constantly thwarted by the obsessive customary racism of whites and a government that abetted these white "cultural" practices. The reduction in black access to elite schools and prestigious jobs that will follow the death of affirmative action is not the same thing as the wholesale denial of access to good schools and good jobs that blacks have historically suffered. After affirmative action dies, black middle-class children will find themselves in a fierce battle with white, Asian, and Hispanic children for access to public schools and universities. Many black children will be at a competitive disadvantage vis-à-vis whites because of residential segregation and the resulting unequal access to high-quality schooling. Nonetheless, black middle-class families now have the resources to create auxiliary educational institutions, including the black equivalent of cram schools and test-breaking enterprises like Stanley Kaplan and The Princeton Review, that can improve the competitive chances of blacks.

Black middle-class parents, whose incomes are quite modest when compared to their white counterparts (as shown in chapter 1) are going to have to choose between enjoying a middle-class standard of consumption or sacrificing their current pleasure in order to invest in their children's human capital. As a practical matter, this will mean that black people will have to live more modestly than their white neighbors in order to finance their children's schooling, so that their children can be smarter, richer, and more secure in the future.

Black middle-class men and women have something to learn from the experience of Asian Americans, whose economic success is partly due to the fact that Asian Americans are a very well-educated population. Table 4.1 compares the educational attainments of Asian Americans and Pacific Islanders, blacks, and whites over the age of 25 as of March 1997. The table shows that Asian Americans are more than three times as likely to have completed four or more years of college or university schooling compared to blacks. Asian Americans' fabled belief in the value of education is sometimes attributed to unique aspects of the various national cultures that together comprise the Asian American community. While this may be so, simple economic sense suggests that middle-class black Americans can greatly improve their lot in the long term by investing in knowledge and schooling, even if it means that current generations of blacks must forego the decidedly mixed benefits of American consumerism for the more substantial benefits of extensive schooling.

The death of affirmative action is certainly a blow to black middle-class aspirations to the extent that these hopes relied on policies that tried to redistribute schooling and jobs to compensate for historic American racism. However, though conservatives' success in ending

Table 4.1 Highest Educational Attainment for Adults over 25, by Race, as of March 1997

Schooling Completed	Asian	Black	White
Less than High School	15.1	25.1	16.9
High School or Some College	42.8	61.5	58.5
College and Beyond	42.1	13.4	24.6

Source: Bureau of the Census Current Population Survey March 1997 CPS Supplement

affirmative action is a reminder that blacks' enemies are still quite busy, blacks can adjust to the new competitive realities by consuming less, studying harder, and investing in an intellectual infrastructure of teachers, scholars, schools, libraries, magazines, booksellers, and test-breaking routines that improve black chances in the merit wars. We have survived slavery, segregation, and the modern jail-industrial complex. We can, in time, win the merit wars too.

On Race, Poverty, and Prisons

Poor and working-class black families, like their white counterparts, need higher wages and steady jobs for their adult members, as well as access to high-quality schools, health care, day care, and housing for all family members. The most pressing problems for black families—low wages, unemployment, and the almost caste-like quality of the under- and mis-education of black children—can only be solved by fundamental changes in American economic policy. Specifically, poor and working-class Americans will only be helped if the United States places the highest priority on limiting the effects of economic inequality on the life chances of those who are judged to be failures in a merit-driven world.

For better or worse, the American work ethic, with its emphasis on honesty, ambition, and persistence, is simply no longer effective in propelling poor and working-class children into the ranks of the prosperous classes so long as these children are condemned to bad schools and unsafe streets. Hard work will yield little reward for adults whose skills are of little value in the modern world, no matter how law abiding, sober, or responsible they may be. Further, the logic of American meritocracy is that some portion of each generation of students *must* fail in the competition for good schools and jobs. The purpose of a merito-cratic schooling system is to allocate access to scarce educational resources on the basis of ability. Some portion of each generation—especially those children who are unlucky enough to come from poor families or families that have modest educational attainments—will perform poorly enough in schools that they are barred from high-wage employment.

This is a problem because it means that the children of poorly educated people are likely to be poorly educated, thereby hardening social class boundaries over time. Reduced social mobility as a result of unequal access to high-quality schooling threatens to push the United States closer to a class system where children inherit the educational and class position of their parents. In an odd way, this is a new situation for black Americans to the degree that there is now a large enough black middle class to permit millions of blacks to pass on their privileged status to their children. However, poor and working-class blacks are still trapped in their historic condition of permanent poverty, where the children of the black poor are assured of being poor themselves.

Color, Class, and Crime

The blend of markets and merit that America has settled on has nasty consequences for young black people. The losers in the merit wars, those who have been shunted into lousy schools, come from families with little formal education, and have few prospects of acquiring adequate schooling in later life, not only form the pool of unskilled labor, but also the army of young people who commit crimes, particularly drug crimes. Chapter 1 showed that the real wages of young American workers with the lowest levels of education have declined between 20 and 30% since 1973. Economist Richard Freeman of Harvard has shown how this decline in the wages and job prospects of young workers, combined with the prospects of higher earnings from criminal activity and the relatively low risk of imprisonment, can plausibly be understood as a cause of growing youth crime, particularly robbery, burglary, and drug crime.[3] No amount of breast beating about moral decay or terrible black families or any other cause of crime can escape the most basic fact of American economic life: the low (and falling) real wages and employment prospects among the young, poor, and modestly educated mean that, short of an economic miracle, American capitalism has a vast pool of largely marginal or even unemployable people who are having trouble sustaining working marriages or stable parenting partnerships, thereby creating the conditions of limited parental and community control over the behavior of the young that results in criminal activity.

The only way to deal with this problem, which is basically a problem of a growing population of economically marginal adults, is either to reduce their numbers (through better and more broadly available education for the children of the poor and working classes, an exceedingly expensive proposition that the American middle class has consistently rejected for a very long time) or to increase the demand for unskilled and modestly educated workers. There is a viable, left-liberal program for raising the income and employment prospects of unskilled workers that can reduce crime, promote social peace, and improve the life chances of poor people. The last section of this chapter briefly reviews the elements of this program. For the moment we must press on with our analysis of the predicament that poor and working blacks face in late twentieth-century America.

Of course, a meritocratic society could choose to use punishment to control the behavior of its unskilled working class, including its black underclass, as an alternative to improving the life chances of the poor. The economic logic of punishment is very clear in the context of a merit-driven society that refuses to reform the crime-creating nature of a free market order. Punishment policy helps deter crime by raising the penalties associated with law breaking.[4] The public invests in police, courts, and prisons in the hope that increases in the certainty (and with longer prison terms, the severity) of punishment will reduce the potential gain from crime and thereby deter criminal activity.

The deterrence function of punishment is not unlike the impact of pollution taxes and charges that a government will impose on activities that damage the environment. The primary purpose of pollution taxes is to force both the buyers and sellers of noxious products to bear the full cost of their activity in the hope that they will either find a better way to make and sell goods or simply reduce the scale of the polluting activity. Similarly, a positive function of punishment is credibly to threaten offenders with loss so that there is no profit in criminal activity.[5] While some people can be dissuaded from breaking the law by the threat of sanctions, others will need to feel the sting of sanctions—including arrest, trial, fines, or, at the extreme, prison—before they change their behavior. If the economic approach to crime and deterrence is correct, then punishment policy contributes to deterring crime by raising the penalties associated with law breaking. Investment by the public in police, courts, and prisons reduces the gain from crime by raising the risk that criminals will be caught, convicted, and sent to prison. Longer prison sentences also deter crime, according to theory, by increasing the costs of incarceration in terms of the income, opportunities, and pleasures that a criminal loses by being incarcerated.[6]

Punishment, particularly imprisonment, is also a social device for removing criminals from society and in that way reducing the incidence of crime. Prisons, from an economic point of view, are warehouses that quarantine or incapacitate those men and women who either cannot be deterred by the threat of sanctions or whose actions are so harmful to society that they are best kept away from the rest of us. In either case, prisons are forms of public capital that insure society against the failure of education, social customs, laws, and intermediate sanctions to deter criminal behavior.

The resources used to operate and maintain prison facilities are funded by taxes, or in the case of governments plagued by budget deficits, borrowing, thereby requiring any rational government to think about its punishment policies in relation to all of its other economic and social policies. Public-sector budgets are tight in the modern world, in part because citizens in all countries chafe at the price tag of the public services they demand, and because taxation and public spending priorities have very important effects on the economic well-being of nations. Governments faced with insistent demands for extensive and high-quality public services and limitations on their taxing and borrowing powers must carefully weigh the costs and benefits of spending extra money on everything, including police and prisons. A government is on solid economic ground in building another prison rather than more schools if the economic benefits from housing more felons exceed those from providing high-quality schooling to the community's children. Conversely, a society that goes on a prison-building binge without carefully considering whether limited funds are better spent on other things, like schools, is being foolish, at best.

A narrow economic perspective on the punishment process shows that a government has to weigh a number of items as it tries to deal with crime. We have already seen that punishment can only deter crime if the threat of arrest, trial, and the imposition of sanctions is credible, which requires significant investments in police and in the court system. In addition, the system of sanctions must be carefully constructed to both deter crime and, where necessary, handle felons in a cost-effective manner. An economically rational punishment policy will match the sanction to the crime in ways that lead to the greatest possible social benefit. This means that there should be a link between the severity of the sanction, in terms of the type of sanction imposed and, in the case of imprisonment, length of sentence, and the social cost of the criminal act *on economic grounds.* Policies that sentence petty drug dealers to long mandatory prison terms ignore the economic logic of using scarce prison resources to maximize safety and social welfare. The cold logic of economics tells us that a greater share of resources should be devoted to offenders who do great social harm, like those who repeatedly commit murder, rape, and other forms of violent crime, with less severe sanctions being meted out to felons whose crimes inflict smaller social costs.

The distinction between the deterrent and incapacitation effects of punishment requires governments to consider the proper balance between deterring crime and warehousing felons when making decisions about punishment policy. As always, the proper balance between deterrence and incapacitation is at that point where the extra social benefits from spending another dollar on deterrence—which may increase the certainty of punishment—is just equal to the additional social benefits from putting an extra dollar toward incapacitation. If societies can reduce crime more by increasing the likelihood of punishment (by spending on police and courts) than by increasing the length of incarceration, then the proper allocation of public resources will shift funds and people toward policing and away from prisons. Similarly, if crime can be prevented by increased long term investments in education, health care, job training, and the development of effective policies to increase the rewards for work among the unskilled, then egalitarian social policy can be said to have a deterrent effect. Simple economics tells us that if we want to maximize social welfare we must choose the right combination of punishment—both deterrence and incapacitation—and employment, welfare, education, and macroeconomic policies in order to realize our goals.

The reader will no doubt object to all of this since it says that punishment policy must be developed in light of all other policy. Since everything in life is related to everything else, the reader will throw up his or her hands in disgust and say that we are proposing an unreasonable standard that requires governments to consider the indirect consequences of their punishment policies on employment, income distribution, and other seemingly separate economic policy matters. It is certainly true that the economic perspective advocated here, a general equilibrium perspective that insists that the full direct *and* indirect effect of policies be assessed when making critical public choices, is asking a lot. But the only way to make sure that punishment policy is not making matters worse is to be sure that it makes sense in light of the other things that the State is trying to do.

The Social Costs and Benefits of Punishment

An economic perspective on punishment asks two questions. First, how large is the deterrent effect of various punishments on offending behavior and second, how large are the net social benefits of incapacitation? If offending behavior is very sensitive to the probability of arrest and conviction, even if punishments are only moderately severe, then policies that tilt toward policing and away from incarceration are called for. If, however, variations in the prospects of arrest and conviction have little effect on offending behavior, then governments should put resources into incarceration and increase the length of prison terms.

The balance between deterrence and incapacitation hinges on the relative strengths of these two effects. A recent survey of the economics literature on crime and punishment reveals mixed findings about the relative importance of the deterrent and incapacitating effects of punishment.[7] Statistical studies by a number of authors imply that, in the US, an increase in the certainty of punishment (that is, in the probability of arrest and conviction) has a greater effect on offending behavior than does an increase in the severity of punishment (as measured by the length of prison sentences). Unfortunately, most statistical studies fail to establish a significant relationship between the size of a police force and the probability of arrest.[8] However, there is evidence that the recent decline in rates of violent crime is due to an increased emphasis on new forms of policing (including the well-documented trend toward "community policing" in major metropolitan areas in the US) and increased police visibility in the enforcement of both major and minor violations of law in deterring crime.[9] For example, an increased police presence on the streets of New York has been matched by investments in the capacity of lower courts and probation authorities to process and supervise felons, thereby both increasing the chances of arrest and conviction for criminal offenses and enabling the State to supervise felons outside prison walls.[10] This particular case suggests that changes in the organization of policing activity, combined with adequate court and supervisory facilities for the management of offenders, may have potentially powerful deterrent effects.[11]

One certain benefit from incarceration is the reduction in crime associated with a larger prison population. Economist Stephen Levitt has estimated that the average crime costs society $3,000 while the average offender commits fifteen crimes per year.[12] If we use Levitt's estimates for the sake of argument, then each imprisoned felon increases social welfare by $45,000 per year: the detention of one more average offender will mean $45,000 less harm due to criminal activity. Of course the gain from punishment, whether through deterrence or through incapacitation, must be set against the cost of deterring crime or incarcerating offenders before we can know the net direct effect of punishment on social welfare. If we once again rely on Levitt's estimates, the operating cost of incarceration is approximately $30,000 per year per inmate (including the cost of maintaining prison facilities), with the consequence that placing one more convicted offender in prison increases net social welfare benefits by approximately $15,000 per year.[13]

Prison Math
The arithmetic of an even greater investment in prisons, for the purposes of both warehousing criminals and deterring crime, is truly daunt-

ing. Assume that Levitt is right, so that putting a "average" felon in prison increases social welfare by $15,000 per year. According to the Bureau of Justice Statistics, the average time served for a violent crime in 1992 was 43 months of an average sentence of 89 months; felons served just over 48% of their sentences. One clear way to reduce crime rates is to keep criminals locked down longer, since so many studies suggest that most prisoners released on probation or parole (two-thirds of the population under supervision by the criminal justice system) will commit crimes within a year of their release. The average turnover rate for violent offenders is 27.95% per year, with an average of 43 months served in prison, that is 27.95% of all prisoners are released from prison each year.[14] Simple arithmetic shows that if the average amount of actual time served in prison is increased by one year (from 43 to 55 months) then only 21.84% of prisoners will be released each year. It is important to note that a rise in the time served by the average felon of one year will mean that the prison population rises by 21.86% (assuming that there is no increase in the number of admissions into the system).[15]

The 1995 edition of the *Sourcebook of Criminal Justice Statistics* (released in October 1996) reports that 1,475,329 people were incarcerated in the US (in prison or jail) in 1994. If the average prison term rose by one year, the number of prisoners released in 1995 would have fallen from 412,354 to 322,506, so that the incarcerated population would *increase* by 89,848 people. If the prison system is already working at capacity when the decision to lengthen prison sentences is made, then the State must make capital investments in prison facilities and in training the required correctional personnel. The most common estimate of the cost of a new prison cell is $50,000. Since Levitt's calculations indicate that incarcerating the average offender yields $15,000 per year in increased social well-being net of the operating costs of incarceration, the social rate of return on investment in a prison cell between 1971 and 1993 is approximately 150%, assuming that each cell houses two felons.[16] This means that the authorities would be able to build jails and thereby improve social welfare (in the narrow economic sense) so long as the cost of borrowed funds, in this case the interest rate on bonds issued by the authorities in order to finance new prison construction, is less than 150%. Since interest rates rarely rise beyond 25% (given the remarkable financial stability of the American economy and the aims of American economic policy), prison building is certainly a "viable" economic undertaking.[17]

Of course, this illustrative calculation is certainly not the most accurate assessment of the economic gain from longer prison terms. A lower estimate on the social costs per crime will certainly lower the rate of return from lengthening prison terms, as would a higher estimate of the cost of a new prison cell. Public-sector cost-benefit analysis is notorious for its inaccuracy; it is very hard to assign the proper monetary value to the many costs and benefits associated with a public-sector capital project that is being provided in a noncompetitive setting by a producer that has little incentive to efficiently provide goods or services. Further, if advances in technology or the privatization of prisons actually reduce the operating costs of incarceration, then the rate of return from lengthening prison sentences must increase.

The foregoing calculation, though sobering and more than a bit frightening, is biased to the extent that it is based on an estimate of the social damage done by the "average criminal." Different types of violent and nonviolent crime impose different costs on society, thereby requiring governments to choose those offenses that warrant prison and those that are better addressed through other forms of punishment. Crimes like murder, manslaughter, and rape are, from an economic perspective, very "expensive" offenses whose prevention through incarceration can be expected to yield great social returns. However, other offenses, like nonviolent drug offenses and petty property crimes, impose much lower social costs and yield correspondingly lower rates of return from imprisonment. John DiIulio and Anne Piehl in "Does Prison Pay, Revisited?" argue that the high costs of violent crime call for long mandatory prison sentences for violent criminals but that economic considerations argue against subjecting nonviolent offenders to long spells of imprisonment.

We should mention one other set of costs that need to be included in any prison calculus before leaving the narrow economics of incarceration. Punishment is, by its very nature, the deliberate use of public power to inflict pain on offenders. Proponents of deterrence hope (without much evidence as noted above) that inflicting pain on inmates will alter the calculations of other offenders and thereby reduce their incentives to commit crimes. For others, especially proponents of incapacitation, the pain that inmates suffer as a result of incarceration is an inevitable by-product of the reduction of crime that comes from ware-housing repeat offenders.

The economic analysis of incarceration requires that the pain associated with punishment be applied up to the point where the social benefits of the additional harm are just equal to the additional costs of administering pain. Any comprehensive economic analysis of punishment must include the costs of incarceration to inmates and their communities into the balance of costs and benefits. There is clear evidence that incarceration imposes such severe mental, emotional, physical, and economic costs on inmates and those who watch them—including everything from violence between inmates, conflict between inmates and prison authorities, and rape—that the State must take affirmative actions to minimize penal harm in the interest of humane treatment of captive populations. Badly run prisons wound people in permanent ways that inevitably affect the lives of men and women outside prison walls, since most prisoners are released from confinement.[18]

There are further hidden costs that, though almost impossible to calculate, must nonetheless be included in the balance in some way. While society has an image of the felon as disconnected social trash, the reality of the lives of men and women who become inmates is much more complex, in part precisely because these people are so ordinary. Most inmates come from impoverished families and communities where they play a variety of social roles. Imprisonment deprives families of husbands and wives, sons and daughters, fathers and mothers, bread-winners and caregivers (of both genders). The disruptions of inmates' mini-communities of families, neighborhoods, and larger social units by virtue of incarceration (especially when punishment is meted out on a mass scale like the current American experiment with imprisonment) surely destroys a portion of the social capital that is one of the bulwarks against social disorganization. Though it is fashionable for economists to talk about social capital in matters of economic growth and business organization, middle-class prejudice (at least among the literate and chattering classes) should not blind us to the fact that incarceration disrupts important patterns of care and association in inmates' communities of origin, thereby undermining these communities' ability to survive and thrive.

The Choice

Americans are not known for their willingness to face up to hard choices before a crisis is upon them. The recent debates about Social Security reform, particularly the need to adjust benefit levels, Social Security taxes, and the age at which retirees are eligible to collect benefits, are a sign that the nation may at last be mature enough to face this deep structural problem in a timely fashion. The position of unskilled workers in the American economy, particularly unskilled black workers, is a structural problem that will require the same kind of fundamental reform as the restructuring of Social Security. The implications of our analysis of the position of poor and working-class people in modern America are simple and very nasty: there are not enough legal jobs for unskilled workers that pay an adequate wage in this country, with the result that many of these workers, especially young men, are choosing to commit crimes in order to supplement their incomes or as an alternative to legal work. This surplus labor problem will not go away as the economy grows, because modern economic growth is driven by forces of technology and globalization that have made unskilled workers redundant. The social problems associated with low wages, sporadic employment, and the lure of illegal activity are permanent features of the economic landscape so long as the nation is willing to tolerate high degrees of economic and social inequality.

The nation will have to make fateful choices about what to do with these "surplus" workers, who are simply that portion of the adult population who cannot support themselves and their families without assistance. The conservative "strategy of inequality" implicitly relies on punishment, especially imprisonment, to limit that fallout from inequality by warehousing some of those unskilled workers who commit crimes and intimidating the rest of them into accepting their plight as intellectual and economic failures. We have already seen that a policy that sanctions growing inequality, and therefore growing crime among the unskilled, as the price of economic growth is economically irrational since it uses prisons to house nonviolent criminals whose offenses are less costly than incarceration. In turn, the "war on drugs," with its emphasis on the incarceration of street-level drug sellers for long periods of time, has resulted in a situation where nearly 7% of black men were under lock and key in 1997, effectively reducing black male civilian unemployment rates by warehousing black men in jail.[19] This kind of regime cannot be sustained indefinitely without contributing to growing black alienation, increasing the distrust and frustration that blacks across the class spectrum feel about American life, gradually setting the stage for a permanent, low-level civil conflict between black people and the rest of the nation.

There is a viable alternative to this depressing scenario. White Americans can choose to abandon the conservative "strategy of inequality" in favor of a policy of fairness that can benefit all poor and working-class Americans, regardless of their color. This alternative policy package is based on the following premise: the best way to deal with the likelihood of a permanent educational and intellectual underclass in a merit-driven capitalist economy, comprised of those who have failed to keep pace with modern technology for whatever reason, is to minimize the class conflict between the winners and losers of the meritocratic game. In turn, the best way to proceed in the near term is to raise the incomes of poorly educated people in ways that make legal work worthwhile, thereby reducing some of the economic incentives among unskilled young men to commit crime, while reducing the size of the pool of unskilled workers in the long term by improving poor people's access to high-quality schooling. The final element of the program is the most radical: end the prohibition on the production and sale of illegal narcotics and other drugs, thereby converting young, unskilled adults, and especially young, black men, from potential criminals into tax-paying workers.

A Quixotic, though Plausible, Egalitarian Program

An effective economic policy that can improve the fortunes of poor and working-class people across the color spectrum must accomplish three goals:

1. *Jobs:* improve the employment prospects of unskilled workers by increasing the demand for modestly educated labor in the short

run while creating widespread access to high-quality schooling for the children of the poor in the long run,

2. *Pay:* raise the wages and incomes of poor workers, thereby offsetting the disastrous slide in the real earnings of unskilled workers and reducing the harmful social consequences of low incomes in poor and minority communities,

3. *Productivity:* increase the rate of growth in overall labor productivity, thereby making it possible for society to finance egalitarian policy through growth rather than through explicitly redistributive policies that run afoul of the white majority's demands for racial separation.

The central problems that poorly educated workers face are low wages and high unemployment rates. William Julius Wilson's *When Work Disappears* argues that poverty, long-term unemployment, and weak labor market attachment have especially damaging effects on the social capital of poor communities. Wilson notes that

work is not simply a way to make a living and support one's family. It also constitutes a framework for daily behavior and patterns of interaction because it imposes discipline and regularities. Thus, in the absence of regular employment, a person lacks not only a place in which to work and the receipt of regular income but also a coherent organization of the present—that is, a system of concrete expectations and goals. Regular employment provides the anchor for the spatial and temporal aspects of daily life. It determines where you are going to be and when you are going to be there. In the absence of regular employment, life, including family life, becomes less coherent. Persistent unemployment and irregular employment hinder rational planning in daily life, the necessary adaptation to an industrial [and post-industrial] economy.[20]

The only clear way to increase the demand for unskilled labor in modern times is for the public sector to promote projects that require manual and modestly educated workers. There is little sense in pretending that the free market will eventually solve the problems of unemployment and low wages for unskilled workers: the collapse in the demand for poorly educated labor is due to long-run factors (globalization and technology) that relentlessly punish the badly schooled. A diverse set of

writers, including William Julius Wilson, Mickey Kaus, Sheldon Danziger, Peter Gottschalk, and Rebecca Blank have argued for the creation
of an extensive system of public-service employment, possibly supple-
mented by a system of wage subsidies to private employers who hire
poor workers, as ways to increase the demand for unskilled labor.[21]
Since unemployment (and, according to some analysts, welfare dependency) undermine the social coherence of poor communities, a public-
sector jobs program combined with more generous income supports
for those who work can effectively replace welfare as a primary form of
relief for adults.

Jobs and Wage Subsidies

A public-sector jobs program that boosts the demand for unskilled
labor will be supported by middle America if it can provide them with
goods and services that they could not otherwise have. Infrastructure
building, repair and maintenance projects that improve the quality of
roads, bridges, airports, water and sewage treatment systems, offer a
prime opportunity for marrying progressive employment policy to the
needs of the middle-class majority. An extensive infrastructure rebuilding program, particularly in and around major urban areas, offers significant prospects for employing large numbers of unskilled workers in
construction and related industries, as well as increasing overall employment rates and tightening all labor markets. Public-service jobs programs have a disappointing record in the United States, in part because
of inadequate funding but also because of serious problems in the
design of various efforts. One difficulty is that many public-sector jobs
require skills that are beyond the reach of many targeted worker populations. Further, job training programs are frequently unable to provide
adequate training for potential workers because these workers' educational and social deficits are so large, thereby increasing the costs of any
effective jobs program.

Another way to boost the demand for low-wage, unskilled workers
whose low levels of productivity make them too expensive for employers
to take on is to provide wage subsidies, that is to pay employers to hire,
train, and retain low-skill adults. A wage subsidy makes it cheaper for
firms to hire certain categories of workers, thereby boosting the demand
for these workers. Wage subsidies allow society to boost the earnings of

modestly educated workers without creating welfare traps. Edmund Phelps of Columbia University, one of the most distinguished economic theorists of our time, has recently proposed that the United States develop a national system of wage subsidies in order to boost the earnings of low-wage workers. Phelps' proposal, presented in great detail in his recent book *Rewarding Work*, explicitly acknowledges the need for modern societies to develop policies that encourage work effort among members of the underclass while simultaneously boosting the rewards from work. Phelps notes that the decline in real wages among the most poorly educated members of the adult population has created conditions of low labor force participation and increasing crime among the underclass.[22] In order to counter the destructive social consequences that low wages and low degrees of labor force participation have on poor communities, Phelps proposes that the government replace most current income support and poor relief programs with a system of wage subsidies where employers receive a subsidy for hiring every employee whose pay is below a level that affords a full-time worker an income above the poverty line (calculated at $7.00 per hour in 1997 dollars).[23] Though Phelps claims that this program would be self-financing (if it fully replaced existing welfare programs and if the resulting rise in real earnings among poorly paid workers reduces crime somewhat), his proposal is rather expensive (on the order of $100 billion per year in 1997 dollars) and, though fully consistent with the ethos of workfare and mandatory work requirements for the poor, is unlikely to pass muster in the current conservative political climate.[24]

The central goal of these two programs is to boost the employment and incomes of unskilled workers in order to overcome the problems that unemployment poses for poor, minority urban communities. A coordinated program of infrastructure construction and repair, wage subsidies for low-wage workers, and the expansion of existing programs like the earned income tax credit (EITC) for those workers who are not covered by wage subsidies could go a long way toward improving the income and employment prospects of poor people. Indeed, a further expansion of the EITC program along lines suggested by Danziger and Gottschalk in *America Unequal* and Wilson in *When Work Disappears* could go a long way toward resolving the damage that welfare "reform" threatens to wreak on poor people.

The reader should note that this proposed program of wage subsidies is meant to be a fundamental and permanent reform of the nature of work and pay that should replace a significant portion of the system of poor relief in this country. The goal of this program is to encourage badly educated people to work for decent wages, thereby fostering their economic independence and improving the possibility of rebuilding a culture of work and achievement in poor neighborhoods. A rational conservative whose primary interest is in fostering self-reliance and initiative should welcome the possibility that wage subsidies offer for improving the welfare of poor communities by bolstering the market for low-skilled labor. Indeed, a wage subsidy can be thought of as a government subsidy that encourages the development of positive externalities—achievement and labor force participation in poor neighborhoods as well as reductions in economically motivated crimes. A rational leftist concerned with promoting social justice and the self-reliance of the poor should also support wage subsidies because they shift the distribution of income and opportunity toward the poor and underpaid in *effective* ways that pro-capitalist conservatives cannot honestly oppose. Indeed, wage subsidies offer leftists a golden opportunity to turn the tables on their conservative opponents by harnessing the power of markets in service of poor people. Finally, a system of wage subsidies is superior to the traditional minimum wage as a means of increasing the incomes of poor workers. While there is substantial debate about whether minimum wages have a negative effect on the employment of low-skill workers, wage subsidies are sure to have a larger positive effect on employment simply because such subsidies make relatively unproductive workers cheaper for employers to hire while a minimum wage increase makes these same workers more expensive.

The Long Run

Any program that raises the demand for and incomes of unskilled workers will almost certainly fail if there is not also a concerted effort to reduce the portion of the labor force that needs help. The program proposed above is likely to be quite expensive, ruinously so if the fraction of the unskilled labor force that needs help continues to grow. Of course, an effective program of educational reform would go a long way to reducing the problem of poverty and structural unemployment. Yet, despite the valiant efforts of teachers, parents, and school officials throughout the country over the past fifteen to twenty years, the improvement in school quality for poor children has been steady but painfully slow. Part of the problem is, as usual, the Gordian knot of racial and class conflict, combined with the peculiar American allegiance to a principle of local control of school funding that prevents a more equitable distribution of school resources across color and class lines. However, a large part of the difficulty is that the problem of low levels of school performance in poor communities is only partly about funding: the social disorganization of poor neighborhoods that is both cause and consequence of poverty and unemployment also eats away at teaching and learning in these neighborhoods.

We have nothing to add to the thoughtful writing of scholars, teachers, and administrators on the trials and tribulations of education reform in America. The wide range of experimentation in this area should yield crucial advances in our understanding of schools and how to teach poor kids. The only note of caution is linked to our discussion of the way race and class conflict twists logic in American economic and social policy. Any successful program of school reform that increases the educational success of poor children is, by definition, also reducing the economic chances of middle America's children. Though genuine improvement in the schooling of poor children certainly improves the economic prospects of the nation, it will also increase the supply of skilled labor. In this sense, a broad-based program of school reform asks middle America to finance the emergence of potential competitors to their own children. Given the considerable economic uncertainty that many Americans already feel about their children's futures, why should middle America consent to increase their own children's economic insecurity by supporting quality schooling for everyone?

In the end, progressive initiatives aimed at reducing inequality and increasing the job prospects of unskilled workers must somehow boost overall economic growth. In one sense, the economic impasse that killed the old program of liberal reform stands in the way of the egalitarian program outlined above. Progressive policies can be pursued if they can appeal to the self-interest of an economically insecure, racially phobic white majority. One way to overcome white resistance to progressive policy is to promote economic growth, thereby creating the extra resources required to finance reform without having to explicitly redistribute income and opportunity across class and color lines.

The only problem with all of this is that no one really knows how to accelerate economic growth. The usual economists' prescriptions for spurring economic growth—increased savings and investment, either through clever manipulation of taxes and subsidies or by a general reduction in the rate of taxation, or better, a reduction in the cost of capital through low-interest-rate monetary policy combined with re-duced budget deficits (as noted in the last chapter) and, over the long term, improvements in the skill level of the labor force—all seem largely unable to consistently spur growth. Indeed, the historic average growth rate of the US economy has been 2 to 2.5% per year. The slower growth of the past couple of decades, on average 1 to 1.5% per year, has provided a stimulus for an outpouring of research on the sources of growth, though no one has been able to coax the economy to grow steadily at its historic 2 to 2.5% average. Clearly, that extra 1% is quite hard to achieve since it involves changes in the structure of economic life, including patterns of business and individual behavior rooted in customs and cultures that completely escape the levers of the State.

One hope for the progressive program outlined above is that it doesn't notably weaken the propensity of the economy to expand. Raising the demand for unskilled workers through massive infrastruc-ture investment could add a bit to economic growth (though most economists doubt that this contribution will be spectacularly large) as well as reduce the social burden that structural unemployment places on society. Infrastructure spending, wage subsidies, income supple-ments (EITC), and a program of real educational reform (along with the financial resources necessary to make it work) could be financed either by cuts in military expenditure (unlikely) or a tax increase (even less likely). It might even make sense for egalitarian politicians to take a hard look at other, favored programs to see if the social benefits of the proposed program outweigh the benefits of other, albeit necessary pro-gressive projects. In the end, though, the ability of a progressive pro-gram to contribute to increasing economic growth is doubtful. A pro-gram for equality will rise or fall—in modern times fall—on its ability to appeal to the majority's sense of solidarity with the less well-off.

Since there is little solidarity across classes, and especially across color lines, egalitarians will have to find ways to promote the interests of the poor people that bypass the racial and class hatreds of middle America.

The End of Prohibition, Again

The reader may wonder how the end of the prohibition on the production and sale of illegal drugs improves the prospects for racial equality in this country.[25] While it is certainly true that anti-drug policy in this country has resulted in absurdly high rates of incarceration for black men, and has contributed to high levels of violence in poor, black neighborhoods (by encouraging disputes over the control of drug markets to be settled violently rather than in court), it may not be immediately clear why ending the drug war will make life for blacks better. One reason for ending the drug war, and indeed for legalizing the market for currently banned substances, is to end the de facto war between the State and poor black people. Poor people sell drugs to each other, and especially to nonpoor buyers, because their earnings from drug sales are high enough to justify taking the risk of getting caught. Though the nation's prisons are full of badly educated men and women who got caught selling drugs, the well-known economic effect of the drug war is to boost the earnings from drug selling for those sellers who have evaded the authorities (which is, and always will be the vast majority of them) by raising the price of drugs. If poor people have opted to become drug sellers because their legal wages are low relative to earnings in drug markets, raising the price of drugs by locking up drug sellers is exactly the wrong thing to do.

The economic logic of the case against the drug war is simple and compelling. Addictive substances are, by their very nature, necessities to addicts, which means that the demand for these substances is not very sensitive to drug prices (in the parlance of economics, the demand for narcotics is quite price inelastic). Drug policies that put an emphasis on the capture and imprisonment of drug sellers may well reduce the number of sellers in the market at a given point in time (at least until the prisons are filled, at which point the State simply recycles offenders from the streets to the jails and back again). However, the smaller number of sellers, and presumably the supply of available drugs, will lead to higher drug prices, which can partially compensate drug sellers for the higher risk associated with selling drugs. Worse, in an economy where the real wages of unskilled workers are stagnant or falling, and where there are limits to the extent to which society is willing to pay for prisons and police, unskilled workers are pushed into the drug market by lousy prospects in the legal labor market and by the State's limited ability to raise the prospects of punishment. Our consideration of the economics of punishment earlier in this chapter make it clear that there are economic constraints on even the most punitive society's capacity to use prisons to control crime. Faced with putting drug sellers in jail at the cost of releasing murderers and rapists, rational people will find other ways to punish drug sellers, or simply stop trying. The problem, however, is that drug selling is a lucrative enterprise because there is a vast demand for these addictive substances and a labor force of low-wage unskilled workers that is willing to work in this illegal sector.

The drug problem is only going to get worse in a world where the process of economic growth not only requires workers to be more and more literate and numerate, but that also rips up the blue-collar road to the middle class. A harsh truth about modern, skill-driven capitalism is that the illegal sector of the economy is a social reservoir for that portion of the population that has been judged to be "inferior" by the schooling process. In turn, so long as there is a demand for "bad" goods and "shameful" services on the part of the skilled and affluent portions of the population, there will be a portion of the poor population that is siphoned off to supply these goods. The free market solution to the problem of surplus unskilled labor is to recruit these workers to sell drugs, and sex (prostitution and pornography) and other services, including the services of professional athletes, to the well-off portions of the population. The attempt to use prisons to punish workers for responding to the economic imperatives of meritocracy in a society where rich and poor alike have powerful illicit desires is rank hypocrisy so long as the poorly paid and unemployed are left without a viable legal alternative. Conservatives who use prisons to manage the social costs of inequality in a market society are fooling themselves: the free market they claim to love has created conditions that they cannot abide.

The only way to reduce the appeal of drug selling as an occupation is to reduce the reward from drug selling, which means that the price of drugs must *fall*, not rise, relative to the wages of unskilled workers. This in turn means that either fewer people are willing to consume illegal substances (perhaps because a successful anti-drug education program has convinced young people to avoid drugs in the same way that social pressure and education have reduced the incidence of drunk driving) or that the supply of drugs has increased. If drugs were legally sold along the same lines as cigarettes, with heavy taxes and tight regulations about the sale of these substances to minors, then there is little doubt that the creative forces of consumer capitalism would provide this dangerous commodity relatively cheaply, thereby undercutting the profits that illegal sellers could earn. Legal sellers, subject to the same consumer product safety laws that govern the sale of alcohol, tobacco, and other addictive commodities, could offer consumers a reliable and "safe" product at a low price through ordinary stores and mail order services, thereby diverting demand from illegal sellers who provide goods of uncertain quality in dangerous places. Alternatively, the government could become the primary supplier of "safe," cheap drugs in measured doses to the addicted population (along the lines of the Dutch model for the control of narcotics), thereby turning a crime problem into a public health issue. This public health approach to drugs has the virtue of providing a legal alternative for drug buyers while depriving illegal sellers of a significant portion of their market, once again reducing the earnings associated with illegal drugs and related crime.

Please note that the purpose of this policy is to drive independent street corner drug sellers out of business, thereby driving a portion of the unskilled work force back into the legal labor market. The only way to keep unskilled workers in the legal labor market is to boost the wages and earnings associated with legal work through wage subsidies and job creation schemes. The end of the prohibition on the sale of drugs would probably be associated with an increase in the number of people who try drugs, and therefore in the number of drug addicts. Curious youth, depressed poor folks, and others lured to try cheap, high quality drugs once the use of drugs is made legal, will be hurt by this policy, though drug treatment and rehabilitation as well as other health costs associated with drug use can be financed by an appropriately heavy tax on drugs that offsets the costs of drug use without encouraging the formation of new illegal markets. The important economic question we must ask ourselves is this: are the costs of the drug war, including the costs of the policy in terms of its effect on racial inequality, greater than the costs of ending the prohibition on drug sales in terms of increased addiction and related social costs? The reader should carefully consider the link between low wages for unskilled workers, the racial composition of the unskilled labor pool, and the resulting racial composition of growing prison populations in formulating his or her answer to this question.

The Next Black Rebellion

Our dissection of the ties between race and well-being in fin-de-siècle America certainly inspires a pessimistic outlook on the future course of racial matters. Derrick Bell's angry eloquence about the permanence of black subordination has been reinforced by our analysis of how markets, technology, and democracy have shredded liberal hopes for a quick and smooth transition from old-style racism to a fair, post-racial republic. A harsh but realistic attitude about the prospects for racial equality in America is a fine antidote to the bewilderment and paralysis that has gripped liberals and leftists in the past decade. The Right's brilliant strategy for destroying the machinery of social justice has had the odd effect of demoralizing the Left, even though a close examination of the conservative program reveals that conservatives have been reduced to jailing the poor as the primary method for dealing with poverty and low wages. Left paralysis in matters of color is baffling because the logic of both the Civil Rights movement and of modern capitalism has swept away old-style, iron fist forms of segregation. The imperatives of liberalism and markets have permanently dashed the hopes of white nationalist conservatives (we hope), yet too many on the Left sit around whining about how awful it is that the old program failed rather than furiously scheming to create a new, sleeker egalitarian program that can survive the vortex of modern global capitalism.

This book has shown why realism should not lead to paralysis and despair in the matter of color. Liberalism's victory over segregation was not the same thing as the defeat of racism, only a hard-earned triumph over State-sponsored racial subordination. It is sad and lousy that the Civil Rights movement cleared the way for market-driven racism, but the belief that liberal racial reform was a path to full social equality for everyone, especially for blacks, represented the triumph of wishful thinking over good sense. Conservative duplicity in racial matters— including the sickening spectacle of social Darwinists loudly proclaiming their commitment to the ideal of a colorblind society while scolding blacks for our bad genes and criminal ways—pays cynical tribute to the power of liberal and leftist ideas. The link between race and well-being is now driven by a complex fugue of class, color, and fear that blocks the creation of a durable, transracial, egalitarian coalition. There is good reason to wonder about the chances of translating a principled commitment to social equality into effective economic and social policy under modern free market conditions. Realism on this score is warranted, not least because conservatives will always be able to make sly appeals to the racial hatreds of whites in their campaign to reverse the assumed cultural and economic depredations of egalitarianism.

But realism is not an excuse for inaction or hand-wringing just because racial liberalism has not proven to be the royal road to social equality. One lesson that should be drawn from our account of the potent mixture of free market racism and rapid technological change is that the deep desire of white Americans for racial distance—really a hankering for some weird type of physical racial "purity," whatever that is—will shape the way American capitalism distributes wealth, income, and opportunity for a very long time to come. A pessimistic outlook on race in modern America is appropriate since it notes that white Americans oppose racial egalitarianism for the simple reason that it asks them to spend money on, and show concern for, people they don't like very much.

Still, our realism need not blind us to the plain fact that America is slowly, painfully, stumbling toward becoming a "creole" country. A clear-eyed reading of the record would note this much: blacks and Latinos are now free to contest white supremacy in every aspect of American life and culture. It is upsetting to think that so many whites seem to want racial separation, without formal segregation, in a society that is formally committed to colorblind government policy. Still, these same whites are ever more deeply enmeshed in a miscegenated national culture that shapes everything, from their styles of movement and dress through the foods they eat to the sports heroes and cultural icons that their children worship. The complete defeat of white cultural separatism will be matched by the gradual destruction of white nationalism in the universities and in politics, as shown by the *belated* capitulation of conservatives to the notion of colorblind government (not matched, to be sure, by an equal commitment to colorblind living among and loving blacks). Blacks and Latinos can now wage a war of attrition against free market racism with the only weapons available: a coherent, transracial progressive program that promotes work, opportunity, and equality for all citizens; a brilliant critique of the absurdities of white racism in a cultural universe where the fusion of "racial" and ethnic traditions is creating a "creole" American culture that the world both fears and envies; a harsh attack on the hypocrisy of white Christians whose racism defames their faith; and hard work and self-love in the face of humiliating attacks by racist-conservatives and others with an inordinate "fear of the dark." If we step back from the brink of despair for a moment, it is perfectly plain that these weapons have always been part of colored folks' arsenal in the war for social equality. The collapse of old-style racial liberalism only means that we need new institutions to pursue a very old dream.

NOTES

Notes to the Preface

1. Gray (1995), pp. 72–73 (emphasis added).

Notes to Chapter 1

1. *United Nations Human Development Report, 1997.*
2. US Census Bureau, *Historical Income Table: Persons,* Tables P-1A, P-1B, and P-1C.
3. *UN Human Development Report, 1997.* These figures are not adjusted for whatever inflation that has occurred between 1994 and the current time in order to make appropriate comparisons to the most recent UN data.
4. The comparative rankings were computed as follows: the ratio of group per capita income to the US population per capita income reported by the Census Bureau in 1994 was then compared to the ratio of per capita income for each nation to US per capita income reported in the *United Nations Human Development Report* for 1994. The closest relative per capita income figures for the UN figures were then matched to the racial group ratios.
5. Massey and Denton (1993), pp. 84–88, especially Table 4.1.
6. Ibid., pp. 67–70.
7. Topel (1997) notes that the returns on a college degree, measured by the ratio of the average wage of college graduates to that of high school graduates in the 25–35 year age group, fell from 1.60 in 1971 (wages for the average college graduate in this age group were 60% higher than those for someone who only completed high school in 1971) to 1.45 or a 45% premium) in 1978. However, the wage premium earned by college graduates in 1992 was around 1.8 (or 80%). Some of the decline in the wage premium in 1970s is due to the rapid expansion in the size of the college-educated work force as a result of the post–World War II baby boom and the increased college attendance by men seeking to avoid military service during the Vietnam War. See Topel (1997), pp. 58–59.
8. Johnson (1997), pp. 47–49.

9. Danziger and Gottschalk (1995) report that 70% of single mothers reported labor market earnings in 1969 compared to 72% in 1991, while the fraction of household income accounted for by the earnings of female heads of families rose from 56.5% in 1973 to 66.9% in 1991. In addition, the cash value of government benefits declined significantly between 1967 and 1996 while wages for unskilled workers also fell, thereby squeezing the living standards of families headed by an unskilled female worker from two directions. See Danziger and Gottschalk (1995), pp. 72–83.

10. Johnson (1997), op. cit.

11. Friedberg and Hunt (1995) provide a convenient summary of the impact of immigration on wage and employment conditions in the United States. Their summary of the literature on the effect of immigration on wage inequality between skilled and unskilled workers indicates that immigration has had a statistically significant, but relatively small, negative effect on the wages of unskilled workers and therefore on wage inequality.

12. The time trend illustrated in the text is a cubic equation of the form

$$R_t = \beta_0 + \beta_1 T + \beta_2 T^2 + \beta_3 T^3$$

where R is the ratio of the fraction of the black adult population that has four or more years of schooling in higher education relative to the white population with similar levels of schooling, and T is time where $T = t - 1967$. As noted in the text, the time trend is a visual aid.

13. Patterson (1997), p. 24.

14. Darity and Goldsmith (1996) present a valuable summary of the effect of unemployment on the psychological well-being of the unemployed that has direct bearing on the economic fortunes of the underclass. In particular, Darity and Goldsmith refer to the work of Martin Seligman (1975) of the University of Pennsylvania whose work on the link between depression and perceived helplessness offers important insights into the psychological effects of failure on individual work effort and initiative.

15. Herrnstein and Murray (1994), Chapters 1–3, pp. 29–125.

16. Ibid. (1994), Chapters 13–14, pp. 269–340.

17. Ibid. (1994), Chapters 21–22, pp. 509–526.

18. Ibid.

19. Historian Eugene Genovese's brilliant analysis of the writing of pro-slavery theorist George Fitzhugh, a leading antebellum Southern intellectual, should be carefully reviewed by all who would support the thesis of *The Bell Curve*. Fitzhugh's defense of slavery as a moral institution, one that he believed should be extended across the color line to apply to whites as well, rests on a number of premises that offend modern, libertarian sensibilities. Fitzhugh saw

the paternalism of slavery, tempered by a "humane" vision of human interdependence and authority rooted in a particular interpretation of Christian love, as the only effective bulwark against the market's tendency to punish the weak and inferior members of society with poverty, employment, and social isolation. In turn, the corrosive power of free markets on the moral character of society, where market values supplant moral and social obligations as the "cement" of society, called for strong patriarchal forms of family life that linked people into extended circles of concern and supervision. Slavery was seen as an extension of the idea of the family that could counter the tendency for capitalism to create moral and social chaos by loosening the grip of church, family, and state on the hearts and minds of society's "weaker" members. One can only be impressed by how similar this all sounds to the basic claims made in *The Bell Curve*. The claim that society's dumber members, especially the black ones, must not be allowed to overextend their limited mental abilities lest social disaster descend upon us is positively "Fitzhughian." See Genovese (1969), pp. 118–244.

20. Heckman (1995) provides an extensive review and assessment of the strengths and weaknesses of *The Bell Curve* from an empirical perspective. Heckman's primary complaints about *The Bell Curve* are

1. the statistical analysis establishes a link between IQ and economic performance that explains a small portion of the overall variation in economic outcomes between persons and racial groups, leaving most of the differences unexplained; and

2. the measure of IQ Murray and Herrnstein use to measure intelligence, the Armed Forces Qualifications Test, has been shown to be affected by investments in education, thereby undermining the authors' claim that his test score primarily reflects innate cognitive ability rather than a complex combination of genetic and environmental factors. Hence, *The Bell Curve*, at best, simply shows that IQ has a substantial degree of inheritance across generations within racial and ethnic groups without disentangling the effects of education, social class, and other environmental factors from genetic influences, thereby rendering any strong statements about the role of genes in the determination of social class suspect.

21. D'Souza presents an extensive summary of *The Bell Curve* debates as well as his reasons for dismissing the genetic arguments of Murray and Herrnstein in Chapter 11, "The Content of Our Chromosomes" in *The End of Racism*, pp. 431–476.

22. Ibid., pp. 477–524.

23. Ibid.

24. Ibid.

25. Preface to the paperback edition of *The End of Racism*, pp. xxvii–xxx.

26. Indeed, recent Census Bureau data suggest that Hispanics, again as a group, have higher rates of teenage births than blacks. One supposes that D'Souza would have to say that Hispanic "culture" has suddenly developed a moral tick when it comes to promoting sexual self-restraint and delayed child-bearing among teenagers, though such an argument would be so ludicrous that even he might have second thoughts . . . maybe.

27. For example, we all know that Stanley Kaplan and The Princeton Review, among other firms, teach students of various ages how to raise their scores on standardized tests and that suburban school districts have an incentive to make sure their teachers instruct their charges in the right sorts of subjects so that they do well on these tests. No suburban school superintendent will keep his or her job if the children of American suburban parents have a brilliant education in science, mathematics, history, literature, and ethics but can't also do well on the SAT and have a good chance of going to a prestigious college. Now, D'Souza's analysis of the links between culture and achievement would have to say that Kaplan and The Princeton Review are manifestations of an academically attuned "culture" rather than helpful aids that rich parents buy to help their children compete for a limited number of positions at highly regarded colleges. Is a bright child who doesn't live in the right suburb and therefore is condemned to a lousy school a victim of a bad "culture," or is he or she just another kid whose life chances are reduced by being born to the wrong parents? Is a dumb child who has rich parents who pay Kaplan lots money to teach their untalented darling how to ace the test the beneficiary of a good "culture"?

28. Oliver and Shapiro (1995) present an excellent summary of the role of wealth disparities between blacks and whites in perpetuating racial inequality. Oliver and Shapiro pay careful attention to the impact of historic racial discrimination in mortgage lending and in federal housing policy on current differences in accumulated wealth across the color line.

29. Sowell (1983), especially pp. 159–182.

30. See ibid., pp. 135–143.

31. Ibid., pp. 128–132.

32. Jones (1992), pp. 238–252.

Notes to Chapter 2

1. Richard Epstein's provocative screed against anti-discrimination law, *Forbidden Grounds*, is the most rigorous statement of the right-libertarian position on race.

2. Thomas Sowell's magnum opus, *Knowledge and Decisions*, extends Hayek's analysis of the role of markets in coordinating the flow of knowledge and human action in society to the analysis of anti-discrimination policy. The Hayekian insistence that markets are better able to make use of "local knowledge" (the specific insights and understandings possessed by specific parties to a transaction that may be invisible to third parties) is transformed into a broad critique of government policy in general, and liberal race policy in particular.

3. This analysis assumes that firms face limits on their ability to substitute labor for capital in response to changes in factor prices, with the consequence that unemployment is possible in circumstances where real wages are extremely low. While nothing of substance hinges on this assumption, it is only right that we allow unemployment to be a possible outcome of markets in societies where despised groups face obstacles to equal opportunities.

4. This situation of monopolistic competition, which can also include elements of oligopoly as well, breaks up the market for legal services into a series of niches that are separately serviced by enterprises offering slightly different products. Individual firms have some control over market prices and some protection from price competition by virtue of the fact that customers view the services of different law firms as imperfect substitutes. Discriminatory law firms who are able to offer legal services to customers in such a setting can protect their hiring practices so long as customers choose them on the basis of quality, reputation, or experience rather than price. This simple consequence of monopolistic competition in product markets undermines most parts of Becker's theory.

5. The important papers on statistical discrimination summarized in the following discussion include Arrow (1972a, 1972b), Phelps (1972), and Aigner and Cain (1977).

6. Social scientists have also shown that young, poor women will engage in status games that are every bit as serious, and increasingly every bit as deadly (as shown by the rising rate of violent crime among young, poor women) as those pursued by men. In a society where beauty and sex appeal are important arenas of competition between women, sociologists have shown that young, poor women will compete for the attention of young men as part of a process of gaining and maintaining power. This competition, like the competition over money and power through the use of force and violence between young men, is simply a form of the broader social commitment to competition for status that animates nearly every part of public life.

7. Some economists go wrong, terribly and maliciously wrong, by con-

veniently forgetting about the social context in which individual choices are made. Further, economists forget that ambition, frustration, resentment, self-hatred, depression, and resignation are powerful motives that can be wedded to narrow economic self-interest in ways that transform the humiliation of lower-class status and relative deprivation into larger, malignant social problems that defy the easy and cheap prescriptions of conventional economic theory.

8. This example illustrates the complications introduced into our thinking about racial matters once we acknowledge the roles of incentives, constraints, and especially *dynamics*, in racial problems. "Dynamics" is a convenient label for the obvious, and sorely neglected, fact that current social conditions are the result of previous economic and social arrangements, and will in turn be the basis for future developments. In particular, the constraints that each of us operates within are largely determined by accident of birth, including race, gender, family, neighborhood, and class. The past exercises a powerful effect on the present and future by presenting each of us with a range of fateful choices that together determine who and what we will be. In recent years, conservative economists have been too eager to downplay the role of constraints, particularly the harsh constraints of poverty and racism, on the choices of the poor and of minority groups. Nonetheless, any serious discussion of racial matters has to confront the ways in which incentives, constraints, and the passage of time give shape to our common life.

9. Loury (1989) in Shulman and Parity (1989), pp. 268–293.

10. Op. cit.

11. Moffitt (1992) provides an excellent summary of the state of research on the incentives effects of welfare. This article is highly recommended to anyone who wants to know what carefully researched empirical studies tell us about the size of welfare disincentives on labor supply, marital stability, program participation, and the "taste" effect of welfare across generations.

12. Ibid., p. 56.

13. Ibid.

14. Ibid.

15. Danziger and Gottschalk (1995), pp. 93–110. The authors make an important point about studies of the role of changes in family composition on the extent of poverty. Danziger and Gottschalk calculate that the poverty rate (adjusted for changes in the poverty line and for inflation) increased by 1.8 points between 1973 and 1991. In addition, the authors provide a statistical breakdown of the sources of the change in poverty rates showing that the 1.8% rise in the poverty rate was due to a variety of factors:

Total Changes in Poverty Rates 1973–1991: 1.8%

Economic Changes	
Growth in mean income	−2.1%
Growth in income inequality	2.0%
Demographic Changes	
Race/ethnic composition	0.7%
Family structure	1.6%
Interaction	−0.3%

Note that the rise in mean income decreases poverty by just about the same amount as growing inequality increases poverty. Changes in family structure certainly contribute to poverty, by the primary problem is that real wage growth was much slower after 1973 than it was in the era of rapid economic growth in the post–World War II period. Danziger and Gottschalk's calculations indicate that real wage growth reduced poverty by 26.9% between 1949 and 1969, while changing family composition raised poverty by 0.7%. Many analysts are right to note that family composition changes are three times more important in their effect on poverty, since 1970 than they were prior to 1969. However, the primary reason for growing poverty is still slow wage growth.

16. Ibid.

17. See Elijah Anderson's brilliant ethnography *Streetwise: Race, Class and Change in an Urban Community* (1990) for a detailed study of predatory sexual status games between members of male peer groups in poor communities. Anderson's account of the sexual cynicism and misogyny that drive young men in a major eastern urban center in the United States to lie, cheat, and engage in abusive behavior to extract sex and emotional dependency from younger (in some cases very young) women is chilling. The combination of teenage sexual energy, limited life prospects, deep hatred of women, and bizarre homoerotic culture of manhood that expresses itself in the sexual humiliation of women leads to unfortunate couplings between predatory young men and foolish or desperate young women that all too often result in teenage pregnancy and childbearing. See Anderson (1990), pp. 114–119.

18. Loury (1983), pp. 49–50.

19. Ibid., p. 50, quoting Martin Luther King (1968), p. 132.

20. Wilson (1987).

21. Cose (1993), pp. 105–106.

22. Ibid., pp. 106–107.

Notes to Chapter 3

1. Murnane, Willet, and Levy (1995).

2. Piore and Sabel (1984) have shown that the success of American capitalism during this period was due to a combination of factors, including the agreement between industrial unions and management to divide productivity gains between workers and firms while granting management a free hand in the operation of firms and the introduction of new technologies. This allowed firms to exploit the efficiencies of mass production without too many labor problems in a world without significant international competition, thereby allowing both firms and workers in key industrial sectors to effectively reap enormous benefits from their unchallenged position of dominance. Piore and Sabel also note that the oligopolistic structure of major American industries—automobiles, steel, transportation, rubber, consumer durables—combined with the cost-plus pricing formula of military production and procurement provided firms with stable markets in which to install and plan large-scale investment in new facilities, thereby providing a stable foundation for economic growth. See Piore and Sabel (1984), pp. 73–76.

3. See Tobin (1982a), pp. 497–517.

4. Ibid., pp. 498–503.

5. Ibid.

6. Ibid.

7. Ibid., pp. 506–508.

8. Ibid.

9. Ibid., pp. 508–514.

10. Ibid.

11. Friedman (1962).

12. Ibid.

13. At the time Tobin wrote "On Improving the Economic Status of the Negro," the US was part of the Bretton Woods exchange rate system which essentially fixed the value of the US dollar in terms of other currencies. In a fixed exchange rate system, a country experiencing inflation has a problem. Higher domestic prices will mean that the country will be pricing itself out of international markets because its goods will be more expensive relative to the goods of its trading partners. Over time, this will inevitably lead to a fall in the level of employment inside the country, as fewer exports are sold abroad and more domestic residents switch from relatively expensive domestic goods to cheaper imports, thereby causing a trade deficit (or worsening one that already exists).

14. Lemann (1992) writes about the considerable political problems that

liberal racial reform created within the Democratic Party. Reform efforts that aimed at increasing black political power at the local level, and that encouraged black participation in the management of anti-poverty, job training, and urban development efforts required a shift in power and authority to blacks and away from white-dominated political machines. Predictably, working-class whites resented being displaced by blacks and subsequently abandoned the Democratic Party.

15. The willingness of bond buyers—primarily banks, insurance companies, colleges and universities managing their endowments, pension funds, and other large financial entities—to purchase government bonds depends on a number of factors, including the returns from holding bonds relative to the returns promised by other assets. For example, if US government bonds promise a 5% rate of return while GM stocks promise a 15% return, then a pension fund manager is going to be sorely tempted to buy GM stock instead of a US government bond. However, GM stock is much riskier than a US government bond for a number of reasons. GM is a private, profit-making venture that must compete with other automobile producers. The risk of GM not making a profit, and therefore not being able to offer a high return to those who lent GM money, is considerable even though the company is far less risky than smaller, less well-established concerns. By contrast, the US government is a considerably safer risk, largely because the US government has a secure source of revenue from which to pay interest to those who have lent it money, namely, future taxes. This makes US government bonds a safer asset than GM stocks or bonds, or most other stocks or bonds. Those who want steady returns with reasonably low risk will buy US government bonds, even if these bonds promise a lower return that private-sector stocks and bonds.

16. A second obvious, but nonetheless underestimated, cost of deficit spending is that each act of borrowing commits the borrower to pay interest on the new debt. In the case of the United States, where persistent budget deficits have been run for the better part of two decades, the mounting national debt brings with it an associated debt burden that must be a part of current public spending. Hence, a $4 trillion national debt with an associated interest rate of, say, 5% will commit the federal government to spend $200 billion to pay interest on *old* debt; any additional deficits simply add to the national debt and to mandatory interest payments. If the perceived benefits of public spending justify this sort of interest burden, fine. But the need to pay interest makes it essential that the long-term consequences of deficits be kept of mind.

17. The extent of the gap between, say, American interest rates and the average level of interest rates around the world may depend on a number of factors, including the tax advantages and disadvantages of parking one's money

in America, the political and economic stability (or lack thereof) of investing in America as against other places, and other important concerns. Nonetheless, if the United States relies on foreign borrowing to finance its budget deficits, it will have to commit itself to maintaining higher interest rates than other countries in order to remain an attractive opportunity for lenders.

18. The demand for dollars on the part of foreign nationals is also determined by their need to buy American goods and services as well as assets. If a German family buys an American car, say a Ford from a dealer in Germany, they will pay for that car in marks. However, the dealer may well want to convert the marks received for the car into dollars, particularly if he or she wants to buy something in the US or simply wants to have dollars handy. In that case, the dealer will trade dollars for marks, meaning that he or she will raise the demand for dollars in exchange for supplying marks. If the German family wanted to buy a US government bond instead of a car, the effect of their desired purchase on the demand for dollars would be identical: they would first convert their marks into dollars in order to then buy the US government bond.

19. Nicholas Barr provides an excellent discussion of the economic principles behind social insurance in *The Economics of the Welfare State*, 2d ed., pp. 111–131.

20. Shklar (1991), p. 93.

21. Ibid., p. 67.

22. Ibid.

23. Ibid., p. 98 (emphasis added).

24. There is overwhelming evidence that the leading citizens of the nation, from the Founding Fathers through statesmen like George Washington, Lincoln, the Roosevelts, to the most important business and cultural leaders in most eras of the nation's history, were committed to creating and maintaining a pan-European, pan-Christian white democracy. See Lind (1995) for an abbreviated analysis of the role of white nationalism as a driving force in American history. In addition, see Takaki (1979) for an extensive discussion of the white supremacist ideology in nineteenth-century American culture and politics.

Notes to Chapter 4

1. Bell (1992), p. 12.

2. Massey and Denton (1993), pp. 65–77.

3. Freeman (1996).

4. The economic logic behind the idea of deterrence, which was first fully

developed by Nobel laureate Gary Becker of the University of Chicago, is quite simple. According to the economic theory of crime and deterrence, criminal acts are simply the result of choices made by self-interested people seeking to maximize the gain or satisfaction they derive from their actions. Just as each of us chooses a product, job, or pursues some other course of action when the benefits from that action exceed the associated costs, so too does a criminal choose to break the law in one area as against another, or maybe even to refrain from criminal acts altogether, depending on the balance of costs and benefits. In one sense, the only difference between the criminal and the law-abiding citizen is that criminals are more willing to violate social taboos and laws if the gain from so doing exceeds the costs, perhaps because criminals come from families or communities that do not instill sufficient respect for social norms and the law (as some conservative analysts insist). Nonetheless, crimes are committed when the gain from crime exceeds the associated costs of criminal actions and vice versa.

5. A second function of pollution taxes and charges is to encourage polluting firms to search for new, less environmentally damaging ways of producing goods and services. The economic theory behind this approach is perfectly sound: governments want to make polluting technologies more costly, thereby giving firms incentives to switch to alternate technologies that yield lower environmental costs. It is perfectly clear that governments do not want punishment policy to encourage technological innovation in criminal activity though, regrettably, the sad history of anti-narcotics policy in the United States shows that harsh punishments may give drug dealers an incentive to increase the technical sophistication of their operations.

6. The economist's tendency to reduce human action to the calculus of rational choice is deeply flawed in at least one important way when it ignores the possibility that people may act without giving much thought to the consequences of their behavior. The economist, like most well-behaved, educated, and well-socialized achievers in modern society, has a deep commitment to the idea that human beings conduct their affairs on the basis of coherent, integrated life plans that reasonably link their objectives and activities in both the short and long term. But the economist's presumption is simple prejudice to the degree that it blinds us to the possibility that many actions may be undertaken with little thought as to their long-run costs and benefits. Compulsion is just as important a force in life as reason, though the typical economic model rarely admits that men and women may be motivated by desires or hatreds that are simply outside the realm of rational thought. There are whole categories of actions and, in our case, criminal offenses, particularly those related to con-

sumption of addictive substances or the commission of sexual offenses, that do not fit easily into the framework of rational decision-making that guides economic thinking.

Compulsions have murky origins, at least from the perspective of economists. More importantly, criminal activities that are driven by compulsions, or at any rate by nonrational sources of motivation, are simply beyond the reach of deterrence. One cannot deter someone from action if they pay no attention to the balance between the costs and benefits of their actions. Punishment can only be a deterrent if one can threaten a potential offender with loss and if this person includes the economic value of punishments in their calculations. There is a great deal of evidence that suggests that a huge volume of crime (perhaps most) is committed by people for reasons that cannot be reduced to narrow economic logic. But this leads us back to the age-old question of the causes of crime. The public, aroused by reports of ever-worsening violent crime (despite ample evidence of falling violent crime rates in major American cities over the past decade), is understandably impatient with the notion that coherent crime policy requires that social scientists answer this seemingly impossible question. Nonetheless, unless we face the fact that crime may not be driven solely, or even primarily, by rational choice, societies that adopt a rational choice view of crime may well commit themselves to policies that do far more harm than good, as we will see below.

7. Erlich (1996).

8. Cameron (1988).

9. Community policing efforts, which try to build strong bonds of trust, respect, and mutual support between the police and residents in particular neighborhoods, are an interesting attempt to build "social capital" as part of an overall crime control policy. From an economic perspective, community policing attempts to deal with problems of imperfect information, particularly the problems of detecting criminal activity and monitoring the behavior of potential offenders especially young men by enlisting the cooperation of neighborhood residents in reporting criminal activity and testifying in criminal trials. These efforts lead to an increase in the certainty of punishment by creating networks where trust between the police and neighbors extends the capacities of the community to monitor behavior. The increased surveillance capacity of the community requires local governments to invest in a number of community services as well as restructure systems for the provision of public services in order to improve a community's incentives to cooperate with the police. Jonathan Eig's report on community policing efforts in Chicago in the December 1996 issue of the *American Prospect* shows the considerable difficulties involved creating this form of social capital.

10. Nonetheless, Erlich (1996) gives good reasons to believe that the claim that the certainty of punishment has a larger effect on crime than the severity of incarceration is problematic, in part because of the complexity of the statistical analyses necessary for disentangling the effects of the likelihood of punishment on the incentives to commit crime from the clear negative effect of incapacitation on crime.

11. One interesting thing to note about the relative effects of deterrence and incapacitation is that policies focusing on particular crimes are less effective than policies that try to reduce crime in general. Economist Steven Levitt (1996) has shown that the attempt to deter particular categories of crime causes offenders to shift their activity into other areas of illegal activity, strongly suggesting that different types of crime are "substitutes" for each other. Incarceration and general increases in deterrence have greater effects on crime than targeted deterrence; incapacitation removes offenders who commit a wide array of crimes, while general deterrence reduces the net benefits from criminal activity across the board.

12. See Levitt (1996). This estimate of the costs that a typical criminal imposes on the public includes the various medical costs, lost wages, higher insurance costs, and greater security expenditures that crime victims must bear as a result of victimization.

13. But there are still more economic benefits from a reduction in crime. Millions of men and women make decisions about where to live, work, and play on the basis of their perceptions of personal safety. Free markets respond to consumer demands for safety by supplying home security devices, anti-theft devices for cars, handguns and handgun training, attack dogs, private security guards for apartment buildings, and private police forces for wealthy residential communities and prosperous urban districts. Businesses pay out enormous sums of money for bank security, retail shop security (against theft by employees, shoplifting, and robbery), security forces in large shopping areas (especially shopping malls) and other protective measures. The money value of private security services and products is both a measure of the public's demand for protection against crime and, in its own way, a type of "tax" that crime imposes on the citizenry. This "crime tax" is the market response to the perceptions of the risk of injury, assault, and theft that individuals and corporations believe they face. In turn, private spending on security is ultimately reflected in the prices of most goods and services produced in the United States, thereby shifting a significant portion of the cost of private efforts at crime prevention onto buyers of goods and services.

14. If the average felon serves a sentence of 43 months, or years, then this must mean that (1/3.5775) or 27.95% of felons are released each year.

15. Note that if the evolution of the prison population over time is represented by the simple dynamic system

$$Z_{t+1} = (1-\delta)Z_t + a_t$$

where Z is the size of the prison population, $0 < \delta < 1$ is the exit rate, and $a > 0$ is the number of new inmates admitted to the system, then the "steady state" or long-term level of the prison population Z^* is

$$Z^* = \frac{a}{\delta}$$

which implies that $\frac{\Delta Z^*}{Z^*} = -\frac{\Delta \delta}{\delta}$, i.e. that the percentage rise in the long-term prison population is equal to the percentage decline in the prison exit rate δ (assuming that $a_t = a$, constant for all values of t).

16. The rate of return on investment in this case is simply the internal rate of return for this project. If n_t is the net social benefit at time t from housing an additional felon for a year (after accounting for all direct operating costs and maintenance charges), x is the price of a new prison cell, and T is the expected lifetime of a prison cell, then the internal rate of return λ is the largest positive root of the equation

$$\sum_{t=0}^{T} \left[\frac{2n_t}{(1 + \lambda)^t} \right]$$

if we assume that there are two felons per cell. Using Levitt's figures, $n_t = \$15,000$ and $x = \$50,000$ for all time t, which lead to a range of different values of the rate of return (λ) for various values of T. Note that if we assume that a prison cell is used for fifty years then the internal rate of return is $\lambda = 1.5$ or 150%.

T	1	3	5	10	20	30	50
$<\lambda>$	0.50	1.39	1.484	1.50	1.50	1.50	1.50

Of course, an increase in the number of prisoners per cell will, all other things equal, increase the rate of return on new prison construction. However, the prospect of lawsuits and regulations against prison overcrowding reduce incentives to increase the average number of occupants in a prison cell.

17. Shichor (1995) notes that the cost of new prisons cells depends on the type of prison facility under consideration. Low-security units cost as little as

$40,000 per cell (in 1988 dollars) while high-security units could cost in excess of $110,000 per cell. Yet if the average prison cell cost as much as $150,000 and was in use for 30 years, the social rate of return would still be 25%. Since the rate of return on the Dow Jones index of the 30 premier common stocks is a little over 10% historically, our calculations suggest that prison building—even of high-security units—is very lucrative in economic terms.

18. Elliott Currie's excellent summary of crime and punishment in America (in a newly published volume of the same name) points out that incarceration has been shown to *raise* the recidivism rates of offenders, especially young offenders, thereby greatly reducing the social benefits of punishment. Indeed, Currie notes that the criminogenic effects of incarceration are a well-known criminological fact that seems to escape the notice of politicians and the public. See Currie (1998) for an excellent discussion of all matters related to the problem of incarceration in the United States.

19. The data on black incarceration are truly depressing. In 1985, 3.5% of adult black males were locked up in prison or jail on any given day. However, in mid-1997 6.9% of all black adults males were in prison or jail. In order to understand the impact of incarceration on black communities, we should note that 742,569 black adults where in prison in 1985 while *1.72 million* were locked up by mid-1997. Back of the envelope calculations suggest that the yearly growth rate of the general prison population was approximately 7% per year. Note that the black population in the United States went from 28.2 million in 1985 to 34.07 million in 1997 (from the *Statistical Abstract of the United States*) which implies an average annual growth rate of 1.6% per year. The black male population grew at an average annual rate of 1.2% between 1985 and 1997, while the black male prison population grew at a *7.4%* annual rate. All of these data are drawn from various editions of the Bureau of Justice Statistics report *Correctional Populations in the United States*.

20. Wilson (1997), p. 73.

21. Ibid., pp. 226–240, and Danziger and Gottschalk (1995), pp. 166–174.

22. Phelps (1997), pp. 38–50.

23. Ibid., pp. 122–143.

24. Ibid., p. 175.

25. This analysis borrows heavily from Miron and Zweibel's superb economic analysis of the absurdities of American drug policy. The reader cannot get a better economic case against current drug policy than Miron and Zweibel (1995) which, in a better world, would be required reading for every politician, columnist, newsreader, clergyman, and other molder of public opinion in these matters.

WORKS CITED

Aigner, Dennis, and Glen Cain. 1977. "Statistical Theories of Discrimination in Labor Markets." *Industrial and Labor Relations Review* (30): 175–187.

Akerlof, George. 1984. "A Theory of Social Custom, of Which Unemployment May Be One Consequence." In *An Economic Theorist's Book of Tales*. Cambridge, UK: Cambridge University Press.

Anderson, Elijah. 1990. *Streetwise: Race, Class, and Change in an Urban Community*. Chicago: University of Chicago Press.

Arrow, Kenneth. 1972a. "Models of Job Discrimination." In *Racial Discrimination in Economic Life*, edited by Anthony Pascal, 83–120. Lexington, MA: D. C. Heath.

———. 1972b. "Some Mathematical Models of Race in the Labor Market." In *Racial Discrimination in Economic Life*, edited by Anthony Pascal, 187–203. Lexington, MA: D. C. Heath.

Barr, Nicholas. 1993. *The Economics of the Welfare State*, 2d ed. Palo Alto, CA: Stanford University Press.

Becker, Gary. 1971. *The Economics of Discrimination*, 2d ed. Chicago: University of Chicago Press.

———. 1975. *Human Capital: A Theoretical and Empirical Analysis, with Special Reference to Education*. New York: Columbia University Press.

Bell, Derrick. 1992. *Faces at the Bottom of the Well: The Permanence of Racism*. New York: Basic Books.

Bernstein, Michael, and David E. Adler. 1994. *Understanding American Economic Decline*. Cambridge, UK: Cambridge University Press.

Blanchflower, David, and Andrew Oswald. 1994. *The Wage Curve*. Cambridge, MA: MIT Press.

Borjas, George J. 1995. "The Economic Benefits of Immigration." *Journal of Economic Perspectives* 9, no. 2 (spring): 3–22.

Branch, Taylor. 1988. *Parting the Waters: America in the King Years, 1954–63*. New York: Simon and Schuster.

Cameron, Samuel. 1988. "The Economics of Crime Deterrence: A Survey of Theory and Evidence." *Kyklos* 41, no. 2: 301–323.

Carnoy, Martin. 1994. *Faded Dreams: The Politics and Economics of Race in America*. New York: Cambridge University Press.

Cose, Ellis. 1993. *The Rage of a Privileged Class*. New York: HarperCollins.

Crouch, Stanley. 1990. *Notes of a Hanging Judge.* New York: Oxford University Press.

Currie, Elliott. 1993. *Reckoning: Drugs, the Cities, and the American Future.* New York: Hill and Wang.

———. 1998. *Crime and Punishment in America.* New York: Metropolitan Books/Henry Holt.

D'Souza, Dinesh. 1995. *The End of Racism: Principles for a Multiracial Society.* New York: Free Press.

Danziger, Sheldon, and Peter Gottschalk. 1995. *America Unequal.* New York: Russell Sage Foundation and Cambridge, MA: Harvard University Press.

Darity, William A. 1991. "Underclass and Overclass: Race, Class, and Economic Inequality in the Managerial Age." In *Essays on the Economics of Discrimination,* edited by Emily P. Hoffman, 67–84. Kalamazoo, MI: W. E. Upjohn Institute for Employment Research.

———. 1995. "An American Dilemma Revisited." *Daedalus: Journal of the American Academy of Arts and Sciences,* 124, no. 1: 145–165.

Darity, William A., and Arthur Goldsmith. 1996. "Social Psychology, Unemployment, and Macroeconomics." *Journal of Economic Perspectives* 10, no. 2 (winter): 121–140.

Darity, William A., and Samuel L. Myers with Emmett D. Carson and William Sabol. 1994. *The Black Underclass: Critical Essays on Race and Unwantedness.* New York: Garland Publishing.

Eig, Jonathan. 1996. "Eyes on the Street: Community Policing in Chicago." *American Prospect,* no. 29: 60–68.

Epstein, Richard. 1992. *Forbidden Grounds: The Case Against Employment Discrimination Laws.* Cambridge, MA: Harvard University Press.

Erlich, Isaac. 1996. "Crime, Punishment, and the Market for Offenses." *Journal of Economic Perspectives* 10, no. 1 (winter): 43–68.

Fitzhugh, George. 1857. *Cannibals All! Or Slaves without Masters.* Richmond, VA: A. Morris. Reproduced by University Microfilm, Ann Arbor, MI, Reel 133.1.

Freeman, Richard. 1996. "Why Do So Many Young American Men Commit Crimes and What Might We Do about It?" *Journal of Economic Perspectives* 10, no. 1 (winter): 25–42.

Friedberg, Rachel, and Jennifer Hunt. 1995. "The Impact of Immigrants on Host Country Wages, Employment, and Growth." *Journal of Economic Perspectives* 9, no. 2 (spring): 23–44.

Friedman, Milton. 1962. *Capitalism and Freedom.* Chicago: University of Chicago Press.

Garrow, David. 1986. *Bearing the Cross: Martin Luther King Jr. and the Southern Christian Leadership Conference.* New York: Vintage Books.

Galbraith, John Kenneth. 1976. *The Affluent Society,* 3d rev. ed. Boston: Houghton Mifflin.

Genovese, Eugene. 1969. "The Logical Outcome of the Slaveholders' Philosophy." In *The World the Slaveholders Made: Two Essays in Interpretation.* New York: Pantheon Books.

Gray, John. 1995. *Liberalism,* 2d ed. Minneapolis: University of Minnesota Press.

Harrison, Lawrence. 1992. *Who Prospers? How Cultural Values Shape Economic and Political Success.* New York: Basic Books.

Haveman, Robert, and Barbara Wolfe. 1993. "Children's Prospects and Children's Policy." *Journal of Economic Perspectives* 7, no. 4 (fall) 153–74.

Hayek, Frederick. 1946. "The Use of Knowledge in Society." In *Individualism and Economic Order.* Chicago: University of Chicago Press.

Heckman, James. 1995. "Lessons from the Bell Curve." *Journal of Political Economy* 103 (October): 1091–1120.

Herrnstein, Richard, and Charles Murray. 1994. *The Bell Curve: Intelligence and Class Structure in American Life.* New York: Free Press.

Hoffman, Emily P. 1991. *Essays on the Economics of Discrimination.* Kalamazoo, MI: W. E. Upjohn Institute for Employment Research.

Howell, David R., and Edward N. Wolff. 1992. "Technical Change and the Demand for Skills in U.S. Industries." *Cambridge Journal of Economics* 16: 127–46.

Jencks, Christopher. 1992. *Rethinking Social Policy: Race, Poverty, and the Underclass.* Cambridge, MA: Harvard University Press.

Johnson, George E. 1997. "Changes in Earnings Inequality: The Role of Demand Shifts." *Journal of Economic Perspectives* 11, no. 2 (spring): 41–54.

Jones, Jacqueline. 1992. *The Dispossessed: America's Underclass from the Civil War to the Present.* New York: Basic Books.

Katz, Jack. 1988. *Seductions of Crime: Moral and Sensual Attractions of Doing Evil.* New York: Basic Books.

Katz, Michael. 1989. *The Undeserving Poor: From the War on Poverty to the War on Welfare.* New York: Pantheon Books.

Kaus, Mickey. 1992. *The End of Equality.* New York: Basic Books.

Kelso, William A. 1994. *Poverty and the Underclass: Changing Perceptions of the Poor in America.* New York: New York University Press.

Lemann, Nicholas. 1992. *The Promised Land: The Great Black Migration and How It Changed America.* New York: Vintage Books.

Levitt, Steven. 1996. "The Effect of Prison Population Size on Crime Rates: Evidence from Prison Overcrowding Litigation." *Quarterly Journal of Economics* 111, no. 2 (May): 319–351.

Lewis, W. Arthur. 1985. *Racial Conflict and Economic Development.* Cambridge, MA: Harvard University Press.

Lind, Michael. 1995. *The Next American Nation: The New Nationalism and the Fourth American Revolution.* New York: Free Press.

Lindbeck, Assar. 1993. *Unemployment and Macroeconomics.* Cambridge, MA: MIT Press.

Loury, Glenn. 1983. "Economics, Politics, and Blacks." *Review of Black Political Economy* 12, no. 3 (spring): 43–54.

———. 1995. *One by One from the Inside Out: Essays and Reviews on Race and Responsibility in America.* New York: Free Press.

Madrick, Jeffrey. 1995. *The End of Affluence: The Causes and Consequences of America's Economic Dilemma.* New York: Random House.

Marshall, Ray, and Marc Tucker. 1992. *Thinking for a Living: Education and the Wealth of Nations.* New York: Basic Books.

Massey, Douglass, and Nancy Denton. 1993. *American Apartheid: Segregation and the Making of the Underclass.* Cambridge, MA: Harvard University Press.

Miron, Jeffrey, and Jeffrey Zweibel. 1995. "The Economic Case against Drug Prohibition." *Journal of Economic Perspectives* 9, no. 4 (fall): 175–192.

Moffitt, Robert. 1992. "Incentive Effects of the U.S. Welfare System." *Journal of Economic Literature* 30, no. 1: 1–61.

Murnane, Richard, John B. Willet, and Frank Levy. 1995. "The Growing Importance of Cognitive Skills in Wage Determination." *Review of Economics and Statistics* 77 (May): 251–266.

Murray, Charles. 1984. *Losing Ground.* New York: Basic Books.

Neiman, Donald. 1991. *Promises to Keep: African-Americans and the Constitutional Order, 1776 to the Present.* New York: Oxford University Press.

Oliver, Melvin, and Thomas Shapiro. 1995. *Black Wealth/White Wealth: A New Perspective on Racial Inequality.* New York: Routledge.

Patterson, Orlando. 1997. *The Ordeal of Integration.* Washington, DC: Civitas/Counterpoint.

Phelps, Edmund. 1972. "The Statistical Theory of Racism and Sexism." *American Economic Review* 62: 659–61.

———. 1997. *Rewarding Work: How to Restore Participation and Self-Support to Free Enterprise.* Cambridge, MA: Harvard University Press.

Piehl, Anne, and John DiIulio. 1995. "Does Prison Pay? Revisited." *Brookings Review* (spring): 21–25.

Piore, Michael J., and Charles F. Sabel. 1984. *The Second Industrial Divide: Possibilities for Prosperity.* New York: Basic Books.

Shichor, David. 1995. *Punishment for Profit: Private Prisons/Public Concerns.* Thousand Oaks, CA: Sage Publications.

Schwarz, John E. 1983. *America's Hidden Success: A Reassessment of Twenty Years of Public Policy.* New York: W. W. Norton.

Seligman, Martin. 1975. *Helplessness: On Depression, Development, and Death.* San Francisco: W. H. Freeman.

Shklar, Judith. 1991. *American Citizenship: The Quest for Inclusion.* Cambridge, MA: Harvard University Press.

Shulman, Steven, and William Parity. 1989. *The Question of Discrimination: Racial Inequality in the U.S. Labor Market.* Middletown, CT: Wesleyan University Press.

Sowell, Thomas. 1980. *Knowledge and Decisions.* New York: Basic Books.

———. 1983. *The Economics and Politics of Race: An International Perspective.* New York: William Morrow.

———. 1994. *Race and Culture.* New York: Basic Books.

Stavans, Ilan. 1995. *The Hispanic Condition: Reflections on Culture and Identity in America.* New York: HarperCollins.

Takaki, Ronald. 1979. *Iron Cages: Race and Culture in Nineteenth-Century America.* New York: Knopf.

———. 1989. *Strangers from a Different Shore: A History of Asian Americans.* Boston: Little, Brown.

———. 1995. *A Different Mirror: History of Multicultural America.* Boston: Little, Brown.

Tobin, James. 1982a. "On Improving the Economic Status of the Negro." In *Essays in Economics: Theory and Policy.* Cambridge, MA: MIT Press.

———. 1982b. "On Limiting the Domain of Inequality." In *Essays in Economics: Theory and Policy.* Cambridge, MA: MIT Press.

Topel, Robert. 1997. "Factor Proportions and Relative Wages: The Supply Side Determinants of Wage Inequality." *Journal of Economic Perspectives* 11 (spring): 55–74.

United Nations Human Development Report. 1997. New York: United Nations.

Wilentz, Sean. 1996. "The Last Integrationist." *The New Republic* 215, no. 1: 19–26.

Wilson, William Julius. 1985. "Cycles of Deprivation and the Underclass Debate." *Social Science Review* 59: 541–559.

———. 1987. *The Truly Disadvantaged: The Inner City, the Underclass, and Public Policy.* Chicago: University of Chicago Press.

————. 1997. *When Work Disappears: The World of the New Urban Poor*. New York: Knopf.

Wood, Adrian. 1994. *North-South Trade, Employment, and Inequality: Changing Fortunes in a Skill-Driven World*. New York: Oxford University Press.

Wright, Gavin. 1986. *Old South, New South: Revolutions in the Southern Economy since the Civil War*. New York: Basic Books.

Yinger, John. 1995. *Close Doors, Opportunities Lost: The Continuing Costs of Housing Discrimination*. New York: Russell Sage Foundation.

INDEX

education *(Continued)*
reform, 190–192; unequal educational opportunity, 2–3, 7, 16–17, 28, 48, 53; wage inequality and, 36
Epstein, Richard, 202n. 1

families: and cultural explanation for inequality, 46–48; female headship, 21; income of, distribution by race, 20–22, 24; income of, and low wages for unskilled men, 22; income of, and mean SAT score by race, 30–31; poverty rates of, for blacks, whites, and Latinos, 17–19; social capital and, 51–54; structure of, and welfare, 86–88, 204n. 11
Fitzhugh, George, 200n. 19
Freeman, Richard, 176
Friedberg, Rachel, 200n. 11
Friedman, Milton, *Capitalism and Freedom*, 6, 128, 151

Genovese, Eugene, 200n. 19
Goldsmith, Arthur, 200n. 14
Gottschalk, Peter, 22, 88, 188–189, 200n. 9, 204nn. 15–16
Gray, John, 8

Harrison, Lawrence, 47
Hayek, Friedrich, 151
Heckman, James, 201n. 20
Hunt, Jennifer, 200n. 11

immigration, 9–12, 20, 23–24, 152–153
incarceration, 175–186, 193–196, 212nn. 15–16; of black men in 1997, number and percentage, 1, 213n. 19
inequality, racial, 3–5, 11, 17, 34, 38–39, 50–55, 57–88, 166–169; cultural roots of, 38–54; genetic basis for (*The Bell Curve*), 5, 32–38, 45–46
inequality, wage, 22–25, 138–162, 185–193

Jones, Jacqueline, 202n. 32

Keynesian policy, 127–129
King, Martin Luther, 2, 30, 205n. 19

Latinos, 59–60, 82–83, 197; changing understanding of racial conflict, 9–12; educational attainment, 174–175; performance of, on standardized tests, 29–31, 39; real income per person by race, 16–17; redefinition of American culture, 26; residential segregation and, 16
Levitt, Steven, 181–182
liberals: black middle-class success and, 26; classical liberalism, 6–9, 45; conservative critique of, 33–35, 39–40, 51, 58–63; and culture of poverty argument, 49; program for racial equality, 19, 30, 57–61, 125–147, 156, 186–92
Lind, Michael, 156
Loury, Glenn, 13, 85–86; critique of D'Souza, 41; critique of liberal social policy, 51; social capital and black underdevelopment, 97–102; 204nn. 9–10, 205n. 18

markets: classical liberalism and, 6–9; cultural modernization and, 48–51; education and market failure, 36–38; inequality and, 27–29, 36; interaction between racism and, 3–4, 11–12, 45, 55, 57–61; and interaction with other social institutions, 51–54; as racially progressive force, 32; racial neutrality of, 39–40, 43–47, 83–88; youth culture and, 44–45
Marx, Karl, 51
Massey, Douglass, 16, 199n. 5
Mill, John Stuart, 7
Murray, Charles: *The Bell Curve* (with Richard Herrnstein), 5, 32–38, 45–46, 72, 77, 84, 104, 160, 200n. 19; *Losing Ground*, 33, 35–36, 48–50

Negrophobia, 17, 30, 57

Oliver, Melvin, 202n. 28

Patterson, Orlando, 27, 200n. 13
Phelps, Edmund, 189–190
Piehl, Anne, 183
poverty, 1, 5, 7, 11, 27–28, 81–88; and crime, 175–180; distribution of family

ABOUT THE AUTHOR

Marcellus Andrews is an associate professor of economics at Wellesley College. Mr. Andrews is currently writing a theoretical book on the macroeconomics of racial and class conflict in economies making the transition from apartheid to capitalist democracy with special reference to South Africa and the United States.